ON THE WAVES OF DESTINY

The Selected Writings of Lili Berger

Edited by Frieda Johles Forman, Sam Blatt, Vivian Felsen, and Judy Nisenholt

Lili Berger wrote about the most traumatic and transformative developments of the twentieth century to which she herself was an eyewitness. *On the Waves of Destiny* presents an anthology that reflects her early life in interwar Poland during the rise of Hitler, her Second World War activities in occupied Paris where she was active in the Communist resistance, and her sojourn in Communist Poland from 1949 to 1968.

The majority of her essays are pen portraits, often based on her own personal recollections, in which she made clear that she considered it her duty to memorialize the tens of thousands of Polish Jewish writers and artists who were murdered during the Holocaust, such as author and painter Bruno Schulz, historian Emanuel Ringelblum, and artist Gela Seksztajn, as well as to preserve their work. Even her short stories are based on actual experiences, not only her own but also those of people around her.

In her stories, her essays, and her allegorical fables, she explored issues such as equality for women, the moral responsibility of a writer, the question of Jewish identity, and the creative process in general. The translations in *On the Waves of Destiny* ensure that Lili Berger's legacy will continue to resonate with future generations of readers.

FRIEDA JOHLES FORMAN was an author, translator, pioneer of feminist Jewish studies, who founded the Women's Educational Resource Centre at the Ontario Institute for Studies in Education at the University of Toronto, and the award-winning editor of *Found Treasures: Stories by Yiddish Women Writers*.

SAM BLATT is a Yiddish educator, translator, and editor, who has served as the coordinator of Yiddish teachers for adult education in the Toronto Jewish community.

VIVIAN FELSEN is an award-winning translator of French and Yiddish, whose published translations include books on Canadian Jewish history, Holocaust memoirs, and short stories.

JUDY NISENHOLT is a Yiddish Book Center translation fellow with extensive experience translating Yiddish memoirs and letters.

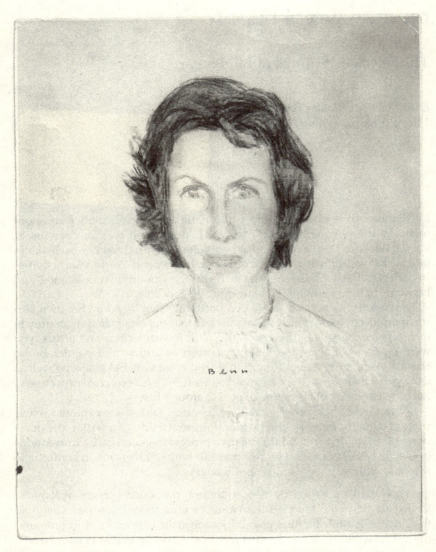

Drawing by Benn [Bension Rabinowicz]. Courtesy Michel Grojnowski.

On the Waves of Destiny

The Selected Writings of Lili Berger

Edited by Frieda Johles Forman, Sam Blatt,
Vivian Felsen, and Judy Nisenholt

UNIVERSITY OF TORONTO PRESS
Toronto Buffalo London

Yiddish of Chapters 1–5, 7–14, and 18–22 © Michel Grojnowski

© University of Toronto Press 2025
Toronto Buffalo London
utppublishing.com
Printed in the USA

ISBN 978-1-4875-5715-7 (cloth) ISBN 978-1-4875-5718-8 (EPUB)
ISBN 978-1-4875-5716-4 (paper) ISBN 978-1-4875-5717-1 (PDF)

Library and Archives Canada Cataloguing in Publication

Title: On the waves of destiny : the selected writings of Lili Berger /
    edited by Frieda Johles Forman, Sam Blatt, Vivian Felsen, and Judy Nisenholt.
Names: Berger, Lili, author | Forman, Frieda, editor | Blatt, Sam, editor. |
    Felsen, Vivian. | Nisenholt, Judy, editor.
Description: Includes bibliographical references and index.
Identifiers: Canadiana (print) 20240478878 | Canadiana (ebook) 20240478959 |
    ISBN 9781487557157 (cloth) | ISBN 9781487557164 (paper) |
    ISBN 9781487557188 (EPUB) | ISBN 9781487557171 (PDF)
Subjects: LCSH: Berger, Lili. | LCSH: Jews – Poland. | LCSH: Holocaust,
    Jewish (1939–1945) | LCSH: Yiddish literature – History and criticism.
Classification: LCC PJ5129.B455 A6 2025 | DDC 839/.134—dc23

Cover design: John Beadle
Cover image: Photographs courtesy of Michel Grojnowski

We wish to acknowledge the land on which the University of Toronto Press operates. This land is the traditional territory of the Wendat, the Anishnaabeg, the Haudenosaunee, the Métis, and the Mississaugas of the Credit First Nation.

This book has been published with the help of a grant from the Federation for the Humanities and Social Sciences, through the Awards to Scholarly Publications Program, using funds provided by the Social Sciences and Humanities Research Council of Canada.

University of Toronto Press acknowledges the financial support of the Government of Canada, the Canada Council for the Arts, and the Ontario Arts Council, an agency of the Government of Ontario, for its publishing activities.

In loving memory of Frieda Johles Forman and Sylvia Lustgarten

Contents

Acknowledgments ix

Introduction xiii

Jewish Life in Poland

We Polish Jews 3
Naftole Herts Kon: The Tragic Enthusiasm 9
Notes and Reflections on the Fate of the Written Word 17
The Yiddish Folk Song in Polish Translation 23

Holocaust

The Hidden Source of a People's Survival: Writings from the
    Ghettos and Camps 33
On the Ninetieth Birthday of Dr. Emanuel Ringelblum:
    Recollections and Summing Up 43
Janusz Korczak, Pedagogical Researcher 52
Anka: To Her Eternal Memory 63
Thoughts on Reading "The Medem Sanatorium Book" 69

Arts and Letters

Bruno Schulz, Artist and Jew 75
Vasily Grossman: The History of a Book or the Path to
    Jewish Identity 88
Reyzl Zhikhlinski: On Her Poetry 99

viii   Contents

A Visit to Chana Orloff 104
Czajka: The Painful Path to Self-Discovery 112
Ber Mark, The Man and the Author: On the Twenty-fifth
   Anniversary of His Death 116
Moyshe Shulshteyn: On the Tenth Anniversary of His Death 124

Fables, Short Stories, and Historic Fiction

All Because of the Wife or The First Quarrel 131
The Rebbetzin's Sense of Justice 134
With Tevye the Dairyman in the Underground 141
Animals and Humans 149
The Jew Who Came Late 156
The Last Night 162
Unfinished Pages: Excerpt 170
The Debate between Paper and Letters: A Tale 175

Epilogue

Notes on the Underground: Lili Berger's Reflections on
   Marranism 181

Cultural Figures Named in the Text 199

Biographies of Editors and Translators 203

Books by Lili Berger 207

Bibliography 209

Acknowledgments

On the Waves of Destiny is a collective creation on several levels: it was driven by the translators and editors, of course, but encompasses as well the wider and diverse community of Yiddish scholars and writers across the globe who are engaged in uniting *mame-loshn* (Yiddish) with an old and new reading public. Long awaited, the volume is the culmination of close to a decade of meetings and discussions on matters ranging from the difficult choices of texts for inclusion to detailed critiques of translations and linguistic decisions. Appreciation and recognition must go to the safekeepers of our cultural, literary, and historical treasures. Over multiple generations and locations the librarians, archivists, and contributors to cultural institutions made their mark: in particular, the Yiddish Book Center, Amherst, Massachusetts, whose digital library allowed us access to many volumes of Lili Berger's books; Maison de la Culture Yiddish–Bibliothèque Medem; YIVO Institute for Jewish Research, New York; Jewish Public Library of Montreal; John Robarts Research Library, Toronto.

The scholars and writers who gave us the *hekhsher* (rabbinical approval) to take on the project of translating the works of the prolific Yiddish writer Lili Berger include Yitzkhok Niborski, Chava Lapin, Irena Klepfisz, Eugene Orenstein, Goldie Morgentaler, and Anna Shternshis.

The late Frieda Forman wished to extend her thanks to friends and family who critiqued various sections of the manuscript and provided a much-needed second review: Anne Shteir, Deborah Heller, Erica Simmons, Mona Kornberg, Nora Gold, and Carol Ann Reid kept up our spirits and never doubted the significance of our project or our dedication in ferrying the works of an almost forgotten writer to a new readership. She felt a deep sense of gratitude to good friends who, over the many years that we worked on the book, provided much encouragement,

x Acknowledgments

enthusiasm and knowledge, without which this much-awaited book would not have been possible. Readers: Rusty S., Deborah H., Erica S., Esther I., Goldie M., Mona K. Good friends of the book: Didi K., Gretchen M., Michelle S. For their care: Kalsang and Rose. And many others too numerous to list.

Sam extends his profound thanks to his caregiver circle and his family, all of whom gave him the space to continue his editorial and translation functions. He notes the extensive collaboration of his partner, Ronnee Jaeger (a translator), upon whom he not infrequently relied to find the exact words to resonate in English. Thank you to Nora Gold for her encouragement and editorial input. Thanks to Stephen Chalastra for his expert "large document" word-processing assistance.

Vivian would like to express her heartfelt gratitude to her friends Nessa Ashtar-Olshansky, for her outstanding scholarly and technical assistance; Gerry Kane, for his constant readiness to discuss language and literature; the late Anna Kremer, who, for over twenty years, generously shared her wisdom and remarkable linguistic skills; and the late Sylvia Lustgarten, for her marvellous sense of language and unwavering enthusiasm. Vivian is especially grateful to her children and grandchildren and to her husband, Shim, for their interest in her work, and their steadfast love and support.

Judy would like to thank Michel Grojnowski, Lili Berger's son, for encouraging and supporting our translation work over the past years, and offering photos from his collection for this volume; Leye/Linda Lipsky for her painstaking work on the Epilogue; Fleur Kuhn Kennedy, who generously shared her academic paper "Les Territoires de Lili Berger" and also provided the contact for Berger's heir and copyright holder, Natalia Krynicka of the Bibliothèque Medem in Paris, for providing access to the Lili Berger archive; Marysia Bucholc for all her assistance with Polish language references and quotes; the late Alisa Poskanzer, who first proposed working together in Yiddish translation; and the late Esther Nisenholt, who passed on her love of words and language and whose Yiddish-speaking voice was always present during the translation process.

Against her protests, Sam, Vivian, and Judy would like to publicly recognize Frieda Forman for her leadership in the discovery of Yiddish women writers. She was the true engine of this and previous translation endeavours, assembling with great devotion the groups of editors and readers for each volume. Frieda took the lead in the process of the selection of works to be translated, always lovingly providing a welcoming table where discussion and reading took place over generous offerings of food and drink.

Acknowledgments xi

The editors and translators of this volume mourn the loss of our friend and colleague Sylvia Lustgarten (1996–2023), an outstanding translator, who, at the age of 96 was still working with us on this book.

We extend our thanks to Stephen Shapiro, of the University of Toronto Press, for continually sustaining our efforts, for his valuable editorial suggestions, and for guiding us through the many steps of the process.

Finally, our thanks go to the prospective readers who expressed their eagerness and enthusiasm, ready to embrace the publication of Lili Berger's selected writings.

Please note: "The Rebbetzin's Sense of Justice," "Animals and Humans," and "The Last Night" have previously been published in *JewishFiction.net*; "The Rebbetzin's Sense of Justice" has also appeared in *18: Jewish Stories Translated from 18 Languages*, edited by Nora Gold and published by Cherry Orchard Books, an imprint of Academic Studies Press.

Frieda Johles Forman, Sam Blatt,
Vivian Felsen, and Judy Nisenholt

I wish to express my profound gratitude to Frieda Johles Forman, Sam Blatt, Vivian Felsen, and Judy Nisenholt, editors, as well as Ronnee Jaeger, Sylvia Lustgarten, and Linda/Leye Lipsky, for their extraordinary efforts in bringing this volume to fruition.

With this volume, the University of Toronto Press has undertaken the first publication in English of a selection of writings by Lili Berger. For that I extend my heartfelt thanks. I am particularly grateful to Stephen Shapiro, acquisitions editor, who carried this project through to completion with devotion and commitment.

I would like to proffer my sincere appreciation to Fleur Kuhn-Kennedy, whose essay "Les Territoires de Lili Berger" (Paris, 2019) helped me tremendously to see my mother's work in a new light.

Michel Grojnowski
Paris, March 2024

Introduction

Lili Berger, herself a translator working in three languages, thought and wrote about translation: its place in world literature, the significance of the translator-creator to the culture of a people in enriching the original language with new concepts and broadening its boundaries. Despite a long and illustrious career, her work was not issued the proverbial life-saving travel visa and she is not widely known beyond the spheres of Yiddish, French, or Polish readers. In this respect her fate is like that of many, indeed most, Yiddish women writers whose works languish untranslated, relegated to oblivion. Every nation strives to make its culture known to people outside its borders. It has even been said that an untranslated book is only half a published book. It is in that spirit that we have undertaken this book of selected translations of Lili Berger's works.

Born 30 December 1916, in Malkin, in the Białystok region of Poland, into a Hasidic family, Berger received a religious education and completed the Polish Jewish gymnasium in Warsaw in 1933. She studied pedagogy in Brussels and then settled in Paris at the end of 1936, where she taught in Yiddish supplementary schools. She contributed to the Yiddish press, including the *Naye prese*, a Communist paper, and later on she wrote for the monthly *Oyfsnay* and the weekly *Di Vokh*, two important Yiddish publications in Paris. During the occupation in France, she edited the underground Resistance newspaper *Unzer vort* (an incarnation of the newly banned *Naye prese*). Her activism extended to the rescue of Jewish children during the Holocaust, smuggling them to the safety of Switzerland.

She managed to survive the war years in France using false papers but living sometimes apart from her husband, Louis Gronowski, a leading figure in the Jewish section of the Communist Party, who was also living clandestinely and frequently on the move. In 1949, denied citizenship

xiv   Introduction

in France, she and her husband decided to return to Poland, and settled in Warsaw. They hoped to rebuild the new Poland and Berger's hope was to participate in the revival of a Jewish culture that had once flourished there. According to Gronowski, Berger was very attentive to injustice and indignant at political abuses, and would engage him in painful discussions regarding the course that Poland was taking, even in the early 1950s. Within eight years of their return, her faith in Polish Socialism had been broken, and she regarded the future in Poland as uncertain.[1] As antisemitism mounted during the 1960s, Berger could no longer sustain her illusions about the possibility for developing a strong Jewish culture in Poland. In 1968 Berger and Gronowski returned to Paris; there she resumed an energetic and productive writing career to the end of her life.

Berger was a presence in the world, a world unto herself yet immersed in the world: the complex social and political present of postwar Poland and the near and distant past of generations of diasporic Jews. Her observations and memories are captured in the many genres in which she wrote: essays, short stories, novels, and plays.

As a writer, Berger is never at rest. She explores archival material, memoirs, works in translation and folklore, searching every surface for weighted layers and omitted moments, opening gates to unexplored terrain. The trajectory of her life is reflected in her writing. Her personal story is one of immigration, activism, persecution, resistance, displacement, and an unflagging commitment to humanism and the power of artistic creation. It follows that her work is deeply entwined with the history and creative drive of the Jewish people.

In exile and stateless, she published her essay "We Polish Jews" in 1969, bearing witness to her disappointment in a Poland that failed to recognize the contributions of Polish Jews who over many centuries had contributed to the country's economic and cultural development. The essay begins with an encomium for the esteemed Polish Jewish poet Julian Tuwim, borrowing its title from his 1944 manifesto. Both in tribute and lament, Berger echoes and expands on Tuwim's refrain in her exposition of the thousand-year history of Jews in Poland. Typical of her essays on culture are extensive lists that name significant individuals from the past or make allusion to possible lists that could be made. In the aftermath of the inconceivable annihilation and cultural erasure

---

1 Louis Gronowski-Brunot, *Le dernier grand soir: Un juif de Pologne* (Éditions du Seuil, 1980), 251.

of Europe's Jews, Berger must resort to enumeration as a necessary act of remembrance and recording.

"The Zionist label is today's yellow star," she writes, framing her analysis of the dire condition of Jewish life in Poland at that time. Her cry is collective but also highly personal. She concludes her elegiac essay with a call for justice, not pity. "Give us what we deserve for our labours! Give the Jewish people the legacy that the massacred Polish Jewry has left behind."

Berger's essay "Naftole Herts Kon: The Tragic Enthusiasm" offers one of her rare personal intimations. She is recalling and paying tribute to Yiddish writer and poet Naftole Herts Kon, her long-suffering friend, initially an enthusiast of Poland's comparative openness, but then unjustly accused by the Polish government of spying in 1960. Berger depicts the apathy of the Polish Writers' Union to the ever-widening encroachment of antisemitism that foreshadowed the expulsion of Jews that was to come.

Cultural loss, a recurrent theme in this collection, figures prominently in "Notes and Reflections on the Fate of the Written Word." Berger takes a historic view of Jewish books, which shared the same fate as its people during wars, migrations, and catastrophes. Every city and town in Poland had a Jewish library. Often at great self-sacrifice, Jews demonstrated their bibliophilic tradition by the rescue of literary and spiritual treasures, the word and soul of a people. Fearing for the fate of Jewish treasures in Poland, Berger collected documents from Warsaw's Jewish Historical Institute. Salvaging the collective memory of her people, she urged vigilance and the return of their intellectual resources to the Jewish people.

In "The Yiddish Folk Song in Polish Translation" Berger reviews the first Polish anthology published after the Shoah. Entitled *Raisins and Almonds*,[2] it is the work of Polish collector, poet, and translator Jerzy Ficowski. Berger takes issue in minor ways with his selections, and acknowledges effects that can be lost in the translation, but applauds this "friend of Jews" for his efforts to create a bridge between two deeply entwined cultures and to leave a memorial to the murdered Jews among whom he once lived.

Alongside the mature, established artists who were murdered in the ghettos and camps, Berger recognizes a cultural inheritance that came from a different source, an "underground spring" as she calls it. This outpouring is the folk literature of ordinary Jews, whose poetry,

---

2 "Raisins and Almonds" is a traditional Jewish lullaby popularized by Abraham Goldfaden.

xvi Introduction

prose, diaries, and memoirs constituted a wellspring of spiritual and psychic resistance. In "The Hidden Source of a People's Survival," Berger provides numerous exemplars of this creative output retrieved from Warsaw's Jewish Historical Institute. The strength that is generated via the creative impulse is front and centre in Berger's essay. Her outrage is roused by a Polish account of the Warsaw Ghetto that appeared in 1968, the year of the Jewish expulsion, in which, among many distortions and lies, Jewish spiritual resistance was labelled as passivity.

Memory, a fundamental concept and character in Jewish life, religion, ritual, and practice, is everywhere in Berger's writings. The *yizkor bukh*, the memorial book, which after the Holocaust became so crucial and enduring an artifact of commemoration and remembrance for the destroyed Jewish communities of Eastern Europe, takes literary shape throughout her essays, stories, and novels. Dedicated to Jewish leaders or colleagues on a *yortsayt*, the anniversary of a death or a birthday, these texts become the synagogue where memorial prayers are recited – her readers become the responsive voices of the *minyan*, the quorum. Remember – *Zakhor!* - is a moral imperative that is central to Jewish life. On the ninetieth anniversary of his birth, Berger recalls Ringelblum, the heroic historian and archivist of the Warsaw Ghetto. "There are few of us alive today who actually knew him," she writes, and she regards it as a "sacred duty" to keep his memory alive. In her essay "On the Ninetieth Birthday of Dr. Emanuel Ringelblum: Recollections and Summing Up" she returns to pre-Holocaust France to paint a different portrait of this iconic figure: Ringelblum is a friend, a visitor to Berger's Yiddish class, where he charms her students with his charismatic personality.

Janusz Korczak, whom Berger also encountered when she was an adolescent, appears in this collection in two essays, a recollection, and a story. She also produced a dramatic piece evoking his last day before deportation. The range of genres gives her latitude to explore a life so consistent in its trajectory yet so versatile it cannot be contained in a single interpretation. "Janusz Korczak, Pedagogical Researcher," one of the more expansive essays, illuminates his development as an educator, researcher, human rights theorist, and, above all, advocate for child welfare over years of cataclysmic historical changes.

The story "Anka: To Her Eternal Memory" follows two friends to Korczak's famed Saturday morning readings to the children in his Warsaw orphanage. It is a story within a story: we overhear the earnest social and political debates argued by the progressive youth, in a glimpse of the prewar period.

Introduction xvii

"Thoughts on Reading the Medem Sanatorium Book" is Berger's memorial to the Socialist healing and education centre serving the needs of Poland's impoverished Jewish children from the 1920s to the 1940s. The comparison with Korczak's children's home, touched upon in this piece, provides a glimpse into the agonizing decision-making that fell to institutional administrators and the many tragic circumstances under which children's lives were claimed during those years.

Berger was fair to all her subjects in their Polish-Jewish interactions, but in her role as literary critic, she addressed the writers and artists as kindred spirits. Their lives were as close to her as their work, with little distance between her and those she brought to life in her essays. She acknowledged Bruno Schulz's universally esteemed artistry, but she probed deeper territory, into his early formative influences and inspiration: the shtetl whose warmth and closeness he introduced into his visual and literary creations. Schulz wrote as a Pole but died as a Jew, Berger reminds her readers. "Bruno Schulz: Artist and Jew" examines Schulz's deeply absorbed Jewish heritage, given light in his prints and drawings. He is often associated with Kafka, with their shared rootless, Jewish fatalism and Schulz's Polish translation of *The Trial*; Berger, however, attaches greater significance to their differences.

In her preface to the essay, republished in Paris, in 1991, Berger continues her engagement with Bruno Schulz's legacy. Years after his death, she comes across the announcement of a multimedia exhibition in Jerusalem, which, to her deep regret, she cannot attend owing to a prolonged illness. Berger casts herself in yet another Schulz-related encounter: at the Polish Literary Society in Warsaw, she meets and befriends the poet and biographer Jerzy Ficowski, who reveals to her his tireless search for and ultimate success in finding traces of Schulz's creative life.

Berger opens her 1968 essay "Vasily Grossman: The History of a Book or the Path to Jewish Identity" by recalling the disappearance and destruction of texts and libraries and linking that history to the near loss of Grossman's novel *Life and Fate*. Recognizing him as one of the greatest writers of twentieth century, Berger views his life and work prismatically, leading her in another, less-travelled direction: his life as a Jew, an identity shaped by the Holocaust and its aftermath, continuing through the Stalinist period. In that light, Grossman emerges as a more complex, protean writer. Raised in an intensely assimilated Jewish Russian family, one could say, the history of the twentieth century forced a reconstructed identity on him. Berger moves between his life and writing, drawing on the research of Simon Markish (son of the martyred poet Peretz Markish), who characterized Grossman as assimilated, to a

xviii   Introduction

surprising extent, until the Nazi period and his embarking on a search for his Jewish roots; ultimately, he became an outspoken opponent of the Communist regime.

Although she may not have proclaimed herself a feminist, understandably given her time and place in history, Berger's elective affinities were certainly in concert with women's rights. Her political sensibility and moral imagination brought her to a deep comprehension of women's social condition, the zones of their exclusion, and the forces maintaining the status quo. She expressed these realities in her opinion pieces. She expressed it too in her choice of female subjects and in the tender treatment she bestowed on them.

In "Reyzl Zhikhlinski: On Her Poetry," Berger, a frequent presence at Paris literary gatherings, introduces Reyzl Zhikhlinski, the guest of the evening, as a true artist and a close friend. Zhikhlinski, a precocious poet, was revered by the luminaries of Yiddish literature and garnered literary awards throughout her long career. However, she did not enjoy acclaim commensurate with her talent and originality in injecting new form, tone, and colour into Yiddish poetry. Fluent in five languages, she wrote exclusively in Yiddish throughout her creative years. After years of wandering, she and her husband and son found their way to New York, where she attended college and continued to write poetry and fiction. Her subjects included the Shoah and the lost world of European Jewry, the world of her murdered family. Zhikhlinski also wrote of New York's disenfranchised, the isolated, the homeless, and the quotidian life of her neighbours.

Berger begins "A Visit to Chana Orloff" by bemoaning the Jewish public's indifference to artists and, more regrettable still, their silence in recognizing women artists. Berger's signature style – her intimate, heartfelt engagement with her subject – is present in her encounter with artist Chana Orloff in her Paris studio. At first, Berger focuses on the setting of the visit; her vivid descriptions of Orloff's sculptures are followed by their conversation about Jewish art, leaving aside details of Orloff's life and many achievements in the art world. Berger is a prodigious namedropper; if we did not hold her in such high regard, we would fault her for that seeming foible. In this essay we commend her for introducing the reader to Chana Orloff's many friends and colleagues, artists whose names, for the most part, have receded into oblivion.

"Czajka: The Painful Path to Self-Discovery" focuses on Izabela Gelbard, an assimilated Jew, or as Berger describes her and others like her, an "alienated Jew," who, prior to World War II was one of the most popular women active in Polish literary and artistic circles. Her experience during the Holocaust was expressed in her poetry, notably, *Mourning*

Songs of the Ghetto. After the war, Gelbard, known as Lieutenant Czajka in the Polish army, was held in high esteem as a writer. In this brief essay, Berger gives us a rare glimpse into her own pain, that of regret.

The Jewish artists Berger writes about, to whatever degree they are Polonized or Russified or Sovietized, cannot escape the classifications that the dominant culture imposes. Berger's own dashed hopes for a Communism where diverse cultures would share common cause are on view in the profile she pens of Czajka and other cultural figures coming to grips with shifting identities.

"Ber Mark, The Man and the Author" is a moving tribute to her colleague at the journal *Yidishe shriftn* (Jewish Writings), her co-editor at the publishing house Yiddish Bukh and the editor-in-chief of the first Yiddish newspaper in post-Holocaust Poland. Among Mark's numerous publications were much-anthologized volumes of poetry, translated into French and English. His highly regarded, meticulously documented historical work *Megiles oyshvits* (The scrolls of Auschwitz) is considered one of the first detailed accounts of the extermination camp.

Berger's individual *yortsayts* and eulogies are always embedded in the context of her grief for the great loss suffered by the Jewish people over millennia, and more particularly, during the twentieth century. Her love of friends and the Jewish people echoes throughout in her frequent Hebrew expressions and references to biblical personages – the matriarch, Mother Rachel weeping for her children comes to mind. Berger's roots in Jewish texts and traditions emerge in her post-Holocaust references to the remnants of a unique people.

There are writers with whom Berger shared not only religious roots and education but also a decades-long embrace of Communism followed by disillusionment. Her friend and comrade in the French resistance, the essayist, memoirist, playwright, and translator, Moyshe Shulshteyn is memorialized in the essay "Moyshe Shulshteyn, On the Tenth Anniversary of His Death." His poems inscribing the Shoah and the murder of Yiddish writers during the Stalinist regime are widely anthologized and translated.

In her fables and folk tales we discover Berger the cosmopolite, one who is also steeped in traditional Judaism. She was raised in a Hasidic family but carries with her the secular world of progressive politics and the modern ethos of artistic expression. She draws on the world she knew in her shtetl stories and enlarges her frame in later years, when she writes as an engaged intellectual examining the triumphs and tragedies of her Polish, Jewish, French, and Yiddish milieux.

"All Because of the Wife" is a return to myth and folk tale. Following the Midrashic tradition of commentary, Berger puts a feminist twist on

xx   Introduction

the Creation story. Eve is presented as lively and assertive, while Adam is the submissive partner of the biblical first family. Perhaps Eve is less a temptress than a risk-taker, prepared to question authority and gain enlightenment, though at a cost.

Berger's moral perception, so evident in her choice of essay subjects, reappears in this short story, where she creates colourful characters entangled in complicated predicaments. Narrated by the only girl in a class of boys, "The Rebbetzin's Sense of Justice" presents the shtetl Hebrew school as the modest stage on which class and gender play a decisive role in a tale of redistributive justice.

Set in Paris during the occupation, "With Tevye the Dairyman in the Underground" is a finely detailed story reflecting Berger's own experience in the Resistance. Despite the tragic context, we find the introduction of Sholem Aleichem's Tevye as protagonist adds a touch of levity and leads to an inevitable comedy of errors.

Ahead of her time, as she so often is, in her short story "Animals and Humans" Berger reveals her deep respect for animals, their intelligence, and their capacity for friendship. In Poland after the war, the shadows of the Holocaust are ever-present, but a visit to a Polish friend in a vacation setting allows for a lighter mood in this witty, well-paced narrative.

"The Jew Who Came Late" is also set in postwar Poland. It is primarily a dialogue between a survivor and a clerk at a Jewish aid organization. With a few strokes, Berger conveys the utter frustration and hopelessness of the claimant, a modern-day Converso, intent on maintaining his Polish Catholic façade, a necessary and all-too-common strategy during those years.

"The Last Night" returns us to Poland under Nazi occupation and the final hours in the life of Janusz Korczak. Berger depicts Korczak's tormented inner life and his nightmares, mirroring the fate that awaits him and the children in his orphanage. It is not surprising that Berger is so deeply drawn to Korczak's life-long dedication to children: she too was a teacher and, as mentioned earlier, devoted herself to the rescue of Jewish children during the Nazi occupation in France.

"Unfinished Pages" ("Nisht farendikte bletlekh"), an excerpt from Berger's eponymous novel, is fashioned as a prison diary kept by Esther Frumkin during her incarceration in a Stalinist forced labour camp in Kazakhstan. It is another of Berger's feminist rescue operations: here, a rare instance of prison writing by a woman, no less in Yiddish. Berger introduces the contemporary reader to Esther Frumkin, the prominent political theorist, astute revolutionary, and educator. In this novel, subject and author find each other: cut from the same cloth, both women are firmly rooted in traditional as well as enlightened

Jewish life and education, integrating the social justice frame of Judaism into Socialist and Communist activism. For both women Yiddish was their life-giving language. However, Frumkin is a contested figure who was reviled by many for her parting of the ways with Bundism, her anti-religious pronouncements as a member of the Jewish section of the Communist Party, and her allegiance to the proletariat over the Jewish nation. Berger brings us the reflections of a tortured soul who ultimately acknowledges her loyalty to a false god yet remains steadfast in her love of the Yiddish language and its people.

"The Debate between Paper and Letters" showcases Berger's talents as a playful teller of tales. Her staging of the dispute between medium and message anticipates our contemporary dilemmas in some measure. In this head-to-head, each reviles the other. As is often the case in Jewish tales, it happens that both sides are right. Is this a moral lesson about the resolution of arguments, or a cautionary tale in which putting the tools of communication in the wrong hands inevitably spells trouble?

To translate Lili Berger's work in our time, at a moment of convergence of two struggling realities, two languages, Yiddish and feminism is to emerge from enforced silence towards the expression of authenticity and freedom. These unchained languages enrich and influence one another in unexpected ways: feminism revitalized worldwide in the latter part of the twentieth century, and Yiddish, returned from near extinction. Feminism advocated for Yiddish women writers, introducing them in translation, carrying them over to a new cohort. Yiddish became a medium and inspiration in the feminist search for historical and literary roots, and was embraced by a younger generation who found resonance in it. Subject and perspective are, finally, the determiner of relevance.

In a 1979 article entitled "For the Public Good"[3] Berger's own perspective is clear. She surveys the place of women in institutions and organizations across the Jewish world and offers numerous instances of women's absence or marginalization in the public sphere. The oversights and sidelining would seem trivial or comic, she tells us, if these were not typical of a general approach depriving women of their due and minimizing their contributions.

The revival of Yiddish coeval with the feminist retrieval of once ignored and rebuffed women's literature has yielded a treasury of moral and literary imagination. Lili Berger, who lived and stood at the nexus of both Yiddish and feminism, used her great gifts to open a

---

3 *Yisroel Shtime*, 5 September 1979, 8.

xxii Introduction

portal to the vital Yiddish culture of the prewar and postwar years. With the probing eye of a journalist and a historian's commitment to fact, she expresses the particulars of her Jewish Polish identity. At the same time, using a colourful Yiddish, replete with biblical and Talmudic phrases and references, she invariably directs the reader to universal concerns: social justice, self-determination, artistic freedom, the rights of children.

Lili Berger is a link in the golden chain, *di goldene keyt*, the glorious history and continuity of the Jewish people. For her work in preserving and illuminating that world, the Yiddish press across the continents honoured and celebrated her.

The Yiddish Press Responds to Lili Berger

Across the more than thirty years of her literary career, Berger was featured widely and frequently in the Yiddish press. Her writing was published and reviewed in newspapers based in Buenos Aires, New York, Paris, Warsaw, South Africa, and Tel Aviv. Her work was given serious attention and overall was warmly received and recognized for its role in illuminating the Holocaust and the sequelae of that shattering destruction.

Among only seven Jewish writers who debuted in the Yiddish literary revival of postwar Poland, Lili Berger was the sole woman. She would have first come to the attention of Yiddish readers with her Yiddish translation in 1953 of "Letters from Death Row," the correspondence of Ethel and Julius Rosenberg. Her first book of original writing did not appear until 1962, when *Yidish Bukh*, the Yiddish publishing house, re-established in Łódź in 1946 and then in Warsaw, brought out *Eseyen un skitsn* (Essays and Sketches). Her essays dealt with works and authors in both contemporary and classic world literature.

In his review in *Yiddishe shriftn*, Ber Mark, the notable Jewish Polish historian, situates Berger within the long-established tradition in Yiddish publishing, of translating, popularizing, and discussing world literature, thus widening the horizons of its Yiddish-speaking audience. He bemoans the fact that in the postwar period Yiddish publishing houses were not undertaking translation and he welcomes Berger's focus on world (largely European) and Polish literature. He applauds her interest in new forms of writing that depart from worn-out literary topoi. She convincingly demonstrates, he notes, that the new voices and ideas of a young, idealistic generation need to be known and shared.[4]

---

4 Boris Pik, "In gang fun tsayt-eseyen fun Lili Berger," *Di Presse*, 1976. (About Lili Berger's book *Eseyen un skitsn* [1962].)

Introduction xxiii

This notion of an important relationship between the Jewish literary world and the larger world recurs in a review of *In gang fun tsayt* (In the Course of Time, 1976), another collection of essays. Boris Pik, a Yiddish editor in Buenos Aires, alludes to the fact that Jews were never cut off from the literature of other peoples, particularly in places with a significant Jewish population. He situates Berger's work within the context of a culture where translation and exposure to international art and literature are expected. Her subjects are as various as French Impressionism, Marc Chagall, Pablo Picasso, Michel Tournier, Curzio Malaparte, and Franz Kafka. Berger's non-fiction deals with specifics of Jewish history and also celebrates, evaluates, and contextualizes the creative work and lives of Jewish and non-Jewish artists. Her fiction is exclusively and solidly anchored in the Jewish moment and Jewish lives. At the heart of her stories, written during the postwar period, are the hidden Polish Jew, the Communist loyalist, the female resistance fighter, the survivor bereft of family - protagonists battling with indecision, resignation, and despair.

Critics praised the psychological insight of Berger's fiction and her sensitive depiction of the uprooting of a people and its culture. Yehudit Kalman, writing as a Parisian Jew in the *Naye prese* about Berger's 1967 novel *Nokhn mabl* (After the Flood),[5] claims that she stands apart from writers who try to shock their readers with horror stories or others who themselves seem broken by the weight of events; Berger approaches her subject with an attitude of responsibility and respect. Reviewers and critics frequently allude to her sense of artistic duty. The critic Akiva Fishbin refers to her as the "guardian of the walls of humanity."[6]

A review of *Opgerisene tsvaygn* (Severed branches), Berger's 1970 collection of stories about Jews struggling to re-establish their lives in Poland after the war, characterizes her as having a "visceral responsibility for all that is sacred to Jewish fate,"[7] and commends her as an *eyshes khayl* (woman of valour) who wants to awaken her people to the resurging antisemitism in postwar Poland. The reviewer contrasts her with those Polish Jewish writers who exoticize and sentimentalize the world of the shtetl, while Berger is distinguished as an "honest witness" of what she has heard and seen in the lives of Poland's Jews, past and present.[8]

---

5 Yehudit Kalman, "Nokhn Mabl' fun Lili Berger, *Naye Prese*, 16 December 1967, 4.
6 Akiva Fishbin, "Geshtaltn un pasirungen fun Lili Berger," *Letzte Nayes*, n.d.
7 L. Bernard, "Ale doyres oyfgelebt mitamol" [source, date not given].
8 Ibid.

xxiv Introduction

Berger's writings belong among the achievements of living witnesses, writes Leyzer Domankevitsh, although he believes the essence of the Holocaust can only be brought to light by researchers, historians, and visual artists. He is not convinced that Berger's stories belong to the *"Belles Lettres-ization"* of the catastrophe, but he does accord her a place at the "ante-chamber" of an artistic salon. He describes the short stories in *Fun haynt un nekhtn* (Present and past) as well-crafted depictions incorporating lived experience and aesthetic sensibility; he values her fictionalized portraits that evoke post-Holocaust conditions and allow a glimpse into the hellish reality of the recent past. Reviewing the same collection, Yekhezkel Kornhendler, a writer and chronicler of Jewish history in Paris, describes Berger as an interesting essayist and as a fine storyteller whose work stands as an important contribution to Jewish history and historiography.[9]

Berger is unable "to escape the trauma of her generation," writes Yosef Friedlander in his review of *In loyf fun tsayt*. He describes Berger as an author whose every story, to a degree, is touched by the poison of "Planet Auschwitz." In her literary role he compares her to a doctor, a skilled specialist, who knows her patients and transmutes their tragic memories into stories that foreground inner conflict and troubled relationships.[10]

Another reviewer, Liber Brenner, writing about *In gang fun tsayt*, describes Berger's work as *refue*, a healing, and accords her an esteemed place among writers of Yiddish literature. He notes, in passing, that few women writers of prose or poetry are represented in Yiddish writing, fewer still as essayists and translators. He admires the narrative skills Berger brings to her profiles and is amazed to find that her research adds new and interesting perspectives even to well-documented subjects such as Janusz Korczak.[11]

Berger's intellectual breadth and erudition is noted in Shimon Kantz's review of *Fun vayt un noent*. She is praised for her realism and the natural fluidity of her language.[12] "A pure literary Yiddish" is how another reviewer describes her writing.[13] Another describes her work as a synthesis of Yiddish folksiness, worldliness, and a deep belief in the value of human life.[14]

---

9 Yekhezkl Kornhendler, "Opgerisene tsvaygn (dertseylungen fun Lili Berger, dershinen in Pariz; hile un ilustratsies fun Benn)" [no source given], 21 July 1971.

10 Yosef Friedlander, *"Lili Bergers tsaytlekhe dertseylungen," Yisroel Shtime*, July 1989.

11 Liber Brener, review of *In gang fun tsayt*, by Lili Berger, *Lebns Fragen*, 1 January 1977.

12 Shimon Kantz, review of *Fun vayt un noent*, by Lili Berger, *Yisroel Shtime*, 9 June 1976.

13 Dr. S. Levenberg, *"In gang fun tsayt: A grus fun Lili Berger," Unzer vort*, 28 August 1976, 2.

14 Chava Slutska Kestin *"Lili Berger," Fray yisroel*, 26 August 1965, 4.

Introduction xxv

According to literary critic and writer Efraim Roytman, Lili Berger is an "enthusiast of the intellect, of reflection, and transparency,"[15] qualities enhanced by her capacity to embrace more than one language and one theme. Her vision and expression are characterized by simplicity, but they are never prosaic or provincial.

Ultimately, Lili Berger writes as a Jewish woman defined by her roots and her historic moment and in conversation with others across time and culture, and with whom she shares deeply felt human values. She writes as a teacher, as a witness, as a journalist, and as an activist. In 1968, deracinated from a Poland that no longer tolerated a Jewish presence, she returned to Paris, a stateless person. There she continued to write in Yiddish until the end of her life for a diminished audience that would participate with her in a world of *Yidishkayt* that lived primarily on the printed page.

Introduction by Frieda Johles Forman
with Judy Nisenholt

---

15 Efraim Roytman, "Mekoyekh 'In gang fun tsayt,'" *Yisroel Shtime*, November 1976.

JEWISH LIFE IN POLAND

We Polish Jews[1]

It has now been over twenty-five years since the greatest contemporary Polish poet, the Jew Julian Tuwim,[2] poured out his great sorrow and pain over the slaughter of Polish Jewry. He wrote under the above title in words that were on fire. It was in 1944, on the first anniversary of the Warsaw Ghetto Uprising. A refugee in America, the poet who had escaped from the massacre sent from afar his passionate call to the suffering Polish Jews with a plea that "the rank of 'Jew Doloris Causa' should be granted to the Polish poet by the nation that had produced him."[3]

Jews gave Poland more than one great poet. Today, as we read again after 25 years Tuwim's shattering cry that he is connected with us not by "the blood that flows in us, but by the blood that flows out of us, ... the blood that is no longer within the arteries, but which has been spilled,"[4] it calls to mind even more forcefully the historic panorama of the Polish Jew.

The past quarter century has left us with new experiences. Today, while the last remnants of the Jewish population, the *sheyres ha-pleyte*,[5] are being driven out [of Poland], would it not be even more appropriate than ever to clarify why "us" and to ask who "we" are? Because once again we are all alike on Polish soil: Polish Jews and "Poles of Jewish origin," Zionists and Jewish Communists, Yiddish speakers and those

---

1 Written in Paris, 1969.
2 Julian Tuwim (1894–1953) was a poet, satirist, translator, and editor from an assimilated family. He was one of Poland's most popular poets of the interwar years and spent the war years in exile in the United States.
3 The full text of Tuwim's manifesto "We Polish Jews" can be found in Polish and English in the book *We Polish Jews* (Jerusalem: Magnes Press, 1984).
4 Ibid.
5 *Sheyres ha-pleyte* שארית הפליטה refers to the Jews who survived the Holocaust.

4   Jewish Life in Poland

who think in Yiddish, and the generations of those estranged from Yiddishkayt, sometimes even a Jew doloris causa like Julian Tuwim – we are all now again, in the land of Po-lin,[6] considered Jews first. And no amount of apportioning shame by artificial categories will mask the disgraceful practice of the present-day government of Poland, which has stuck the label of Zionist on the handful of surviving Polish Jews in the same way they affixed the *mogn dovid* on our clothes just over a quarter century ago. And just as in those times, when we were stamped with the ancient marking of Zion, in order to put us outside the law so as to be able to annihilate us, now the added label of Zionist is used to demonstrate our detrimental character and make of us a modern-day scapegoat.

So, who are we and how many are we, the "Zionists" in Poland?

We are Polish Jews. We are many – who knows how many tens of millions? We are hundreds and hundreds of bygone generations, who with their toil and sweat, the exertions of their bodies and minds, built up the country, helped to accumulate property, and to enrich and to enhance the once backward land. We built homes and factories, huts and workshops, as well as theatres and philharmonic orchestras and other temples to culture. With all our might we put our share into spiritual and intellectual capital.

We, Polish Jews, we are the shadows of long generations of Jewish working people: farmers, trades people, merchants and entrepreneurs, rabbis and religious scholars, among whom are famous doctors, mathematicians, glorious writers, philosophers, and many kinds of scientists. Our bones are spread across the whole of Polish ground, from east to west, from south to north. We are the breath of great spirits, from a great many creators and from countless martyrs and warrior heroes. We are knots of suffering and pain. We are more than three million annihilated and a handful of survivors from Hitler's ovens, now tormented, pursued, robbed, and driven away.

We, Polish Jews, have written our long history on Polish soil with our heart's blood and have not yet recorded all of it. We have an old, old history and an old, old lineage. Our history on Polish soil is older than the history of the Polish Catholic people and of the Polish nationhood. Jewish migrants set up their tents on Polish soil back in the year 800. They had come from distant Babylon, Byzantium, and from Khazaria.

---

6 *YIVO*, s.v. "Relations between Jews and Non-Jews: Historical Overview," accessed July 23, 2021. Poland being referred to as פּוֹה־לין/*Po-lin* from the Hebrew is a "false etymology" maintained in Jewish folklore which Berger alludes to in her essay.

In the later centuries they came streaming in from western and eastern European lands, bringing with them knowledge, skills, capital, and a mix of cultures. The Polish princes and later the kings gladly took them in because they needed their hands and their minds; they needed their capital, their experience, and their initiative. With their knowledge acquired in more developed civilizations, they helped to till and to fertilize the rough earth of the Polish plains, to build cities, towns, and villages and to connect the unfamiliar land to the wider world.

A legend is told: a wandering Jew, having escaped from the massacres at the time of the first crusade landed somewhere on Polish soil, and being tired, fell asleep. In his dream he heard a voice from the heavens: Po-lin! Here you shall stay the night!

Even back then when our grandfathers began to spend the nights and the days there, they would come upon scattered Jewish settlements each with its own individual Jewish culture. Gradually, the two cultures, the one brought from the east and the other of the western European lands, amalgamated and simultaneously enriched the culture of the new land, and built their own national and spiritual life. And as historical sources tell it, the Polish Jews back then were not hunched and fearful. On the contrary, they were occupied in managing the land; they rode horses, knew how to handle weapons, and knew how to defend the soil and their rights when it was necessary.

We, Polish Jews, in those days of old, brought to Poland an advanced skill in keeping orchards and gardening. We were the first to build silk-weaving workshops, to introduce furriers and glass-making. Jewish trade paved the way for manufacturing and played a pioneering role in the development of Polish cities.

The Jewish migrants brought with them new forms of exchange and helped to transform the barter economy into an economy based on merchandise and currency. Jewish merchants helped to create commercial ties with other lands. The first news of Poland reached the Western world through the Spanish Jew Avraham Ben Yaacov, a diplomat of the Cordoba Caliphate who was versed in languages. During a trip to the German lands in the year 966 he first came to have intelligence about the land on the other side of the Oder River.

We, Polish Jews, are co-builders and co-creators of all the wealth of the land – both material and intellectual. We are the great wood carvers and graphic artists, the printers and bookbinders, inventors and entrepreneurs. The first book from the printing press of the Radziwills was illustrated by the Polish Jew Lejb Lejbowicz: dozens of his portraits of nobility decorated their palaces. A painter by the name of Shmuel painted the portrait of King Jan the Third. The miniaturist Chaim

6   Jewish Life in Poland

Ben Isaac Segal introduced the art of the miniature. The forerunner of Jan Matejko, and the pioneer of Polish historic painting, was the Jew Aleksander Lesser. It was also he who began to research documents on the earlier Polish artistic creation and laid the foundations for Polish art history. As well, he immortalized in painting Poland's martyrdom and its patriotic resistance against tsarist tyranny. His father and his grandfather, the Lessers, brought Poland into the world markets in the eighteenth and nineteenth centuries. Jewish antiquarians distinguished themselves by finding, rescuing, and popularizing rare books of Polish writing. Under their influence, Polish antiquarians then began to collect Judaic antiquities. The mathematician Avraham Shtern, that Jew with the patriarchal beard and a yarmulke on his head, was the first to invent the calculating machine and acquired a reputation in the Warsaw Scientific Society for his knowledge. The Jew Aleksander Sochaczewski, the painter and fighter, went to Siberia in chains as a Polish resistance fighter and rebel. There, "In the Snowy Desert," as one of his canvasses is called, he immortalized the suffering of the Polish soldier in dozens and dozens of oil paintings that were gathered into the temple of Polish national art.

We, Polish Jews, have a great share in all the intellectual and cultural wealth of Po-lin. We gave the country such masters as Maurycy Gottleib, Buchbinder, Pilichowski, Weinles, Markowicz, Wachtel, Nadelman, Glicenstein, Kuna, Abraham Ostrzega, and hundreds of other famous and lesser-known artists.

We, Polish Jews, gave Polish literature Klaczko and Lange, Kraushar, and Feldman, Leśmian and many others. The literary field has been tilled and seeded by constellations of Polish writers, critics of literature, and art of "Jewish origin"; on account of this they would today be stamped with the label *Zionist*. The most outstanding of the prewar historians was the Jew Szymon Ashkenazy. Ludwig Zamenhof, the virtuoso brothers Wieniawski, Arthur Rubinstein, Leopold Infeld, and many other scholars and artists brought fame to the land of their birth.

We, Polish Jews, have a long dual lineage. We have our own intimate, specifically national spiritual treasures; it was here on Polish soil that our Polish-Jewish national nature was forged. Here, in Po-lin over the course of our long glorious and martyred history we have amassed an enormous cultural and material fortune, great cultural works that drew their inspiration from both our biblical prophets and from the Vilna Goan, from the Baal Shem Tov down to Nachman Krochmal and I.L. Peretz. Polish Jewry has produced generations of authors in both national languages and they are part of the pantheon of universal values. It is here on Polish soil that our modern Yiddish language

We Polish Jews   7

crystallized and developed. Great Polish writers have sampled it and have kneaded some of its essence, like raisins, here and there into their work. This is the extent to which both literatures and cultures have influenced one another.

We, Polish Jews, have been on all the killing fields, wherever it was necessary to defend the land. In the destroyed old cemetery in the Praga district of Warsaw there were still sunken graves with the old head-stones of Jewish rebels of the past century. In the cemetery[7] on Gęsia Street stand headstones with still legible inscriptions: "Fallen for the glory of the fatherland." Thousands of our sons and daughters gave their young lives just like Hirsh Lekert and Naftali Botvin so that life on Polish soil would be better and more beautiful.

We, Polish Jews, tortured in the ghettos and in the camps, confined behind the ghetto walls, were the first on Polish soil to stage an armed uprising, attacking Nazi tanks with grenades and old rifles. The Polish flag waved alongside the blue and white over the resisting Warsaw Ghetto. Then too we struggled "for our freedom and yours." Today people try to forget that the commander of the uprising, Mordekhai Anielewicz, was a Zionist.

We, Polish Jews, Zionists, Communists, Socialists, Bundists, religious and atheists, generations of the abased and persecuted, condemned to death in Hitler's genocide, we all played a great part in freeing Polish soil from its former enemies and from the Nazi plague, just as we have a share in the richness of the land that we have helped to build for over a thousand years.

In Polish cities and towns stand Jewish homes, hospitals, orphanages, old people's homes, and an assortment of buildings and institutions, built with Jewish toil, with Jewish – or according to the new terminology – with "Zionist" money from abroad. On all of these there is no stamp saying "Zionist," while we, the few survivors, inheritors of glorious Polish Jewry are all marked as "Zionists" – a synonym for "damned Jew" so as to deny us all basic human rights, to rob us and chase us out of the land where we worked and were creative for over a thousand years.

We, Polish Jews, we the small handful of hunted and afflicted, wandering blindly in all directions, and we, the shadows of long generations, we the dispersed, scattered bones and the ash of Auschwitz, Treblinka, Majdanek, Sobibor, Chelmno, we the mass graves spread over the whole of Polish soil – we call you, today's rulers of Poland, we call you to judgment for defamation, for slander, for humiliation, for the

---

7 Warsaw's largest Jewish cemetery.

8 Jewish Life in Poland

past injustice to the few survivors and on behalf of the memory of the ones who perished.

We, Polish Jews, we are legions of accusers. Among us are Berek Joselewicz with his heroic Jewish regiment, Abraham Shtern and his inventions, Janusz Korczak and his children, the famed resisters in the ghettos and the camps, the Zionist and martyr Ringelblum, and the Communists Levartovski and Szmidt. And along with us as accusers, others step forward: Tadeusz Kościusko, who called his "brother Israelites" to battle against the common enemy, and Adam Mickiewicz with his character Jankiel Cymbalist, and Gomulicki with a new "El Maleh Rachamim,"[8] and Maria Konopnicką with her Mendel Gdanski,[9] and Eliza Orzeszkowa, leading Meir Ezofowicz with one hand and Eli Makower with the other.[10] And we hear her cry anew to the Polish poets, just as in 1881, at a time when tsarist Russia's pogroms burst out in Warsaw, she then called to Konopnicką: "Take your lyre in your hand and pluck the strings of human love and harmony ..." By our side stands the great Polish poet Władisław Broniewski, who in his poem "To Polish Jews" expressed the belief that "the spilled blood makes us brothers." With these shadows, we have on our side the finest spirits of the Polish people.

We, Polish Jews, we rivers of blood and tears ... we mountains of ash and scattered bones, and we, miraculously still alive, orphaned, our wounds still fresh, once again humiliated and robbed of our human rights – we all plead not for charity and not for pity. We demand justice: Give us back our rights! Give us back what we deserve for our labours! Return to the Jewish people the legacy that this gutted Polish Jewry have left behind.

Translated by Judy Nisenholt
In gang fun tsayt, Paris 1976

---

8 The poem bearing a Hebrew title describes the wedding of a Jewish orphan girl during which the prayer for the dead is chanted.

9 In her story "Mendel Gdański," Konopnicką (1840–1910) takes a stand against the rise of antisemitism. https://culture.pl/pl/tworca/maria-konopnicka, accessed 4 July 2021.

10 Eliza Orzeszkowa (1841–1910), Polish writer, sometimes publisher and social activist, twice nominated for the Nobel prize. Her novel *Meir Ezofowicz* (1878) portrays a Jewish community in conflict over religious orthodoxy and depicts the pull towards a more open society. Translated into English as *An Obscure Apostle*, it is available via Project Gutenberg and in Yiddish translation via the Yiddish Book Center's Spielberg Digital Yiddish library. *Eli Makower* (1875) deals with relations between Jews and the Polish nobility. https://culture.pl/pl/tworca/eliza-orzeszkowa, accessed 4 July 2021; https://www.encyclopedia.com/religion/encyclopedias-almanacs-transcripts-and-maps/orzeszkowa-orzeszko-elizadeg, accessed 5 July 2021.

Naftole Herts Kon: The Tragic Enthusiasm

(On the first anniversary of the death of Naftole Herts Kon)[1]

It was the end of April 1971. Sitting in the car which had taken me from Tel Aviv to Jerusalem, I began to have some misgivings about having gone directly to the Western Wall, where Naftole Herts Kon was supposed to be waiting for me. I would be more than an hour late. Arriving and not finding him at the agreed-upon place, I was ready to get back into the car. Suddenly I spotted him in the distance.

After reprimanding me, he expressed his surprise that I had been able to recognize him from so far away. In fact, I had identified him from his nervous gait, and his head turned skyward. Knowing very well that here, too, his life was not easy and that neither his tired mind nor his tattered spirit had found peace, I was pleasantly surprised because I had never seen him looking so well. In his usual hurried manner, he began telling me about his literary work, his future plans, and his worries. However, when he showed me the marvels of Jerusalem, his face beamed.

"Look, take a good look! Have you ever before seen such splendour, such enchantment? Have you ever seen hills enveloped in such a mysterious, silver mist?" He did not forget to show me his collection of stones, of pebbles of various shapes and colours, of dried twigs and pieces of bark that looked as though they had been sculpted by human hands. "Nature is a great artist. No artist can compare with nature," he

---

1 Although Lili Berger used the name Cohen instead of Kon, I have used the spelling chosen by Kon's daughter, Ina Lancman, who, having devoted many years to the preservation of her father's literary legacy, in 2017 published a new edition of his book *Farshribn in zikorn* in Tel Aviv, together with Vita Serf and the assistance of the National Authority for Yiddish culture in Israel. This edition was digitized by the Yiddish Book Center in July 2018.

10   Jewish Life in Poland

assured me enthusiastically. We both regretted that our time together was so short, and that he could not show me all the beauties of Jerusalem. Jumping from one subject to the next, he told me that on my next visit, I should reserve more time for Jerusalem.

Six weeks later I received the news that Naftole Herts Kon was no more. His death, as the family later informed me, had happened as suddenly as had each of the other misfortunes that had accompanied him throughout his life. "In death," they later told me, "his face had an expression of deliverance."

It was my fate to witness first-hand one period in Naftole's life of martyrdom, and to live through it with him and his family. Those were his years in Poland, when he returned from Soviet Russia. I had not known him prior to that time, although the Polish security police "knew" that I had known him from way back. Over the course of my interrogation after his arrest, I was barraged with questions for eleven hours straight, including some about his "sin" of long ago.[2]

We met in the fall of 1959. It was the end of the second repatriation,[3] during which several Jewish intellectuals, after being liberated from camps – or simply belatedly – had returned to Poland from the Soviet Union. To me, Naftole Herts Kon seemed different than the rest because of his openness about his self-imposed mission to recount what had happened, and his ardent enthusiasm. After learning about all the seven levels of hell that he had endured, which had damaged his health and frayed his nerves, I was astonished at the way he was able to throw himself with such passion into his literary, journalistic, and community work. It was also astounding how someone who had suffered so much had found such courage, determination, and faith in his own strengths.

Naftole told me that after the war he had slept on a bunk with a knife concealed on his chest because on that same camp bunk was a Nazi prisoner who did not hide his savage hatred of Jews. Aware that his neighbour was a Jew, this Nazi would torment him with descriptions of how Jews had been murdered. Naftole was convinced that one night

---

2 Berger fictionalized her interrogation by Polish investigators in a story called *Oyf der oysforshung*, which appears in her collection *Fun vayt un noent* (*Du Lointain et du Proche*) (Paris, 1978).

3 This occurred between 1955 and 1959.

Naftole Herts Kon: The Tragic Enthusiasm   11

this bloodthirsty animal would grab him by the throat and strangle him. He kept his knife for self-defence.

More often than not, his nights were sleepless. During those nights he also found within himself the strength to describe in verse the depths of human pain, and etched these verses into his memory because ...

> There is no power
> that can overcome
> the fortress
> of my brain –
> no power!

Once, during a visit to my home in Warsaw shortly after we had become acquainted, Naftole confided to me that he was ready to publish a collection of his poetry, most of which had been composed in the camps. I already knew that in the Soviet camps it was impossible to write, especially poetry. As he explained to me how he had "recorded" his poems in his memory, he began reciting a poem which is now in his book. I am reproducing a few verses here:

> Though every bite was precious
> I would have given away
> two-thirds of my bread
> for a piece of paper
> and the stump of a pencil ...

And later:

> Had I possessed
> pencil and paper
> the guards at the gates
> would have noticed
> and taken them away
> and added another accusation
> to my misdeeds
> and to my hands and feet,
> another chain –another chain ...

I sat distraught as I listened to other similar poems which he recited off by heart.

"Do you really think this will be published here?" I asked him. My question did not upset him. He would only include part of his camp

12 Jewish Life in Poland

poems in the book, interspersed with others. I asked him to recite the poem about Russia again. Without having to be asked twice, he declaimed with more even emotion and anguish (I'm quoting here from his book):

O Russia! O October!
Your light drew me from far, far away.
Its brightness lit my eyes,
I fled far, far away,
And fell before you on my knees.
I surrendered my entire self to you.
Like a butterfly drawn to the sun
I fluttered and glided towards you,
and I thought: on your earth I am born anew ...
Though on my own face
I could feel both the fire and the light,
and though I was choking on the smoke,
I was still enraptured.

It was not easy to discuss Poland with those who returned from Russia. They were "still enraptured," some with being able to move about freely and receive a place to live with a kitchen of one's own, some with the existence of public Jewish institutions, and some with both. Apart from that, the "Polish October"[4] had reverberated in the Soviet republics like a bell of freedom. As the saying went, "Poland is the most pleasant barrack in the whole camp."

In the case of Naftole Herts Kon, it was clear that he had just begun to live for the first time. For thirty years he had been a nomad, and the more he roamed, the more he strayed into the circles of hell. Born in Bukovina, he arrived in Poland at the age of eighteen in 1928. According to his family, he had come with the intention of working with YIVO. During his four-year stay on Polish soil, his life had not been easy. The

---

4 Stalin's death in 1953 and Nikita Khrushchev's famous speech in February 1956 denouncing Stalin's "cult of personality" led to a series of events in Poland that culminated in October of that year in the Polish October, or Polish Thaw, when Władysław Gomułka was confirmed as leader of the Polish Communist Party and for a brief time brought liberalizing changes in Poland. See Antony Polonsky and Leszek W. Gluchowski, Leszek, "1968, Forty Years After," in *Polin: Studies in Polish Jewry*, Littman Library of Jewish Civilization, vol. 21 (Oxford: Oxford University Press, 2008).

Naftole Herts Kon: The Tragic Enthusiasm   13

entire time he was there illegally. He was finally arrested and given a taste of Polish prisons. Afterwards, like a moth to the light, he fled to a "free land" to spread his youthful wings. In 1932 he succeeded in crossing the eastern border. He had barely begun to fly when his wings were clipped. He was arrested for the first time in 1937, and in 1948 for the second. Thus began the great "demonic game," as he calls it in one of his poems. In another poem he sings in anguish:

Sun!
I cannot look you
In the face.
Leaving this place –
Strictly forbidden.
My best friends
my worst enemies
kneaded together
as one.
My shadow
Hangs and writhes
on barbed
wire.

Kon was behind barbed wire until 1956. Only those closest to him knew the truth about the condition in which he returned from that "hellish place." In 1959, after three years of "being free," he arrived in Poland.

Should we be surprised that after more than thirty years of being tossed on a raging sea that was about to swallow him up, after weathering all the storms, he thought he had finally reached a peaceful shore? Only a flicker remained of the flame of freedom which had ignited the "Polish October" in 1956, and this flicker had also begun to fade. It seems, however, that when one emerges from dense darkness, a flicker is also light.

Naftole Herts Kon summoned all his strength to pitch his tent on Polish soil. His natural zest for life, his renewed enthusiasm, helped him more than his physical strength. During a year and a half of working for the *Folksshtime*,[5] he had managed to write numerous articles and reports, to visit and become acquainted with various parts of a country which was not his birthplace, to immerse himself in Jewish life, to

---

5 Yiddish weekly newspaper in Communist Poland.

14 Jewish Life in Poland

compile a book of poems which that was soon to be printed, to travel to Romania to investigate the sad situation of the Jews there, to take notes, collect material, make contacts abroad, and make great plans.

I am reminded of two very different states of mind. Naftole came to visit Kraków when the Jewish Museum was opened in the famous Old Synagogue. Although he had already poured his enthusiasm into his reports, he was brimming with excitement and still felt the need to provide more specifics. But he had just returned from Romania shaken. With anguish and indignation, he described in detail Jewish life there, and probably not just to me. Nor did he refrain from making notes about his trip, like the notes he had begun to make about the places where he had "hung on barbed wire."

Now another memory is coming back to me. It was the spring of 1960. With a group of friends, I had gone for a Sunday walk in the forest in the Warsaw suburb of Bielany. Naftole and I walked on ahead. He talked, I listened, and finally I made up my mind and asked him, "Do you really think it's worth staying in Poland? Has it ever crossed your mind ...? Don't you see ...?"

"I have too many plans. I don't see why I can't realize them here."

He did not realize them. Soon afterward came his arrest. A new circle of hell opened for him. When, prior to his trial, I visited one of his two lawyers, the latter consoled me by saying, "The diagnosis is now less serious. Before it was cancer (he had been charged with espionage), now is it's only a cold." The cold, however, had after-effects, even once he was released from jail. In 1964, after many interventions, he finally got permission to leave the country.

It seems to me that the tragedy of his enthusiasm, his faith, lasted until the end of his stay in Poland. In an afterword to his poetry collection entitled *Farshribn in zikorn* (Inscribed in memory),[6] published in 1966 in Israel, Naftole revealed the hardships he suffered after his release. It was generous on his part to acknowledge that the Polish Writers' Union had given him material and moral support. In truth the relationship was not always like that. The support did not come spontaneously, and it was only from a certain segment of membership of the Writers' Union.

I mention this not just for the sake of truth, but because of subsequent developments, when the Writers' Union proved to be much less magnanimous than it had appeared to Naftole Herts Kon. Not only did the leadership of the Polish Writers' Union fail to say a word during the

---

6 *Farshribn in zikorn* (Tel Aviv: Aliye, 1966).

great "bacchanal" of 1968 leading up to the expulsion of the Jews from Poland,[7] but other prominent writers remained silent as well.

In this connection, I shall limit myself to two incidents. The first took place in February 1968, during the famous meeting of the Polish Writers in response to the closing down of Mickiewicz's play *Dziady*. When someone from the podium mentioned the antisemitism being incited at the time, the writer Jerzy Putrament, the General Secretary of the Writers Union, thundered from the podium: "The party is fighting antisemitism!"

It was left to my humble self to intervene with that same Putrament on behalf of Naftole Herts Kon while the latter was in jail. We met, just the two of us, I, a member of the Writers' Union, an outsider, and Putrament a well-known personality. The intervention was done secretly. I reviewed with him the entire human tragedy of the Jewish writer who had suffered so much, an innocent man incarcerated for so many years in a camp. I touched upon every aspect to show that his arrest was incomprehensible. I described his physical condition, his psychological state, and underlined that it was not acceptable to allow him to be locked up again.

Putrament, who had the whole union in his pocket, listened and answered as though it were completely natural, that the arrest was surely because of "a Jewish matter." It appeared that he did not take this "Jewish matter" very much to heart, although under persistent pressure he did send a short letter about it to a party higher-up. He refused to intervene with Gomułka. Another Polish writer did not even appear at a scheduled appointment, although more out of cowardice than ill will.

A second incident. Before I left Poland, in the summer of 1968, a few courageous Polish writers interceded on my behalf to enable me to take my manuscripts. A Polish writer, a woman, appealed to the President of the Polish Writers' Union, the famous elderly writer Jarosław Iwaszkiewicz, to use his influence to help me take out of the country with me my manuscripts, my notes, and my two typewriters, a Yiddish one and a Polish one. At the time it was forbidden to take even one typewriter. Iwaszkiewicz was not very concerned about the whole matter, but only asked, surprised: "Why are you leaving? This will blow over." However, that same Iwaszkiewicz did not utter one word of protest against the "bacchanal."

---

7 The great "bacchanal" refers to the antisemitic campaign instigated in 1968 by the Polish Ministry of the Interior, which forced most of the Jews remaining in Poland to leave the country, including Lili Berger.

16   Jewish Life in Poland

During the many interventions on behalf of Kon in 1960, the author of these lines, with the agreement of the arrested man and his signature, had sent a long letter to Iwaszkiewicz. The story about the letter is tragicomic. Kon was taken from the jail to a psychiatric hospital. This was an achievement. His conditions improved, and he considered himself a free man. The director of the hospital was sympathetic and friendly to him, especially in allowing family to visit him without supervision and without restrictions. In these new conditions, Naftole wrote Iwaszkiewicz a thirty-page letter and gave it to someone who had visited him to deliver to me so I could translate it into Polish and send it to him. Had that manuscript – heaven forbid – not reached me, it would have been a windfall for the security police and another piece of evidence for the indictment. Had the translated letter reached Jarosław Iwaszkiewicz, who was known as a coward, nothing good would have come of it, not to mention the fact that he would have felt insulted. After consulting with Kon's family, we destroyed the letter. Instead, I wrote another letter. The "secret mail service," *di heymishe post*, delivered it to the patient in hospital. The patient liked it and signed it. Now a new challenge presented itself: how to deliver the letter directly to the president of the Writers Union. I learned that it did in fact reach him, but, according to my sources, Iwaszkiewicz, had shown little interest in the whole matter. Who knows whether he "liquidated" this letter, the way we had destroyed the Yiddish original.

Thus, we kept going around in circles.

The material support and the good relations with the Polish Writers Union came only after Kon's release. When he had needed money for lawyers, he could not count on any support from official sources. What is more, the people who took up the cause of the imprisoned writer found themselves increasingly isolated.

The extent to which Naftole Herts Kon was by nature both naïve and enthusiastic, always seeing the best in people, is also evidenced by how highly he valued the support of the Polish Writers Union. This is a fine quality, but also the tragedy of misplaced enthusiasm.

Also tragic is the fact that when he finally reached the land he had longed for, where he desired with all his being to participate in the Jewish rebirth, and where, despite all difficulties, he had enthusiastically prepared a comprehensive work, believing that he would be recompensed for all his suffering, a dark night suddenly descended upon him. Death came to him in an hour of great despair.

Translated by Vivian Felsen
In gang fun tsayt (Au fils des années), Paris 1976

Notes and Reflections on the Fate of the Written Word

This article was written at the start of the summer of 1963, after I had been given particulars about the fate of Jewish books, libraries, and archives in Soviet Russia. It was not possible then to write about it openly. I made an attempt to weave it into a historical overview, to "smuggle" it into a collection of writings about the persecution of books. But even that could not be printed. Finally, I "smuggled" it to Paris with the aim of having it published under a pseudonym. However, the manuscript got buried somewhere. The one remaining copy that was in my possession I destroyed before leaving Poland.

The work being sent out has gone through a lot of peregrinations. It turned up only a few months ago. After six years, it still seems to retain its timeliness, especially when the break with Poland occurred, which obliged me to extend the earlier work. Aside from the short added section at the end about Poland, no modifications were introduced into the text. Even the title remains the same [...]

… Someone has said the fate of books and writing is similar to the fate of people. There have been no catastrophes – no natural and historic cataclysms, no upheavals and persecutions in which the written word, the book, has not suffered precisely as much as mankind. One could write gripping novels about the fate of books, of writings, and of whole libraries, just as one could of humanity, its convulsions and its struggles to hold onto life by the narrowest of margins.

In his great historic and biographical novel about Goya, Lion Feuchtwanger describes an inquisitorial tribunal of four heretics. The tribunal takes place in the church of Domingo el Real in Madrid.

18   Jewish Life in Poland

Among the defendants is a woman; in the yellow prisoner's garb and in the long conical cap of the disgraced, she hardly looks any different from the other accused. The defendant, Constancia Rodriguez, is the proprietor of a book business and the agents of the "holy inquisition" discover seventeen forbidden books in her keeping. Three were hidden behind false title pages under innocuous titles. Feuchtwanger doesn't tell us what happens to the forbidden books. He knew that the reader would easily understand.

This was in the 1790s. The great French revolution had already begun to cast its light across Europe. Following her former Golden Age of science and free thought, Spain had sunk into medieval obscurantism and was caught in the evil grip of the Inquisition. Here the persecution of the written and the printed word was more extensive and more brutal than in other European countries and the transgressing writers often perished with their works.

With great religiosity and holy passion, books and assorted writings were judged and condemned and, on grounds of the least suspicion, were destroyed everywhere that the medieval church had extended its unbounded might. It is sufficient to remember that much that the great Italian philosopher Giordano Bruno had written was destroyed either before or after he himself was burned at the stake in 1600 in Rome. If one were to calculate the losses that various despotic autocrats, driven by a medieval insanity, perpetrated in the name of spiritual and cultural values, one would arrive at a gruesome portrait of intellectual and spiritual mass graves.

There are enough accounts, documents, descriptions, and sometimes intimations of how the word was persecuted, and how books were destroyed in various horrible ways. To have a notion of this, one has only to linger on the lost intellectual works of ancient Greece from which European culture drew in great measure. Not all the works of the ancient poets, writers, thinkers, and philosophers were passed on to later generations. The truth is, that such treasures went missing during wars and natural catastrophes, immigrations, and upheavals. In those times there were few copies of a work. It is known, however, that in antiquity, there were famous collections and compilations that contained the creative work of many hundreds of years. Such collections were in Rome, in Alexandria, and in other places. Little remains of them.

More damage, however, has been done through religious or political fanaticism than through war, natural disaster, or upheaval. Under

Notes and Reflections on the Fate of the Written Word   19

the reign of fanaticism and obscurantism the fruits of the human spirit are dishonoured and disgraced. Over the course of hundreds of years, libraries rotted in the cellars of cloisters, in dark rooms of monasteries and cathedrals, or even in holes somewhere. Precious writings lay about in the dust; no one knew how they got there or who brought them there. The mysteries that envelop the actions of each and every despotic power, whether religious or secular, and in particular the secret ways in which the Inquisition was used, have created a thick fog of forgetfulness around such deeds.

At the start of the European Renaissance, and especially at the time of the early Italian Renaissance, the great humanists of the time began to search out lost intellectual treasures. Great Renaissance minds such as Petrarch, Boccaccio, and Bracciolini dedicated time and effort to find abandoned and forgotten collections, books, and archives. They would make their way inside cloisters and cathedrals, searching cellars, rummaging through disordered archives. They would travel around Europe, attracting ambassadors and assorted statesmen to their mission, and with their support, would infiltrate wherever necessary to save mouldering, moisture-damaged volumes from destruction. Experienced copyists would then recopy them. Thanks to them, the works of Tacitus, Cicero, and many other masters of the written word were saved.

Boccaccio became aware that there was a great old library hidden away in Monte Cassino. He made his way there like a starved man in search of food. When he arrived he asked the first monk he met to lead him to the library and unlock the door for him.

"Go on your own. You'll find it without an escort; the door is open," the holy brother told him without civility. Boccaccio quickened his step happily and was pleased that soon he would be at the temple of human creativity where cruel time certainly had no dominion. But he was seized by a shudder when he entered the little house. The door and windows were torn off; it was open to the rain and the wind. Between four mouldering walls, in the middle of grass-covered earth, and under a thick layer of dust lay stacks of volumes, writings, manuscripts. Boccaccio began to pull volume after volume out from under the mould and the mud. He was greatly pained, however, when he saw that many pages had been ripped from the bound writings. The narrator tells us that when Boccaccio came out of the library, he cried like a child, and sobbed over the fate of man and of people whose intellectual creations had been turned into piles of refuse.

Boccaccio then sorrowfully made his way to a second monk and asked how it could happen that pages would be torn out, whole pieces

20   Jewish Life in Poland

of a book. The holy man answered that the pages were needed by the brothers to write prayers books for the peasants.

In those days the monks would often search for lost or hidden libraries. Paper was then a very dear and scarce commodity. They would tear out pieces of abandoned manuscripts, wash away the script with a special fluid, and use the washed paper for "holy" purposes.

This was not the only circumstance in which the written word was destroyed. To this day we don't know precisely how considerable portions of the intellectual inheritance of various nations and individuals were torn away, though literary historians and other researchers are engaged in this pursuit. Only in a few, well-established cases can one know how much has gone missing. So, for instance, we know that Sophocles wrote nearly a hundred dramatic pieces and only seven have come down to us. Aeschylus lost no less. Only a third of Euripides remains. Aristophanes was robbed of nine-tenths of his creative work. There are only a few fragments from the famous Greek poet Sappho, who would have written a great deal. There is hardly a memory or a name that remains of many creative minds.

Since the invention of the printing press, a book can survive the greatest persecution and catastrophes. And yet, there are numerous libraries, books, archives, and manuscripts – not to mention other creative work – that have been destroyed in our time. Is there any record that would show how many libraries, archives, and completed books that did not manage to see the light of day were annihilated in Eastern Europe at the time of Hitler's death march?

In all the darkest times, the harshest fate has always befallen us Jews. This is not the place to give even a superficial overview of the burned, destroyed, defiled holy books and various works, from the time of the decrees and expulsions from France, England, Germany, Spain, and Portugal, from the time of the Crusades and other persecutions. In the ghettos of Warsaw, Łódź, Białystock, and Vilnius the libraries perished along with the readers, the manuscripts along with the writers. Once there were Jewish libraries in all the Polish cities and towns. The tide of Nazism swept them away.

~

With the greatest of self-sacrifice, Jews have always rescued their intellectual and spiritual treasures. Fleeing the persecutions and fires of the Middle Ages, they saved first of all their Torahs, their holy books. We have long been a people of the book; the book, the art of the word, has always been our greatest intellectual asset, going back to ancient

Notes and Reflections on the Fate of the Written Word 21

times. Jews have rescued the art of the written word – the soul of its people – like a living body.

At the time of Hitler, in the ghettos and death camps, saving a manuscript, a page of writing, a drawing, was exactly like saving a soul. It is not blind chance that so many people standing on the verge of death created something singular in human history, such as the Ringelblum Archive. And how many similar collective and individual self-sacrificing challenges were undertaken?

Rescuing written and printed words has in all times meant rescuing the memory of a people. Because the word is continuity, it will not let itself be wiped away and forgotten, even after the greatest catastrophes. Perhaps no branch of human culture – especially among Jews – has such force to halt time in its diabolical course as the preserved, creative word. Every self-aware collective, every nation jealously guards its written pages, digs into the depths of the past, in order to find the merest traces of memory. A papyrus from ancient Egypt, wherever found, is considered to be a precious gem. If today we knew that libraries and archives were hidden away somewhere, lying about without supervision, or were in danger of being destroyed, imagine how many volunteers would be found to lend a hand! To the hidden and threatened Jewish intellectual inheritance, however, no saving hand is extended.

In the mountainous region behind the Ukrainian capital stood an old monastery – I don't know if it is still standing. The collected treasures of Jewish writing had for years been thrown in its dark and damp rooms or cellars.

So I was told. The silent witness, pretending not to see or know, informed me in greatest secrecy that valuable Jewish books and documents were rotting in the well-known catacombs of this same city.

I was also told that there were times when libraries, book collections, and archives – anything that you could label "Judaica" – were gathered together, far off in an empty field, or in an improvised barn building, and set on fire, the way you burn fallen, withered leaves in the autumn.

In Odessa they secretly – how else but in greatest secrecy? – threw books and religious texts into the basement of the city library: entire libraries, condemned, as one condemns people to a slow death in a prison cell. I don't know what happened to all these treasures, I searched but did not discover anything further about their fate.

For the past two years it has been Poland's turn. Despite the Nazis' diabolical talent for annihilation, Poland was left considerable Jewish

22 Jewish Life in Poland

intellectual wealth, most of it gathered together in the Jewish Institute in Warsaw. No, in Poland they don't set fires and they don't relegate Jewish holy books to dark cellars. But I myself have been witness to how the archives of the murdered Jewish communities were taken out of the Jewish Institute. To what end, if not once and for all, to erase all traces of the over-thousand-year history of Polish Jewry?

For long months excited specialists sat and searched, checked documents, and rummaged among the treasures of the Jewish Institute in Warsaw. To what purpose?

No, in today's Poland, where the last few remaining Jews are being hounded and robbed, they don't burn, and they don't toss Jewish books and archives into dark basements. However, the leaders of present-day Poland have carried out that which no other reactionary regime has dared to carry out – to make the land *Judenrein*. The flood of anti-Jewish writing, which smacks of medieval obscurantism, acts as a springboard to medieval practices to this end.

Who knows what will be done, under sundry "Socialistic" pretexts, to the salvaged intellectual inheritance left by Polish Jewry after living and creating on Polish soil for a thousand years?

Let us be on our watch and let us demand the return of the Jewish intellectual heritage to the Jewish people.

1969
Abridged and translated by Judy Nisenholt
In gang fun tsayt, Paris 1976

The Yiddish Folk Song in Polish Translation

> We are a nation that loves to sing
> We sing songs about ourselves
> Gather yourselves, sisters and brothers
> Help each other to understand.

We do not know when and where the anonymous folk singer, or folk poet, or perhaps troubadour, composed his song that is found in an old Jewish-Soviet folklore collection, and from which we bring you the above first stanza. But whenever or wherever he may have lived, he expressed in his simple verses a deep truth. Yes, we are a nation that writes poetry and is forever singing, under all conditions, even in the ghettos and in the death camps; not only poets but also plain folk, composed poetry and sang songs both old and new.

From early on, Jewish poetry, or even simple Jewish rhymes, were woven together with Jewish music and various melodies. Thus over many generations great treasures of folk songs from various locations and genres were assembled.

In general, we define a folk song as having been created anonymously. This definition is probably too narrow and can lead to error. The creative sphere is broad and varied and does not lend itself to being forced into a narrow framework of definitions.

Folk songs were composed by ordinary, often unsophisticated, people, as well as by professional writers, both famous and less famous. At times, the folk song of a well-known writer so tightly connected with the people, so deeply penetrated their soul, that the writer himself was forgotten. The song was widely sung, and forever pealed out from the mouths of the folk as though it was their own creation. This is what

24   Jewish Life in Poland

happened with M.M. Warshawsky's[1] "Oyfn Pripitchik," with Shneour's[2] "Margaritkelekh," and Reyzen's[3] "Tsum Hemerl."

It could also have happened that a folk song by a known writer, who polished and shaped his song until he made a diamond of it, alluded to another folk song by an anonymous writer that the people created, as we say. Because both, the proficient writer and the anonymous, unsophisticated writer, drew from the same source – from the folk, from its sufferings and joys, from its tribulations and its exaltations.

Themes of the Jewish folk song are unlimited and always pluck at the human and Jewish heart, starting with the lullaby which the Jewish mother spun with so much tender love in her heart, and with her sadness. Themes include love songs, and songs of poverty, dire need, prosperity, yearning, loneliness, dreams, rebellion, struggle and hope. These songs express a wide range of feelings, emotions, and reflections, delivered in diverse tonalities and colorations. The same can be said, even more so, of the national, religious, and Hasidic folk songs, with their rich and varied melodies. From such a prolific and diverse musical folklore other nations would have created more than one symphony, more than one opera.

How Jewish folk songs were born is another chapter. It is told, for example, that Reb Levi Yitzchak of Berdichev[4] melodies would be intermingled with traditional Hebrew songs; he would sing songs about our people, as in the above quoted verse by the anonymous poet. It was only later that musicians were found to transcribe them.

Mark Markovitch Warshavski, the modest, small-town attorney, also never sat down specifically to write a song. The songs sang themselves from within; in modern parlance we would say he improvised, sang out words, verses. It is only thanks to Sholem Aleichem, who was captivated by his "wandering" improvisations, that Warshavski's songs were collected, catalogued, and published.

---

1 Mark Warshawski (1848–1907). Yiddish songwriter. First collection: *Yidishe Folkslider mit Notn* (Yiddish folk songs with music notes), 1900. Most famously known for his song "Oyfn Pripitchik." *YIVO*, s.v. "Varshavski, Mark," accessed 15 September 2021.
2 Zalman Shneour (1886–1959). Hebrew and Yiddish poet and novelist. First collection of Hebrew poems published 1906. Among his Yiddish poems is the well-known song "Margaritkelekh." *YIVO*, s.v. "Shneour, Zalman," accessed 15 September 2021.
3 Avrom Reyzen (1876–1953). Writer, poet, editor. Contributed regularly to *Forverts, Tsukunft, Der Tog,* and *Frayhayt YIVO,* s.v. "Reyzen, Avrom," accessed 15 September 2021.
4 Reb Levi Yitzchak of Berdichev (ca 1740–1809). Rabbi, Hasidic leader, Jewish folk hero. *YIVO*, s.v. "Levi Yitshak of Barditshev," accessed 15 September 2021. Note: There are many spellings of this name.

The Carpenter from Kraków, Mordkhe Gebirtig,[5] that gifted folk poet, composed while at work in his carpentry shop. After committing the song to memory, he transcribed the lyrics to paper, and then began composing a complementary melody. He had never studied music, and as a friend of his told me, he had no idea of musical notation. However, along with the poetic words, streamed a wealth of melodies. The words and the music flowed together.

And under what conditions did we not write our songs! I would have to say that we are not yet aware of the vast number of our folk-song composers. Though we have many folk-song collections, we probably have not assembled all that exist. In the Library of the Warsaw Jewish Historical Institute,[6] there is a thick bound volume of notebooks, with the stamp of the former Jewish Library in Poland, in which appear almost two hundred folk songs, both popular and not well known, written in a fine handwriting. Reading these, I concluded that a folklorist, or perhaps just a lover of folk songs, had been preparing to assemble a large collection. The transcribed songs encompass many pages, but a large number of pages remained blank. Who knows what happened to that collector of folk songs?

For over a thousand years, Jews and Poles have been living under one roof, under the same sky, breathing the same air. For over a thousand years, while living among their non-Jewish neighbours, Jews created great literary works. What do the Poles, even the learned classes, the intelligentsia, know about our creative treasures? Little, very little has been translated, and it is doubtful if even this reaches the Polish reader. But the Jewish melody, which the Jew was always humming, at home, at work, probably did reach the ears of Polish neighbours. The Jewish tradesman – the tailor at his sewing machine or threading a needle, the shoemaker hammering was always humming, certainly religious melodies of the Sabbath and other holiday songs. What did the non-Jewish neighbour understand of the meaning of the words?

Jerzy Ficowski,[7] the Polish poet, strove to overcome this distance, and through the folk song to create a bridge to repair this estrangement. And I emphasize the word repair, because Ficowski had assembled

---

5 Mordkhe Gebirtig (1877–1942). Yiddish poet and songwriter. Some of his most well-known songs include *Reyzeleh, Kinderyorn, and Es Brent. YIVO*, s.v. "Gebirtig, Mordkhe," accessed 15 September 2021.
6 Created 1947 to spread knowledge about the heritage of the thousands of years of Jewish presence on Polish lands.
7 Jerzy Ficowski (1924–2006). Poet, fiction writer, essayist, and translator; the world's most renowned expert on Bruno Schulz.

26 Jewish Life in Poland

the anthology of Yiddish folk songs, translated them into Polish, and crowned the anthology with the name "Raisins and Almonds"[8] – his acknowledgment of a debt.

In addition to his poetic talent, the poet Ficowski became known for his books about Gypsies, many of whom lived in Poland. Among his achievements are *The Polish Gypsies*, the *Papusza Songs* folklore collection,[9] and, very soon to be published, a historic book about Gypsy life.

I used to think – and not only I – that this poet actually had Gypsy roots. "Some think of me as a Gypsy, others – as a Jew," he told me. As to the question why he devoted so much effort to the theme of Gypsies, he answered, "The occupation, the concentration camps – I saw how they were exterminated."

Ficowski described to me at great length how he became so involved with Jewish folk song. Before the war he lived in a shtetl, where he was brought up among Jewish children. Even as a youth he was captivated by Yiddish songs, by the melodies. He caught not only the sounds but also the words. The slaughter of Polish Jewry horrified him. After the war he wrote a moving song dedicated to the annihilated. In memory of the murdered he also composed an epistolary poem in honour of Chagall.

He undertook the anthology of the Yiddish folk song many years ago – not an easy undertaking. He had learned the Gypsy language from being among the Gypsies during the occupation, but Yiddish had stayed in his memory as an echo of Jewish street life. He still understood Yiddish, but could not read it, and needed to ask for help for an accurate translation, or for a transcription into Polish. The project stretched out over a long period; Ficowski told me that, based on the many letters he received and discussions he had concerning the anthology, there was enough material to publish another book. It is unfortunate that he did not have the needed resources, that is, assistants and advisers.

The anthology includes ninety-eight folk songs, divided into five parts (categories): love songs, satirical and humorous songs; and songs about conscription, about lifestyle and philosophy of life, about work and poverty.[10]

---

8 *Rodzynki z Migdałami*, published by Ossolineum in 1964.

9 The name given to songs written by Bronislawa Wajs. www.romarchive.eu/en/collection/p/bronislawa-wajs/, accessed 15 September 2021.

10 Jerzy Ficowski, *Rodzynki z migdałami: Antologia poezji ludowej Zydow polskich w przekadach* (Wrocław: Zaklad Narodowy im. Ossolinkich Wydawnictwo, 1988).

The Yiddish Folk Song in Polish Translation 27

It is clear that Ficowski approached his work with reverence and invested much creative energy. I will not be disclosing anything new when I say that if poetry is in general hard to translate – it is often quicker to rewrite a poem than to translate it – then folklore also belongs to that most difficult genre for the translator. And more difficult yet is Jewish folklore. Yiddish literary works are in general not among the easiest works to translate into another language.

Our poor neglected language is so rich that it is difficult to translate Mendele, Sholem Aleichem, and of course Peretz even into the most complex languages. The richness and depth of a language is measured not only by the abundance of its vocabulary but also by its spirit, the soul of the people who speak it, its vibrancy, and its unique inner life. Those who, with a wave of their hand, show such disdain and are so dismissive of our Yiddish language should carefully reconsider.

In short, it is not easy to translate the Yiddish folk song and folklore. And it seems to me that, even with the best translation, it's impossible never to lose a touch of elegance, a twist, a nuance; something is just lost in translation. Ficowski, however, was successful in maintaining the essence of the poetry, the Yiddish charm and appeal. He was successful in this regard – and it seems he was passionate to stay faithful to the original text, which, as already noted, is not easy in poetry. Most faithfully realized, it seems to me, are the lullabies. "Under the Child's Cradle Stands a Golden Lamb," "Sleep My Child," and similar songs sound like true musical poetry in Polish, truly heartfelt in his Polish translation. Like a professional poet, or experienced translator of folklore, Ficowski magically imparts Jewish humour into the Polish language, the playfulness, and also Jewish sadness and anguish, the crying through laughter.

However, not all the translations are equally successful. For example, his translation fails to convey the deep sorrow and seething rebellion of Rabbi Yitzchak of Berdichev when he presents his grievances to God. The playfulness and depth of "Come Here, You Philosopher," "Oh, How He Prayed," and "Miracles, Miracles" do not come through. At times the satire remains – at best, a gentle irony. I would say the same of the many songs about righteous rabbis and Hasidim. The issue is not only the difficulties of translating; the fault lies also in the selection.

In his short introduction, Ficowski writes that the anthology is the first attempt to give the Polish reader an exposure to the folk song of the decimated Polish Jewry. Hence the importance of being selective. Songs such as "A Young Hasid," "Shhh, Quiet, the Rabbi Comes," or even a song about Jewish poverty such as "Bread, Meat, Fish, and Tasty

28 Jewish Life in Poland

Dishes," certain songs about holy men and rabbis, could have been excluded. Not only because they are difficult to translate – the song "The Rebbe Elimelekh" does, in fact, read lyrically and playfully – but because they are too exotic for the Polish reader, especially with the omission of musical notes. Without the melody, without the heartfelt music, they risk remaining just dry exotica. In Poland more than elsewhere, we must consider the reader, who has limited familiarity with Jewish life in the past – or none at all.

I made the same observation when the collection *Jewish Wit*,[11] by Aleksander Drozdzynski,[12] was published. That little book truly does contain many fine and clever Jewish vignettes; it was sold off by the booksellers, and passed from hand to hand, because it was soon unavailable. And it seems to me that the average Polish reader relished mostly those – luckily just a few – tasteless jokes and anecdotes such as "Deposit," in which the town Rabbi shows that everyone in the community is a swindler. It is nicely told, but very unsavoury; you won't find anything similar in Ficowski's work. Quite the opposite, the spiritual takes precedence. Nevertheless, certain folk songs could have been omitted.

And one more short remark: we find in page after page of the anthology songs by anonymous writers and folk songs by such writers as I.L. Peretz, Zalman Shneour, Avraham Reyzen, Morris Rosenfeld,[13] Frug,[14] Kulback,[15] Nadir,[16] and Manger.[17] It is fitting that their creations be especially noted. True, in his Introduction, Shlomo Lastik mentions them,

---

11 *Jiddische Witze und Schmonzes* (Düsseldorf: Droste Verlag GmbH, 1976).

12 Aleksander Drozdzynski (1925–1981). Journalist, columnist, writer, satirist. Jewish, given name Aleksander Kahane. https://pl.wikipedia.org/wiki/Aleksander_Drozdzynski, accessed September 2021.

13 Morris Rosenfeld (1862–1923). Yiddish poet. His work sheds light on the life circumstances of emigrants from Eastern Europe in New York's tailoring workshops. https://www.poemhunter.com/morris-rosenfeld/biography/, accessed September 2021.

14 Shimen Shmuel Frug (1860–1916). Russian and Yiddish poet and essayist. *YIVO*, s.v. "Frig, Shimen Shmuel," accessed September 2021. Berger profiles Frug in *Oyf di khvalyes fun goyrl* (Paris, 1986).

15 Moyshe Kulbak (1896–1937). Yiddish poet, novelist, and dramatist. *YIVO*, s.v. "Kulbak, Moyshe," accessed September 2021.

16 Moyshe Nadir (1885–1943). Pseudonym of Yitskhok Rayz. Published poetry, satire, articles in several Yiddish language newspapers. Also translated works from English. *YL*, s.v. "Moyshe (Moishe) Nadir," accessed September 2021.

17 Itsik Manger (1901–1969). Yiddish poet, playwright, prose writer, essayist. Popularly known for his Khumish Lider (Bible stories/songs) and Megilah Lider – a rewrite of the Purim Megilah. *YIVO*, s.v. "Manger, Itsik," accessed September 2021.

The Yiddish Folk Song in Polish Translation   29

but the reader doesn't necessarily read the Introduction. These illustrious writers should at least have been acknowledged in the collection, and it would have been even better for short biographies to have been included. It is no less important to identify Peretz or Reyzen than to explain the meaning of the words *kugl* or *Shabes*.

Incidentally, the word *Shabes* is translated as "the sixth day of the week"; as for *kugl*, which is translated as a dish eaten in the shtetl during holidays as a special dessert, it is, in fact, a dish regularly served for Shabes. I wouldn't pay much attention to such picayune errors if the annotations had also included the important and necessary explanations. And one must wonder what else Lastik,[18] who had been a Jewish teacher and literary intellectual, might have omitted.

To sum up: Despite these minor reservations, the anthology of Yiddish folk song in the Polish language is a great achievement by the poet Jerzy Ficowski. From what I know, he is now undertaking an anthology of Yiddish folk songs of the ghettos and camps.*

The anthology *Raisins and Almonds* will, one hopes, build the first bridge between the Yiddish folk songs and the Polish reading public. The informative, well-conceived introduction by Shlomo Lastik leads the Polish reader through the problems of translation. The finely illustrated cover and charming drawings by Wanda Ficowska embellish the book.

Warsaw, January 1967

*The later savage attack against the handful of Jews in Poland effectively paralysed Ficowski's efforts. I am not aware whether this Polish poet and friend of the Jews Jerzy Ficowski later found the necessary resources and environment to begin realizing his plan.

Paris 1975
Translated by Sam Blatt
In gang fun tsayt, Paris, 1976.

---

18 Salomon Lastik (1907–1977). Literary historian, writer, journalist, publisher, teacher. *YL*, s.v. "Sholyme (Salomon) Lastik," accessed September 2021.

HOLOCAUST

The Hidden Source of a People's Survival: Writings from the Ghettos and Camps

So as not to be misleading, I have to stipulate at the outset that this will not be an exhaustive look at an enormous body of material: these are rather attempts to classify, as far as possible, the creations of ordinary people, works that erupted spontaneously from Jewish hearts in a mighty outcry of pain and suffering.

I collected the materials and documentation on the current theme of vernacular writing years ago from the Jewish Historical Institute in Warsaw. The title as well derives from a source in the Jewish Historical Institute. A literary essay by an unknown author was found in Ringelblum's Archive. It dealt with both an evening in the Warsaw Ghetto dedicated to Vaysenberg[1] and to works created in the ghetto. The author had given no title to his paper. The historian Professor Ber Mark of blessed memory[2] took some of the wording of the essay and gave it a title: *The Hidden Underground Source*.[3] This title, which I have borrowed in part, lends itself very well to my subject: it was a mighty underground spring, which flowed with its various streams and rivulets and which is unique in the history of human collectives.

In unimaginable circumstances, at the narrow margin between life and hundreds of deaths, people wrote and kept records, and they were not only literary people. They were also the ordinary people. Someone once said that an entire people, sentenced to death, was writing. In those dark years an immense amount of "folk writing" was born, the likes of which has never been seen and of which only a small part remains.

---

1 I.M. Vaysenberg (Weissenberg) (1881–1938), a writer, disciple of I.L. Peretz, a major force in Polish Yiddish publishing. *YIVO*, s.v "Vaysenberg, Itshe Meyer," accessed 19 July 2021.

2 See Lili Berger's profile on Ber Mark in this collection.

3 *Der oysbehaltener vaser kval fun unter der erd.*

34 Holocaust

Only in passing will I note that in Poland the war affected a great number of well-known writers: poets and writers of prose, essayists, dramatists, and a variety of other literary people such as historians and researchers. I will not list all of them here. But one can't overlook or fail to remember that among forty murdered writers from Poland alone were people like Yitzhak Katzenelson, the author of "The Song of the Massacred Jewish People," the poet Kalmen Lis, Yisroel Shtern, Miriam Ulinover, Yosef Kirman, Mordkhe Gebirtig, Yekhiel Lerer, Borekh Olitski, Fayvl Garfinkel, the young Hirsh Glik, author of "Zog nisht keynmol az du geyst dem letsten veg." Among the prose writers were such talents as Yehoshua Perle, Alter Kacyzne, Zalmen Skalov, Peretz Opoczynski, Berenshteyn, and so on. During those bloody years, new talents were emerging. Under inhuman conditions they all wrote, cried out, bewailed the great catastrophe, and captured it in prose and in verse. Unfortunately, very little remains of it. In his writings, Ringelblum tells of many lost works that he and his helpers in the Oyneg Shabes should have saved and for each of which they were too late. Hillel Zeitlin, for example, sat writing day and night keeping a systematic diary until he was led away to the Umschlagplatz. The historian Meir Balaban, aside from his academic work, wrote a memoir, beginning with his earliest childhood recollections. The famous ethnographer and folklorist Shmuel Lehman unremittingly collected sayings, jokes, and curses and over several years compiled great treasuries of folklore, which went missing.

Parallel to this source of mature, artistic creativity flowed a second underground spring of a primal sort: stormy, dynamic, and unruly, it came leaping from the Jewish heart with immense power. From the depths of the soul came words of grief and anger, of pain and angst, of protest and the urge for revenge. Ringelblum describes it with these words: "Everyone wrote – the intelligentsia and the public intellectuals, writers, teachers, community activists, youth and children." It was the same among the common people: old and young, women and men, and even children. They kept diaries, drew pictures, wrote about what they survived. Most of the persecuted poured out their hearts in verse. At first, they wrote in the confined spaces inside the ghettos, later they wrote while hiding in cellars and bunkers, in the forests and in the camps. Just as pious Jews went to the gas chambers with a prayer on their lips, so Jews in general, on the brink of death, used any scrap of paper to express the great catastrophe.

So was born an enormous body of folk literature, which has no equal in any historic period, and among any other people. In the postwar years, as we know, a certain number of diaries, memoirs, and song collections from the ghettos and camps appeared. But we have to estimate

The Hidden Source of a People's Survival   35

that this is just a small part of what was written by the captives. The largest part was probably lost along with its authors. Some of it is presumed to have been stashed away, concealed in various holes. We can suppose that only a certain portion of the hidden works was found. Twelve-year-old Dovidl Rabinovitch,[4] who left behind a diary, was likely not the only child who wrote his experiences down in a school notebook. And Dovidl's diary was only found in 1959, hidden in an attic. In 1958 someone brought the diary of thirteen-year-old Rena Kroll of the Kraków Ghetto to the Jewish Historical Institute in Warsaw. It emerged that Rena's diary had wandered from Kraków to a large paper factory in Jeziorna, a small town near Warsaw. The Germans would bring libraries, holy books, and manuscripts to be milled for raw materials to make paper. How the child's scribbler was not milled and why it came to be delivered to the institute is a story of its own. But from these particular cases – and there were a lot of them – we have a notion of how powerful the underground current of creativity was.

Here is yet another specific case: many years after the war, the Warsaw evening paper, *Express Wieczorny*, printed a letter from a Polish woman who wrote that either after or during the occupation, she had found in the Warsaw Ghetto a notebook with fifty pages of writing bearing the title "Szarti na Karti" (Jokes on cards, such as bread ration cards). She believed, she wrote in her letter, that it was too important a document to remain in private hands. These were satiric verses, about how people "lived" during those times.

No discourse by professional historians can convey the abyss of anguish felt by the unfortunates as well as they themselves could. Theirs was the most intimate expression of pain that they were capable of. I read several pages of notes by a young man of twenty-two, who, having saved himself, hid in a mine, and after digging a kind of cave for himself out of the sandy wall, set down his experiences. Among other things, he recorded that he didn't know how many days and nights were left to him. He hurried to record what he had witnessed and endured, and his last wish was that his record should come to someone's attention somewhere, when he would no longer be living, and that the events be remembered for generations to come. His are short notes, written in a fever. As well, as already mentioned, there are recovered diaries that take up several notebooks. There is the case of the Polish militia man in Żelechów who, many years after the war while undertaking

---

4 https://www.holocaustedu.org/this-week-in-history/november-1-1941-dawid -rubinowicz/.

36 Holocaust

renovations in his apartment (it would appear formerly a Jewish apartment), discovered three thick notebooks sealed up in the walls. They were in a woman's nervous Yiddish handwriting.

In the Jewish Historic Institute in Warsaw I have leafed through seventy such diaries.

~

Concurrent with the memoir, the diaries, the accounts, and other works, a people's poetry arose. It appears that a great number of the captives wrote poetry, presumably because a poem is the most direct means to express profound experiences. Through the poetry, which often went by word of mouth in the ghetto from one to another in changing form, they wept, sobbed, and expressed hatred of the enemy; they expressed hope, encouraged endurance, called for resistance, called for revenge, and also mocked the enemy, joking in order to make it easier to carry on. A tremendous number of parodies were written during those dark times. In Warsaw's Jewish Historical Institute alone, over a thousand poems, created just in Poland, were collected from 121 authors.

I could tell of similar cases in occupied France, though on a smaller scale.

In 1943, by circuitous means, two pages of a notebook in a fine, very clear hand found their way to me. These were the sixth and seventh pages of a longer poem by the journalist and poet Munye Nadler, who was with me in the resistance movement. He wrote these pages either in prison or the Compiègne Internment Camp, knowing that he would never get out of there alive. Under sentence of death, he wrote poetry.

But it was not only poets who wrote poetry in the face of death. I cannot forget how, shortly after the liberation of Paris, a Jew came to me in the editorial office telling me how he had escaped from a camp and survived the last months in a farmer's barn, where he had written down a song. Let me publish the poem, I proposed to him.

"I haven't written it down yet; I've committed it to memory." And right away he movingly recited it for me.

Thus, I am a witness that in occupied France, confronting death, both a poet and a simple Jew wrote poetry. And this is not a unique instance. There were no ghettos in France, but there were camps. It was mainly in Poland where there were both ghettos and camps and a population of over three million Jews. It was Poland that the

The Hidden Source of a People's Survival   37

Nazis chose as a fitting place to carry out "the Final Solution." Under those conditions in the Eastern European countries a very particular literature emerged, a genre of folk poetry that has no parallel anywhere. We know that a large part of the poetry that was discovered and saved was published in several volumes. The largest of these was put together by Shmerke Kaczerginski. But this is only a small part of what was produced during those bloody years. Young and old wrote songs. This is confirmed in the verse itself of a ghetto poet named Lerka Rosenblum, who, in one of his long poems, expressed the urge to grab the pen:

> A tumult, a commotion
> Ghetto writing in full motion
> From dawn till after day is done
> They think they're poets, every one.

Understandably, it is not a matter here of the poet making a critique; the author just cited, is being ironic. That literature, in particular the genre of vernacular writing, cannot be evaluated using normal criteria. There were naïve *and also* artful works. It is rather a matter of the phenomenon itself, of an entire people writing in different ways; at times the most primitive of songs, showing barely a hint of lyricism, revealed the soul of a martyred people: its vitality, its stamina, its protest, and its will to live and survive. It was recorded that there was a young man in the Warsaw Ghetto named Rubinsztajn,[5] a bit disturbed, who went around the ghetto streets and courtyards calling out in improvised fashion things like:

> We have them on the run
> We have them on the run
> We will outlast them!
> We'll live to see that yet!

At the start, he recited his improvisations; later he sang them to the tune of Sabbath hymns. He invented jokes and sayings that any folklorist would have delighted in recording.

---

5 The Ghetto Fighter's House Archive (catalogue 389, Holdings Registry File 9420) includes a photo and an entry for Rubinsztajn, describing him as "crazy or pretending to be."

38   Holocaust

Another folk poet from the Kovno ghetto proclaimed with furious pathos in a long bitter poem of which these are just a few lines:

Sing us, sing us ghetto songs
Join our ghetto dance-along
Brothers let's lock horns and dance!

These are noteworthy songs of simple people that arouse courage and call for endurance, when enduring was already so difficult. This is how it sounds coming from the pen of an unknown folk poet from Vilnius named Kasriel Broydo:

Moyshe hold on
Don't break down
Hold fast hold fast Moyshe
Moyshe hold out,
Don't slip up
Know this – we must get out!

What's more, the closer to the tragic end, the more forcefully charged the tragic tone became. There is an immense drive in the songs of revenge, truly the voices of long generations that echo with a dramatic and historic resonance. But it is not only an urge for vengeance. These are deep feelings that come from a people's belief in justice and fairness and their call must be heeded. It is the great passion to ensure that the enormous destruction does not go unpunished; otherwise the world cannot go on.

Here are a few poems by anonymous writers:

You live no more, my heart,
My consolation, life, and solace
But before me floats your holy spirit
Your blood that urges vengeance.

And a poem by another unknown folk-poet:

Hear the voices of children
Put down like herds of cattle
Blood around and all around
It boils, it seethes, it shouts:
Revenge! Revenge! Revenge!

The Hidden Source of a People's Survival   39

Or this lyrical poem from another unknown folk poet:

> I see you, eyes, mournful and wet
> Expressing only sorrow, suffering, pain
> I see you, pale tormented faces,
> That long for joyful sunshine.
> Yes, unfortunate sisters, brothers,
> You lie there mute, you speak no more.
> Your limbs no longer tremble
> Your tears no longer flow.
> But two eyes are gazing out
> from every single soul
> Fixed in an immensity of woe
> They call demanding vengeance.

Another unknown folk poet, stuck away in hiding, expresses his angst-ridden anticipation and calls out with great nationalistic feeling for armed struggle to defend the people's honour in the following simple lines:

> Tomorrow they plan to lead us at last to our death
> So, heroic comrades
> Get into pairs and go
> To fight, to fight the foe!
> Oh mother, oh mother, I will be back
> Those bandits will hang with the rope round their necks!

I have purposely presented several of the weaker improvisations and use the last, quite unsophisticated, example to show that poetic glory did not come to rest on all of them. For that reason, it is even more remarkable and raises the puzzling question: how is it that simple people, the common folk, wrote songs and poems, when they were being driven to the slaughter? How was it possible? It would be normal to wonder how, at such a time, it could occur to anyone, even to a genuine poet, to write poems? Would even the professional writer pay any mind to his pen?

Of course, there is a simple answer: the troubled had to unburden their hearts, to cry, to lament on a scrap of paper; it is easier to carry on,

40 Holocaust

maybe easier to die. And this is probably true. It is in man's nature. But it is even truer that writing is a powerful, though silent, spiritual resistance, a deeply interior summons, and though in truth passive, a form of spiritual courage nonetheless.

It has so often been thrown in our faces that the ghetto captives went like lambs to the slaughter. At times, we have been reproached gently. In certain quarters and under various circumstances some have denied the great and multi-faceted Jewish resistance, here remaining silent, there disclaiming, or even saying that Jewish fighters were a mere component of others. In Eastern Europe they were with the Russians, in the south it was Yugoslavs and Romanians, in Poland it was the Poles, just as the Jewish dead are reckoned among the total of those killed in the Polish population. Only those who remained alive were counted as Jews. From the outset this was done quietly; where it could be done, one kept silent about the various forms of Jewish resistance. There was a period in Poland when they even wanted to reclaim the Warsaw Ghetto Uprising. At various opportunities the press in its public opining, and sometimes books, would ceaselessly point out how the Polish Underground and also the Polish people strenuously made all efforts to help prepare the uprising in the Warsaw Ghetto and how the ghetto's Jews had to be pushed into that great historic act.

Before me sits a book entitled *The Warsaw Ghetto*. The author is one Wacław Poteranski.[6] This book appeared in the summer of 1968, when the handful of Polish Jews were preparing themselves for expulsion from Poland. For this reason, it was necessary to issue even more plainly ugly lies, defamations, and deliberate historical falsehoods. Poteranski goes to great lengths to show how the Warsaw Ghetto Uprising was supported on the Polish side and was truly inspired by the great solidarity with the Polish resistance movement. He writes, "Because of the passivity of by far the largest part of the Jews, the contacts between the ghetto and the Polish side were made exceptionally difficult, especially when it came to placing arms in the ghetto, which would have permitted them to put up an armed resistance much earlier." And further, "At least a million Poles actively brought help to the Jews in the ghettos and were intimately involved in trying to rescue them."

These are just some of the choice lines taken from the more mendacious passages. Poteranski emerged as a historian at a time that was auspicious for him. The same tainted goods were peddled by not a few

---

6 Wacław Poteranski, *Warszawskie Getto: W 25-lecie walki zbrojnej w getcie w 1943 roku* (Kraków: Książka I Wiedza, 1968).

The Hidden Source of a People's Survival   41

commentators and even by Polish historians. But this is not the place to settle accounts. That is not our subject. Nor is the superhuman active Jewish resistance of the whole community and of individuals within the scope of this work.

Today, more than forty years after those bloody events, when one looks deeply at the ghetto and camp Jews, and thinks about the strangely unique phenomenon of ghetto and camp writing, one must affirm that the secret writing of the captives, even the passing of the writings, sayings, and jokes by word of mouth, the mockery of the bloodthirsty enemy (and others of his like) were an immense psychic and spiritual resistance. It could only have come from a great inner courage. Perhaps no other people could have withstood what the Jews withstood in the ghettos. The multi-faceted, underground creative source quite likely nourished and shielded them. Resistance takes different forms and the exhaustive writing was one of these forms. The Germans had counted on a swift extinction of the Jews and also on mass suicide. The ghetto inhabitant and the Jew in the camp made a psychic revolt from the start. Those who were not strong enough to make it perished quickly. Still another aspect: when there was no longer a shred of hope in a rescue, they found a faith in the immortality of the Yiddish word. "We will no longer be here, but after us the word will remain. Our written word will inform the world; the remnants of our people and the word will continue to add links to the golden chain of Jewish national survival. The murdered people have left behind something that will ensure continuity.

Emanuel Ringelblum assures us in his writings that all those who laboured selflessly on the Oyneg Shabes, which is, by the way, a unique event in world history, saw their efforts as holy service. And yet the entire Oyneg Shabes was considered a great national responsibility. The same applies to all those who on the face of it made no such calculation. Evidently, we feel that the nearer the tragic end, the larger grows the passion and the perseverance to take up arms in resistance in an unequal contest; and with the knowledge that the odds are stacked, the national aspirations and responsibility grow. We will perish, but the writing will extend the thread of a people's survival, as the young partisan poet Hirsh Glik sang out:

> And if the dawn fails to break
> The song will go from one generation to the next
> Like a watchword

What does this signify – "from one generation to the next?" This is the historical memory of a people. There is an old Jewish motto: "Israel and

42 Holocaust

its Torah are one." In the Yiddish language it means that the people and its cultural treasure, its national consciousness, the people and its word, its culture are one, not to be divided.

It is no coincidence that wherever someone pits themselves against the Jewish people on whatever account, they begin, as was done in the Soviet Union, by undermining the Jewish spiritual foundation. It starts, first of all, by demolishing national values, expunging Jewish knowledge and culture, and crippling Jewish religion, as for example in "Judaism without Embellishment" from the sadly famous Kichko[7] and his like. They do it by denying, or simply extirpating, Jewish history. Take it all away, you wipe out a people's historic memory, and with that you remove their stability. You break the spiritual backbone, make the people lame, a people without a history and a past. Then you jabber on about the Jewish masses, about a people as an abstraction, without a yesterday, without a tomorrow, and gradually you begin to revoke not only national rights, but also human rights, both for the Jews at large and for the individual Jew.

In view of all these transformations and vivisections done to and still being done to the organism that is the Jewish people, and especially as we think more deeply on the phenomenon of a people writing on the narrow margin between life and death, we feel more strongly the great responsibility. We perceive more clearly the pulsing drive and stubborn will of a people not to let themselves be torn apart, or to have the thread of their continuity forever broken.

Today, more than forty years since they tried to wipe us off the earth, in the face of new threats that are surfacing, there is a command, a spirit, a national aspiration left by the annihilated in their works, in the simple sometimes primitive words, in the song that must pass from generation to generation. They are precious to us; they are our own. They should remind us and rouse us to gather up our spiritual legacy, which the exterminated of Eastern Europe, mainly Polish Jewry, have left us in various forms, and to save what remains on a Polish soil without Jews.

Translated by Judy Nisenholt
In loyf fun tsayt, Paris 1988

---

7 An antisemitic propaganda brochure by Trofim Kichko, *Iudaizm bez prikras*, was published in 1963 by the Ukrainian Academy of Sciences.

On the Ninetieth Birthday of Dr. Emanuel Ringelblum: Recollections and Summing Up

We Jews are a people with a long memory. However, when it comes to commemorating the dates of birth or dates of death of great Jewish personalities, or individuals of epoch-making significance, we either forget or else we acknowledge them with a standard little article. I was reminded of this undesirable tendency when I found among my files some yellowing pages relating to the teacher Dr. Emanuel Ringelblum.

Today marks ninety years since the birth of that passionate historian, the youngest of a group of Jewish historians who shouldered the huge and heavy responsibility of chronicling the Holocaust for posterity. There are few of us alive today who knew him personally. Thus, I believe it to be the sacred duty of those few to keep his memory alive by sharing our recollections of even the smallest details. I can still picture him as he looked when I was teenager: slim, always smiling, relaxed and easy-going in conversation. Among children, he became a playful child. With teenagers he became a fun-loving adolescent.

After graduating from the University of Warsaw and receiving his doctorate in 1927, Ringelblum became a teacher in Vilnius before teaching for ten years in three Warsaw Polish-language Jewish high schools for girls. As a secondary student from the countryside, I had the privilege of studying in the high school where he was one of the teachers. In accordance with the official government curriculum, a subject called "religion" was obligatory in the higher grades. Prior to the eighth grade it had appeared to us to be a waste of time, except that without a passing mark in religion, one could not take the matriculation examinations. With Dr. Ringelblum, however, that subject because entirely different.

My class was assigned a teacher who was an older woman, in that category of Jews who called themselves Poles of the Mosaic faith. She expounded at length on the Jewish religion, especially Jewish religious laws, and, after the lesson, we would laugh into our sleeves.

44   Holocaust

At the oral examination, the eighth graders would often get flustered. The teacher would then turn red in exasperation, although she was not really an angry person. Quite the opposite. However, I was a source of pride for her, because at the examination I knew more about religious laws from my Hasidic home than she had taught us. Occasionally, I would tell my classmates that our teacher had been mistaken about some detail or other.

We were very jealous of the two lower classes because they had Dr. Ringelblum as their teacher. He managed to sneak Jewish history into his religion classes without leaving out Jewish laws. We, the eighth graders, used to ask his students about his lessons, strongly regretting that we had not had the good fortune of having him as our teacher.

But he was no stranger to us. On the contrary, he was very friendly. We were already "young ladies," and he would greet each of us with a charming smile. He was the favourite teacher in the school. We knew which girls were in love with him, and when we sometimes got together as a group to discuss the teachers, Ringelblum turned out to be a true hero.

Among the incidents that I can still recall is the following. The German teacher, who was from Germany, used to remind us in every lesson to read German books in order to perfect our German. Searching for a German book at a friend's place, my glance fell upon a volume by Graetz[1] in the original. It would be doubly useful. It was late at night so I had had no chance to look at it before taking it with me the next morning to show to my German teacher, who also happened be Jewish. She, however, was sick that day and had not come to class. During the long break, which I always used to full advantage, I took my copy of Graetz, found a little corner in the large hall away from all the tumult, and began leafing through it. At that very moment Ringelblum came by. His sharp eye caught the title. He stopped beside me and asked, "Are you studying Jewish history in German?" I told him the whole story of the book, adding that in our class we were not learning Jewish history, but only Jewish religion. Hence, I was trying to learn Jewish history whenever I had a chance. Ringelblum responded to me in a low voice, "They think Jews have no history, only a religion! You know whom I mean by 'they'?" I nodded that, yes, I knew.

Quite a few years went by. It was now late summer, 1937. Jewish Paris was preparing for the International Jewish Culture Congress. A temporary office had been set up in Montmartre, where I was working as a secretary. On a Wednesday morning I was sitting at my typewriter

---

1 Heinrich Graetz (1817–1891) was one of the earliest Jewish historians to write a multi-volume history of the Jewish people.

transcribing dictated letters, when there was a knock at the door and in walked a slim young man. I stared at him in amazement. I could not believe my eyes. He recognized me first. Smiling, he came over to me, extended his hand, and exclaimed, "You here, of all places!" I began to mumble in Polish, but soon realized that he was speaking Yiddish. It was the first time I had ever heard him speak Yiddish.

"Where is the troika?" he asked. He was referring to Professor Kiveliovitch, Ben-Adir, and Dr. Sloves,[2] with whom he had corresponded, but they were not coming to the office until the late afternoon. "Well, the time won't be wasted," he said. I stopped typing. He sat opposite me bombarding me with questions. What was I doing in the office? What was I doing generally? He kept repeating, "Who would have imagined that I would meet a former student from the gymnasium here!" I answered all his questions at great length, told him that I had studied pedagogy in Belgium and was now working in that field.

Upon discovering that on Thursdays and Sundays I worked as a Yiddish teacher in a supplementary school, and since the following day was Thursday, Ringelblum again began asking questions. How many Jewish supplementary schools are there? Who organizes them? He insisted that I give him the address of my school because he had indeed wanted to visit such a school. I did not really want to give him the address. I prayed that the next day he would find something better to do because the school, which was on Belleville Boulevard, was in a large, abandoned building. I was working there temporarily, the children were new, and everything else – woe is me! I told Ringelblum that I would take him on Sunday to my regular school in Livry-Gargan, which had a wonderful space in the Socialist Centre, and delightful children, almost all of whom spoke Yiddish. I even had a pupil there who wrote Yiddish well and assisted me by taking over a group of the youngest children. (That was Henri Binstock who was shot in 1943 as a partisan.) That school was something to see, but the other was not very interesting. First of all, Ringelblum said to me, he would no longer be in Paris on Sunday. He had come here from Geneva, where he had coincidentally been at a meeting of the Joint.[3] The next evening he was leaving Paris. Secondly, the first school interested him more.

---

2 For further information on the Jewish Culture Congress of 1937 see Gennady Estraikh, "A Quest for Yiddishland: The 1937 World Yiddish Cultural Congress," in *Quest: Issues in Contemporary Jewish History* (Journal of the Centro di Documentazione Ebraica Contemporanea (CDEC onlus), no. 17 (September 2020), https://www.quest-cdecjournal.it/.

3 Joint Distribution Committee.

46 Holocaust

I gave him the address and was immediately seized with anxiety. I, the young beginner teacher, would be hosting Dr. Ringelblum! Late into the night I prepared materials for over forty children of various ages. I usually divided them up into three groups. For the youngest I prepared sheets of paper and coloured pencils – that was the best way to keep them quiet – and something else for the other two groups. The next day, my heart pounding, I arrived at the Belleville school an hour early to create some order, while still praying to God that Dr. Ringelblum would unexpectedly have to attend to other important business.

The Master of the Universe took little interest in my trepidation. Dr. Ringelblum arrived punctually. The children also arrived on time. A ten-year-old girl, as always leading her five-year-old brother by the hand, a thirteen-year-old boy, as usual bringing his four-year-old little sister – these were the children of the Jewish artisans of Belleville who worked from home. A large percentage of them were among the new immigrants who had begun streaming into the country in early 1930s. On Thursdays, when the French school was not open, these hard-working parents were happy that their little ones were not underfoot.

The children were seated at three long well-worn tables, according to their age. Dr. Ringelblum sat down on a chair that stood against the opposite wall. I divided the large blackboard in half. I wrote a dozen short sentences for the older children. First, of course, I introduced them to our guest before reading the sentences, which they then were to copy in their notebooks. Apart from the little ones, who were charmingly occupied with the coloured pencils and paper which I had put on the last table, the eyes of my pupils were directed more at the guest than at the blackboard. I felt that I was headed for failure. Suddenly, Ringelblum took his chair and sat down discreetly in the same row as the pupils. Looking intently at the sentences, he took a pad of paper and a pencil from his pocket, and began writing so enthusiastically that all the children turned towards the blackboard and diligently copied down the sentences in their notebooks. Afterwards, a few pupils whom I called upon, after stealing a glance at our guest, proudly and willingly read the sentences which connected to make a story.

After the first forty-five minutes, I felt that my face was flushed. The children surrounded Ringelblum and interrupted him as he was complimenting me for controlling such a gang. He patted their heads, and they, especially the older children, kept asking him, half in Yiddish, half in French, whether he was going to remain in Paris and become a teacher. Ringelblum, laughing heartily, replied that he had to go back to Poland, because there were many, many more Jewish children there,

On the Ninetieth Birthday of Dr. Emanuel Ringelblum   47

and he had to be with them. He asked the children various questions, which they all answered at the same time.

The break had been longer than usual. We said goodbye. As I led him out, he stopped as though he had just remembered something, and asked me, "In what language do the parents speak to the children at home? You said they had recently immigrated."

"They speak to them in their broken French, and that's why the children speak Yiddish so poorly."

"I surmised," he said, "that it was not from the street. But Jewish education must start with the parents. We'll talk more about this when I'm at the Congress." Again we said goodbye to each other. That was the last time I spoke to Ringelblum. He did not attend the Congress. Only a detailed letter arrived, explaining the disruptions.

At the time, Emanuel Ringelblum was not quite thirty-seven years old, but the young historian's creativity was already multi-faceted.

His childhood and youth coincided with an era of Jewish migration. He was born in the town of Buczacz, Galicia, in November of 1900. During World War I, the family migrated to Kolomea, and then to Nowy Sącz, where he completed the gymnasium before leaving to study history in Warsaw. In 1927 he received his doctorate from the University of Warsaw based on his dissertation, which was an in-depth study of the history of the Jews in medieval Warsaw to their expulsion in 1527. He remained a scholarly historian until the final tragic days of his life.

Immediately after completing his study of the Jews in Warsaw, which at the same time mirrored the then unknown history of the Jews in the entire Kingdom of Poland, he undertook, together with historian Raphael Mahler, to find source material about the history of the Jews in Poland and Eastern Europe, which, at the time, was an almost completely unexplored field. His particular research was about the Jews of Poland in the nineteenth century. He had already embarked upon an exhaustive study of Jewish participation in the Kościuszko Uprising,[4] and after that, one about the history of the Jews in Warsaw up to the end of the

---

4 The Kościuszko Uprising against the Russian Empire and the Kingdom of Prussia, led by Tadeusz Kościuszko, was a failed attempt to liberate the Polish Lithuanian Commonwealth from Russian influence after the Second Partition of Poland (1793).

48 Holocaust

eighteenth century. His goal was to produce a comprehensive study of the Jews in all of Poland. He wrote a separate volume about Jews living in the countryside, such as those who leased mills or inns. Not one single aspect of Jewish life was unfamiliar to him.

The young historian Ringelblum was an exceptionally devoted researcher. He was constantly collecting more material, discovering important new sources, and writing comprehensive historical works about the more recent Jewish past. His scholarly work, whether already in print or being prepared for publication, traced the development of Jewish life from its very roots. Most of his books were published either in Polish or Yiddish. Although it would require too much space to list all his research papers, it is worth noting that for the German-language Encyclopedia Judaica alone he contributed over thirty monographs about Jewish communities in Poland. About Jews in Poland in the nineteenth century, he managed to publish twenty-five lengthy essays.

Dr. Emanuel Ringelblum, the eminent historian and researcher, did not limit himself to history. It is rare to find a scholar, totally engaged in his research, who is also involved in a variety of fields – cultural, literary, sociological. Ringelblum also participated in various periodicals and community institutions such as the Joint, Tsysho,[5] and YIVO. In addition to spearheading the group of young Jewish historians in YIVO, he was also a community activist. He was concerned about every aspect of Jewish life. Wherever there was a need, he lent a hand. That was a tradition carried over from his early youth. As a member of the Left Poalei Zion Party in his hometown, he organized and actively led the youth there. He was a rare example of a young scholar who combined his academic research with his community activities. The active, creative person went hand in hand with the caring person.

When war broke out, he found himself in Zurich at a meeting of the Joint. He moved heaven and earth to get back to Warsaw. When the dark, diabolical plan of the Nazis began to reveal itself, he still had the opportunity to save himself. Other prominent people accepted help to leave Poland, but Ringelblum categorically refused.

He immediately put himself at the service of the beleaguered Jewish population. He was among those who took the initiative to organize the self-help organization and the various social institutions in the ghetto. He was one of the organizers of cultural work, and a pillar of the

---

5 Di Tsentrale Yidishe Shul-Organizatsye (Central Yiddish School Organization), known by its acronym, TSYSHO or CYSHO, was founded in Warsaw in June 1921 by members of the Bund and Left Zionists to create a network of secular Yiddish schools.

On the Ninetieth Birthday of Dr. Emanuel Ringelblum   49

Yiddish Cultural Organization, the IKOR. Later he was involved in the campaign to mobilize the ghetto population to active resistance.

Ringelblum was a born historian. The tragic times had to be recorded for future generations. Even prior to the ghetto period, in October 1939, he began describing current events. Being locked into a ghetto created horrific new situations. One person was not enough to document them all. Thus, Dr. Ringelblum created an association unique in human history. Amid the direst poverty, the bloodiest persecution, the most numerous and diverse types of killings, he created an extensive underground organization by the name of Oyneg Shabes, which served as a headquarters for dozens of dedicated correspondents who recorded everything that was happening not only in the Warsaw Ghetto but in ghettos all over Poland.

Among them were writers, teachers, and community activists, but most were people without any prior experience as writers. Thanks to his social welfare activities, Ringelblum came into contact with many people, prominent personalities as well as ordinary Jews, whom he was able to recruit for this sacred task. The members of the Oyneg Shabes chronicled, described, and wrote essays about events in the ghetto. Sometimes Ringelblum assigned the same event to two or three correspondents to be able to better expose the reality of what had happened. In this way, a giant underground archive was born.

Ringelblum created his own archive, using every free hour of daylight and every evening to record, in his tiny handwriting, on both sides of small pieces of paper, bits of information. Under the worst possible circumstances, in every conceivable hiding place, Ringelblum was constantly writing. His work was twofold. In addition to making notes, almost on a daily basis, in the form of a letter or a journal entry, he wrote treatises, composed on the spot, yet thoughtfully conceived and based on facts, with such titles as "The German War Strategy as Applied to the Jews in Warsaw," "The Problem of the Jewish Police and the Judenrat," "How the Creative Jewish Intelligentsia Was Murdered," "Jewish-Polish Relations during the Second World War," and "Why the Jews Did Not Stage an Uprising at the Very Beginning."

We must remember that the materials in the underground archive also served – indeed they were meant to serve – to alert the world. Ringelblum managed to send warnings through the Polish Underground to the Polish government in London, which were also intended to reach the Jewish world. The world, however, kept silent. Nonetheless, Ringelblum did not stop. He recruited people in the ghetto and continued his dedicated work.

50 Holocaust

In the ghetto, the committed scholar Dr. Emanuel Ringelblum became a master organizer in all areas. He communicated with headquarters, conveyed accurate information, drew attention to specific topics and events, while constantly directing his co-workers in the Oyneg Shabbes as to where and how to conduct their investigations. Sometimes he suggested, for legal reasons, giving the reports the title "For a Competition."

He remained vigilant day and night lest any event be lost to history. At the same time, he made it his goal to ensure that the reports, at least in part, reached the outside world. In the tragic days of the second half of 1942, when the Nazis rounded up over 300,000 men, women, and children in the Warsaw Ghetto, loaded them into sealed train cars, and sent them directly to the gas chambers of Treblinka, Ringelblum, without stopping to rest, drafted a "radio bulletin" and succeeded in sending it to London. His numerous initiatives and his extensive creative endeavours (he even portrayed wartime occurrences as a continuation of prewar themes) were conducted without neglecting the safety and immediate needs of the ghetto population, always a tremendous concern. In the hell that was the Warsaw Ghetto, his creative mind worked in tandem with his deeply compassionate heart.

Under Ringelblum's leadership, numerous documents, reports, and other materials were collected and packed into milk cans and iron boxes, before being buried. Rescued from their burial sites, these documents even included artwork such as the paintings and drawings of the talented artist Gela Seksztajn,[6] as well as her moving letters. The materials prepared by Ringelblum personally have now been published in two thick volumes entitled *Notes from the Warsaw Ghetto*.[7] For this alone we owe the young historian our eternal gratitude.

Not everything that was buried has been found. One part was unearthed in 1946, another in 1950. As of now, the third part has not yet been discovered. I was told by historian Ber Mark that presumably some of the material collected during the final days of the Warsaw Ghetto Uprising could not be hidden.

Dr. Emanuel Ringelblum fell into the hands of the Nazis when the Ghetto Uprising began. The Nazis dragged him off to the Trawniki camp near Lublin, where he languished for a few months. Thanks to

---

6 Gela Seksztajn (1907–1943) a Polish Jewish artist and painter, whose portraits and other paintings were hidden in the Ringelblum Archive and found after World War II, are now held mostly in the archive of the Jewish Historical Institute, in Warsaw.

7 E. Ringelblum, *Ksuvim fun geto* (Yiddish) (Warsaw, 1961–3). Translated into English as *Notes from the Warsaw Ghetto* (New York: McGraw-Hill, 1958).

On the Ninetieth Birthday of Dr. Emanuel Ringelblum 51

the efforts of his close friends, and with the help of the Polish Underground, he managed to escape, dressed as a railway worker, and return to Warsaw. His last hiding place was a large bunker in a garden on Grójecka Street, where over thirty Jews were hiding.

In that living grave Ringelblum went right back to work. Within a short time he had written a long monograph about the Trawniki camp. Unfortunately, that monograph, like other material, was never found. There is a theory that Ringelblum had written a great deal in the bunker, but only two pieces of his writing were saved: "Jewish-Polish Relations during the Second World War"[8] and several short monographs about certain intellectuals as well as a few of the activists in the anti-Fascist bloc. Thanks to efforts of the Polish Marczak[9] family, these were given to Berman,[10] who was on the Aryan side.

On 7 March 1944, thanks to an informant, the bunker on Grójecka Street was discovered. Ringelblum, his wife, and fourteen-year-old son, along with over thirty other Jews, were taken to the notorious Pawiak Prison, where they were shot. Shot together with them were Ludomir Marczak and Mieczysław Wolski, noble Polish rescuers who had been assisting Ringelblum for a long time. They all deserve our everlasting reverence.[11]

Translated by Vivian Felsen
Ekhos fun a vaytn nekhtn
(Echos des temps lointains), Tel Aviv 1993

---

8 Published in English by Yad Vashem in Jerusalem in 1974.

9 Władysław Marczak constructed the hiding place.

10 Adolf Berman (1906–1978), a leader of the Warsaw Ghetto underground, together with his wife, Batya Temkin-Berman, collected letters, memoirs, and diaries during the war and initiated extensive documentation activity. In September 1942, he was sent to the Aryan side of Warsaw, where he represented Żydowski Komitet Narodowy (Jewish National Committee) and served as a secretary of the presidium of Żegota, the Polish Council for Aid to Jews. Berman transferred relief funds to Jews in hiding and to the Jewish underground in camps and ghettos. He also helped to save written records hidden on the Aryan side, including materials gathered by Ringelblum. See https://www.haaretz.com/jewish/news/for-first-time-rare-warsaw -ghetto-uprising-diaries-unveiled.premium-1.494599 (accessed 25 November 2017).

11 Malgorzata Wolska and her children, Mieczyslaw, Halina (Michalecka-Wolska), and Wanda (Szandurska-Wolska), and nephew Janusz Wysocki were recognized as righteous gentiles by Yad Vashem in Jerusalem. https://www.yadvashem.org/ righteous/stories/wolska-wysocki.html (accessed 21 June 2021).

Janusz Korczak, Pedagogical Researcher

On the Thirtieth Anniversary of His Death

It is puzzling that Janusz Korczak's last tragic path, his great martyrdom, overshadows his multifaceted literary and pedagogic achievements ...

During his lifetime, Henryk Goldszmit, known as Janusz Korczak, was a legendary figure recognized for his lifelong devotion to child research, and at the same time he was a guardian, a friend, and a father to the most neglected child, the Jewish orphan. By the time he was thirty, he had already made a name for himself as a pediatrician of the first rank and as a talented author of scholarly works and children's literature. A life of wealth and honour awaited him, yet he left the hospital and his private patients to care for poor children. In summer camps his pedagogic theories crystallized and took shape ... using his literary and medical gifts in the development of the new thinking on education and child-rearing ...

Education took hold of him as a mission, a mission to alleviate the suffering of the abandoned child ... His decision to be a pediatrician was not accidental; it was as a physician at the children's hospital in Warsaw that he first encountered Jewish poverty ... The care and education of the neglected child answered a profound need in him; the pedagogue and educator went hand in hand with the committed physician and writer ...

Korczak based his pedagogy on the sciences of medicine, psychology, sociology, and demography ... As a social reformer, he was closely tied to the Polish Workers' Movement against tsarist enslavement and oppression ...

As a Polish freedom fighter, he shared a prison cell with the Polish scholar Krzywicki,[1] who influenced him both as a socialist and a

---

1 Ludwik Krzywicki (1859–1941), a Marxist thinker who took a particular interest in how systems of ideas alongside innovations in material culture produce change. https://culture .pl/en/article/a-museum-of-scientific-pathology-polands-most-influential-sociologists.

sociologist. Like so many others, Korczak had anticipated that with emancipation, Poland would be freed from the yoke of foreigners and liberated from her native oppressors. The expected did not happen; the same individuals who had fought against national and social oppression became the oppressors. These new oppressors were just as harsh as the earlier ones, giving Korczak much to ponder. Completely distancing himself from his one-time comrades, he searched for root causes in both external conditions and in the inner life of the individual ... He came to the conclusion that the best and finest beliefs were worthless if the essence of humanity was absent. Therefore, to change the order of the world, we must change the person; we must educate, starting with early childhood ...

"A child is not merely a future person, it is already a person, with a developing physical constitution and a different way of thinking. A young, immature person, thinks, observes, dreams, suffers, hopes, loves, and hates. This little human being has worries, secrets, and tragedies; loneliness and sadness bite more deeply into his heart than into the heart of an adult. It is not true that a child forgets quickly: a humiliation, an insult, an injustice take root in the child's heart for a lifetime."[2] ...

The late Polish Jewish writer Hanna Mortkovicz-Olczakowa,[3] a childhood friend, relates the following in her book about "the old doctor." In 1919, Korczak lectured at the Special Pedagogic Institute and brought with him a little boy. He then invited the students into the radiology lecture hall. He led the little one into the darkened room, undressed him, and placed him behind an x-ray screen. The child became frightened and clung to the doctor. The students behind the screen could observe the child's heart beating convulsively, his breathing abnormally rapid and his muscles cramping. Korczak turned to the class and said, "What you are seeing, you must never forget: when you are tired and distraught, when the children are unbearable, drive you out of your mind and you become angry, yell at them and want to punish them, remind yourself then, of the boy's heart you have seen today."

This lecture not only was meant for students, future teachers, and educators, but was also an appeal to parents and the community to

---

2 The author does not provide a source for these quotes. We have to assume they are from Korczak's writings.

3 Hanna Mortkowicz-Olczakova (1905–1968) was born in Warsaw to an illustrious publishing family. A precocious author of poetry, novels, children's books, she survived the war in hiding in Poland.

54 Holocaust

promote a respectful approach towards the child. Korczak demanded that physical punishment be prohibited at school, at home, or anywhere else ... Humane societies have been established for the prevention of cruelty to animals, but the abuse of children is met with passivity and indifference. Korczak proposed a solution, the creation of a comprehensive legal code to protect the child. In 1919–20, he published two books on pedagogy: *Moments of Education* and *How to Love a Child*.[4] This was before the First World Congress on the Protection of the Child, and who knows if Korczak did not provide an impetus for that conference. It is certain that he was among the first to lay the foundation of today's organizations for the protection of children. In 1929, when his monograph *The Right of the Child to Respect*[5] was published, it was a breakthrough in educational theory.

Though these concepts are now accepted, they were then boldly innovative, and his influence was significant. He taught that children and youth are as much an oppressed class as workers, women, and colonial peoples, who are ruled under the pretext that they lack the competence to manage their own affairs. In the context of that time and even ours, few of his proposed changes have been realized ...

Using his medical experience, Korczak was able to create his own comprehensive method; it was said of him that as a doctor he was a pedagogue, and as a pedagogue a doctor. This was not a play on words. In his *Sketches on Education*, he established the connection between medicine and pedagogy: ... "If pedagogy is to follow on the path of medicine, it must develop a diagnostic method based on understanding symptoms. The smile, the laugh, the tears, the rosy cheeks, all display emotion to the educator; they are what a fever, a cough, a rash are to the physician" ... To be understood, the child must be observed in many aspects: crying, yelling, shrugging shoulders, dragging feet, running, crawling, hunched over, standing erect. From all these signs, we can learn what is in his heart" ... Korczak observed and researched, achieving rare insight into the child. Even so, he believed the child remained a secret, hiding corners of his soul, his rich fantasy life.

Korczak believed the child's education should begin before birth. Drawing on medicine, he linked education to genetics and eugenics. In Poland he was the first proponent of birth control and premarital

---

4 *How to Love a Child: And Other Selected Works*, vol. 1 (London: Vallentine Mitchell, 2018).

5 5 *A Child's Right to Respect*, first published at the end of 1928, is a synthesis of Korczak's thinking and educational activities. https://brpd.gov.pl/sites/default/files/a_childs_right_to_respect_-_book.pdf Accessed 3 June 2024.

chastity. For him these practices were also associated with the improvement of the human species. He advocated against alcoholics, syphilitics, and parenthood for the mentally ill. We may agree or disagree with such a position, but Korczak put the problem on the agenda ...

In his philosophical-psychological novel *Bobo* he expresses with pure lyricism the child's reactions on coming into the world; childbirth brings pain to both the mother and the child. The light, the air, the change in temperature and in breathing, the entire new world falls on the newborn like a heavy weight, eliciting a cry, a scream, which Korczak the doctor and psychologist recognizes as a scream of pain. He observes the psychic evolution of the tiny infant and concludes that nature is never at rest as she shapes the little human ...

Korczak was first and foremost a practitioner, not only a theoretical pedagogue. As educator and director of children's colonies, he was able to extract the essence of his theories in order to test and develop them. When he required a more spacious research facility, he settled in the orphanage on Krochmalna 92, in Warsaw, which included his laboratory and the educational clinic. In this large white house which he himself had built, he lived with the children from 1911, sharing their joys and pains; he was one of them. He also directed a second orphanage for Polish children and held many other pedagogic appointments as a professor.

My first visit to the orphanage is etched in memory forever: it was a Saturday morning, and Korczak was reading the wall newspapers to the children and the staff. I was a secondary school student from Warsaw, coming with preconceived notions of the children's home and of Korczak. We, the Young Eagles, who rebelled against everything and everyone, were inspired by Korczak's books. After all, he too was a rebel, a great rebel who had accomplished so much. To me he was a giant ...

How taken aback I was when I entered the great hall and saw before me a slender man of average height, his head totally shaven, his friendly face framed by a short, blond beard. He was reading quietly; he lifted his head from time to time, turning his intelligent blue eyes towards the young audience, and then continued reading. The children, older, younger, even the really young, were seated on benches, alert and attentive. When Korczak occasionally directed a knowing look towards them, the gang of children burst into laughter. But as soon as Korczak bent his head to the page, they grew silent, listening intently to the lovely tales ...

After the reading, a bunch of children surround Korczak; all have questions, all want to know more; the very young ones cling to him

56   Holocaust

as to a mother. And he, in the green work apron he always wore in the children's house, looking more like a modest clerk than a professor, continues to speak to them calmly, slowly. He answers this one with a joke, another with a pat on the head. Among the children he looks like one of the family, but with more knowledge, more experience, and a greater devotion to all.

Through the years, hundreds of children from various backgrounds lived in the orphanage: some from poor homes, some from broken homes, and some who had never had a home. These troubled children between the ages of seven and fourteen years had seen more bad than good in their short lives. And a great miracle happened: Korczak brought all these unfortunate children into one family, creating a happy children's republic where each child could live freely and develop. In his ghetto memoir, he quoted a letter he received from a young boy after leaving the orphanage: "If I hadn't been in this house, I wouldn't have known that there are honourable people in the world, people who don't steal. I wouldn't have known that anyone can speak the truth. I would also not have known that there are laws about justice in the world." ... What pedagogic magic brought about such transformation? Actually, we can express this in a few words: self-education, self-discipline, and autonomy, concepts that are widely accepted today, but were unfamiliar and strange at the beginning of the century ... We must acknowledge, however, that Korczak's pedagogy was not completely new. He began his practice at the dawn of the century when, even then, the names Pestalozzi[6] and Froebel[7] had long been known. Maria Montessori,[8] a pediatrician, was working with abandoned children in her own country, Italy, and had already championed independent, free education. Korczak went further, a great deal further than these three theoreticians of modern pedagogy. He accomplished this in a country under a tsarist educational system with its militaristic discipline, with the whip ...

Today, we speak of humanistic education; here and there we attempt methods that Korczak had introduced, tested, and for which he had laid the cornerstone ...

---

6 Johann Heinrich Pestalozzi (1746–1827). Swiss pedagogue, eminent reformer, advocate of education for poor children. His methods, based on student capabilities are now integral to modern elementary education.

7 Friedrich Froebel (1782–1852). German pedagogue, student, and disciple of Pestalozzi. Froebel developed the concept of kindergarten.

8 Maria Montessori (1870–1952). Italian physician, feminist, early childhood educator who championed education for poor children. Her methods, based on the child's natural spirit of learning, are widely accepted and used.

Korczak understood how to utilize the children's need to be in constant motion, their fantasies, their wish to be responsible, and, most important, their desire to be trusted. The child's innate qualities allowed for self-education, for self-discipline, and for the development of individual interests, of course under the guidance of a skilled adult. Korczak maintained that a child must never be treated as a passive object, presented with established rules, but as an active individual who naturally observes the appropriate limits of social behaviour. There is no ready-made model for education, and here it seems, Korczak went further than today's educators. According to him, any model that disturbs the child's independent development is wrong. Alongside a basic education the child must be given an understanding of good and evil, a feeling for justice and good works, a desire to be useful. These values appear in his children's books *The Stubborn Boy*[9] and *Glory*.[10]

He was not a proponent of education being provided exclusively by an institution; in his opinion, no institution could replace the home and parents. However, where there is no choice, we must create institutions where children feel themselves at home. But how to feel at home in an orphanage? When children participate in managing their new home, they will become a part of it, learn to love it, and care for it. How to run it well, and who should run it? The children themselves. "Show what you can do! Here you have a large home, look after it, make it more beautiful and better," said Korczak. In general, he did not like to talk too much. He did the work himself as an example to others of how things needed to be done.

From its beginning, the orphanage on 92 Krochmalna was managed by a children's council, a sort of parliament, comprising twenty-two elected girls and boys of varying ages. It was guided and headed throughout the years by Korczak and the devoted pedagogue Stefania Wilczynska,[11] who handled all the affairs of the communal house. She was not content to encourage responsibility only with words, as is

---

9 The biographical story *The Stubborn Boy* was published in 1938 – although a shorter version of story about the main character, Louis Pasteur, was published by Korczak as early as 1923.

10 Published in 1913 in Polish as *Sława*.

11 Stefania Wilczynska (1886–1942), educator and Janusz Korczak's closest associate for three decades, was the guardian angel of the orphanage, maintaining its spirit and administering the daily necessities of life. In 1934 she spent months in Palestine, visiting former students and participating in kibbutz life. When the deportations of the orphanage in the Warsaw Ghetto began, she and other staff who could have avoided the gas chambers accompanied the children to Treblinka.

58   Holocaust

common with adults, but by vigilance and example. The children had a hand in all tasks of the orphanage: they helped in the kitchen, in the tailoring workshop, in keeping order and cleanliness. The older ones cared for the younger, the better students helped the weaker prepare for their classes, the more experienced ones became monitors, librarians. Many responsibilities were carried out exclusively by the children, including library work, publishing the wall newspapers, serving and clearing the tables, keeping their belongings in order. The children also tended to the courtyard, keeping watch that neither trees nor walls suffered from destructive hands.

The entire organization of the children's house was based on daily schedules and assignments. Korczak, himself, with all his responsibilities, took part in the "menial" work. In his ghetto diary, he explained why he helped in clearing the table after meals; certain staff members disapproved, maintaining it was a waste of time for such a creative person. But Korczak, the creative pedagogue, claimed the opposite: his notes indicated his wish to discourage such thoughts by his own example, demonstrating his basic belief that no work was "menial" or unfit for delicate, human hands. This was also an opportunity to see up close how his method worked. But he did not participate as a supervisor but rather as an experienced leader with a keen eye who could see imperfections that others missed; and they could learn from him.

Korczak also knew that, like grown-ups, children were far from angels. So, what should be done if a child refuses an assignment, or injures or hurts another? There are children who love to provoke, especially if they expect no punishment. In these instances, the opinion of the children played the major role: the entire collective watched lest members lead others astray and bring suffering to everyone. These individuals had to be healed for their own good. To defend the collective good, there were the wall newspapers, reflecting the life of the collective, and there was the children's court. The court, a powerful protector of the ethical and moral life of the community was run by children who demonstrated good behaviour and fellowship ...

The court was guided by justice and righteousness, but also by compassion and forgiveness ... By helping the child search for ways to correct bad deeds, the court became a great contributor to education and self-awareness.

On hearing of the children's participation in the management and work of the collective, some people might have had the impression that it was complicated, that the children were overburdened or mishandled their assignments; in either event, it was thought, the pressure should be lifted. But whoever was familiar with the entire system

Janusz Korczak, Pedagogical Researcher 59

knew that the orphanage was a model of order and cleanliness. The children performed their tasks with love and dedication, trying hard to earn the special "appreciation card" with the signature of their "Pan Doktor."[12] Korczak's leadership, magnetism, intelligence, and kindness inspired the children as did his diligence. The entire organization of the children's house worked like a well-regulated clock. Supervising the home was the remarkable Stefania Wilczynska, who left her parents' affluent home upon completing university, to devote herself to the impoverished orphans. First in the foundling home on Franciszkańska Street, and later on 92 Krochmalna, she carried the full administrative responsibility, was a devoted mother to the orphans, and along with Korczak, accompanied the two hundred children into the gas chambers of Treblinka.

The children's house on Krochmalna Street was a great experiment in modern pedagogy. Even today, certain aspects are little understood or completely unknown. For example, Korczak recognized that children, just like adults, needed to be alone from time to time, to find themselves a quiet corner. This was even more urgent for a child in a collective than in the family home. For that purpose, Korczak established a "silent room" in the orphanage where any child could be alone with his own thoughts for as long as necessary. And more than a few took part. Korczak never considered all children as cast from the same mould.

Korczak believed that children from a religious background must be given the opportunity to live according to their beliefs; suppressing their religious feelings would be harmful. The child's inclination had to be respected. For every child who prayed regularly or just wanted to pray, there was a special room, a sort of holy site, where no one was allowed to interfere and inappropriate behaviour was deemed a great sin.

The child's spiritual needs and individual development were realized in varied ways. Korczak created the first newspaper for children, managed and edited primarily by them. The weekly paper, *The Little Review* (*Mały Przegląd*), was the first experiment of such an educational resource. The chief editor was Korczak's secretary at the time, the well-known Polish writer and Judeophile Igor Newerly.[13] Every child, not

---

12 Editors' footnote: These two words became the one word, Pandoktor, with which the children always addressed him.

13 Igor Abramov-Newerly (1903–1987), born into a Polish-Russian family, was a social activist, a close associate of Janusz Korczak, with whom he participated in joint publishing projects. During the Holocaust he hid Jews and was sent to various concentration camps. In 1982, he was named Righteous Among the Nations by Israel.

60 Holocaust

only those from the children's house, could publish an article, a poem, or any other creative work. In their articles the young authors dealt with problems, polemicized, and gave advice, proving that children have their own issues, which adults often do not recognize.

The singular closeness that Korczak established with the children was fundamental to his pedagogic system. It was instructive to see and hear how a close connection was established from the moment of arrival. Korczak himself received every child who arrived in the children's house; soon a bonding conversation took place: if Korczak recognized that he had before him a wise guy, someone who would not hesitate to trip another child, he would ask him mischievously, "Are you something of a rascal? Tell the truth, don't be ashamed. Don't you sometimes fight too much?" On the other hand, speaking to an apathetic, depressed child, he would use a very different tone: "Do you know how to run? Do you know how to tramp around? You probably also know how to fight with the boys?" Such conversations also had another purpose: Korczak knew that among children there were wolves and lambs, and one must disarm the little wolves and encourage the lambs to protect themselves. "Boys," he wrote, "will always test their strength by fighting." In such cases, close contact between child and educator was essential.

The relationship between the children and Korczak was remarkable. It would happen that on a summer day, when Korczak was sitting on a bench under the shade of a tree, the youngest would fall upon him, one child sitting on his lap, another at his feet: several standing at each side of the bench, patting his bald head and whispering a secret in his ear. After such playfulness with the young ones, Korczak would say, "I am an old, overgrown tree on whose branches young birds leap and sing." The informal intimacy did not diminish his authority or his influence one iota. Familiarity came naturally; it flowed from constant concern and devotion to the young. The children felt his dedication, commitment, his love, 24 hours a day, even in their dreams. In the evening, when the rooms were sunk in sleep, Korczak would descend from his third floor "residence" and with very quiet steps he would pass between the beds, notice which child was uncovered or lying in an uncomfortable position, which child couldn't fall asleep or cried silently, head buried in the pillow, perhaps a homesick newcomer. A tender hand would pat the head, a soft word calmed the child, chasing away the sadness, and the child fell asleep.

After a hard day's work with the children, the doctor and educator would sit down to his creative pursuits in his isolated room. The capacious room on the third floor was a scientific laboratory and an artist's studio, sparsely furnished but enhanced by a rich library. Here Korczak wrote his pedagogic works, and here he perfected his wonderful books for children and adults. Here, using every free hour, he prepared his lectures, corresponded with teachers, educators, and parents, and deliberated on his day-to-day obligations. In addition to directing the two children's homes, he was a professor at the Institute for Special Pedagogy in the Free University and lectured in the orphanage dormitory to new cohorts of educators. He was a consultant to the Warsaw Juvenile Court, and for many years he broadcast a weekly radio program for children and interested adults.

Korczak's pedagogic system underwent the severest ordeal in the dark years of the ghetto. During the Nazi attacks on Warsaw, the house was set on fire by bomb shrapnel, then attacked by local vandals. Korczak and Wilczynska withstood the first trials through their own perseverance and that of the entire orphanage, which demonstrated the exemplary maturity of the children.

It wasn't long before Korczak and the children restored the house to order; then, right after the outbreak of war, they were forced to vacate it. Krochmalna Street remained outside the boundaries of the ghetto, and again the staff and the children faced another challenge: to re-establish the orphanage in a location on Chlodna Street. As it happened, Korczak was arrested while moving the children's house because he refused to wear the badge of shame[14] on his arm; then he was imprisoned for some time in the Pawiak prison,[15] notorious for its brutality. But the orphanage was soon chased from its new refuge when Chlodna Street was cut off from the ghetto. Korczak and the children were remarkably resilient in reorganizing the children's republic in a cramped, unsuitable location on Sienna Street. Despite those hellish conditions, the children's republic functioned as in the good days: until the last day, a children's parliament and the children's court continued, as did the wall newspaper, artistic circles, and children's performances. The children worked and studied, learned Hebrew and Yiddish, and, as witnesses told me, the children themselves maintained order.

This is how, in 1948, former educator Irena Chmiyelewska,[16] an associate of Korczak in the ghetto, who visited him right after the move to Sienna Street, described the children's house:

---

14 Badge of shame: the yellow badge Jews were forced to wear during the Middle Ages in Europe and, centuries later, during the Nazi period, to stigmatize and identify them.
15 Pawiak prison, built in 1835 in Warsaw as a transit camp for Poles sentenced to Siberia in tsarist Russia. In World War II, it was used by the Gestapo during the Warsaw Ghetto Uprising as a Nazi base.
16 Irena Chmiyelewska, a young Polish educator, helped many Jews in Warsaw during the Holocaust.

62 Holocaust

A crowdedness, a terrible crush, and yet order, hardly imaginable under such circumstances. Everything was calm, clean, in its place. If all the walls were covered, they found other places to hang notices, and tabloids – on cupboards or other furnishings. On display were scraps of paper: here a child's thanks for a favour, there a request for pardon from a friend ...

The tribunal's code of laws and the wall newspaper are prominent. At the side of a table sits an elderly, exhausted man wearing a wrinkled military coat. On his bald head sits a Jewish cap; his eyes emit an unusual sadness. Suddenly, the youngest ones rush into his room. And he's on his feet already; he goes from one room to another with them. One child holds his hand, another holds on to his coat, another cuddles up to him. Near him, with him, all signs of insecurity, of angry thoughts, vanish. Their carefree faces shine, their childish chatter is full of trust. On a terrace by a window, in an earthen pot, sits a plant, its two twigs broken in half; skilfully, the doctor bandages them. In a whisper, he begins to explain the mystery of his work to the young ones; the children watch, curious and attentive.

Korczak's educational system defied and endured the most severe trial by fire. In today's times of confusion and insanity, when many lovely ideas to reform the world have come to naught, to ashes and mud, Korczak's method of effecting change from early childhood has lost none of its validity.

Paris 1972
Translated and abridged by Frieda Johles Forman,
Ronnee Jaeger, and Sylvia Lustgarten.
In gang fun tsayt, Paris 1976

Anka: To Her Eternal Memory

"We're going to Krochmalna, hurry – we still have to get seats. This time, I'll go with you. After that – you'll go alone. One visit to Krochmalna, and you'll want to go every Saturday morning."[1]

Krochmalna meant a lot to Anka, much more than just a Jewish street, with its poverty and exoticism. Krochmalna meant the large white house, the warm, brightly lit home for abandoned Jewish children. Krochmalna most importantly meant Doctor Janusz Korczak. For Anka and her friends it also meant a university, a place where they gained experience while preparing for the calling that Korczak inspired. In my provincial imagination, all this blended with my future vocation, dreams of fairness and justice, my youthful ideals for a brighter future.

"I must introduce you to him. We might even arrive before it starts, and if not, I'll introduce you later."

Anka pulled me from my hard iron bed, from my Sabbath sleep, a sleep which made up for my sleepless week nights, and rushed me along.

Still sleepy, I hurried. I had been waiting a long time for that Saturday morning, hoping to see with my own eyes everything that Anka had been telling me, wanting to have a look at the author of those wonderful books, that great children's advocate. I wanted to see the man himself. What did he really look like? When I read his books, or when Anka described his accomplishments, he appeared as a giant, sometimes a mythological god, but most often as a biblical prophet. Most

---

1 The cornerstone for the orphanage at 92 Krochmalna was laid in June 1911 and the building opened in October 1912. It is still in use today as an orphanage. The building also contains the Korczakianum Documentation and Research Centre, an arm of the Museum of Warsaw. https://culture.pl/en/article/12-things-worth-knowing-about -janusz-korczak, accessed 15 September 2021.

64   Holocaust

importantly, he was a rescuer of children, and was always among children. It didn't please me that he devoted his time and knowledge only to children, that he concerned himself too little with the unjust world of adults. I didn't hide this from Anka. Korczak fascinated us. He ignited our youthful dreams, gave them wings, taught us to soar.

Was I ever happy to be going with Anka! My dear older friend was well known there, and knew everyone and everything. For me, it was the first time I would be setting foot there. I will always remember that golden Polish morning: mild, almost warm, awash with sunlight. The air had a scent of spring. The Jewish streets and alleys of Warsaw were steeped in Sabbath. We cut across Krasinski Gardens. Young Jewish mothers were strolling, pushing their little ones in prams, or leading them by the hand. Jewish men, in long *kapotes*,[2] their beards carefully combed for Shabes, hurried to their small synagogues. That it was Shabes was clearly visible in the Jewish streets. The bright rays of the late morning sun, spread across the sky, contributing to the holy day.

My heart was beating. Amazing that I was going to the Korczak house. As usual, Anka took my hand as though leading a younger sister, showing her the wonders of the world. She recounted, described, explained; I listened attentively. As she spoke, she joked, laughing aloud. She could tell the saddest story with humour, with a joke, and that's how a vivid picture would emerge.

"Oy, was he full of lice! His dishevelled hair practically stood up on his head. And out of his nose dribbled two fat drops of snot, which he kept in check with his tongue. On no account did he want to go with me; he tore himself away from me, and tried to bite my hand. We washed him, bathed him – the two of us – one (of us) alone could not have managed." With resounding laughter she told me the details about the orphan who was left with a poor, sick grandmother. "He was a homeless beggar, but in the white house on Krochmalna, he turned into a good, well-mannered, boy."

Anka was also my angel, spreading her protective wings over me. In Warsaw I felt myself cast away to the end of the world. My attic room felt like a bird cage, crowded with small-town, provincial high school students like me. I also disliked the big city, with all its noise; everything appeared threatening and strange. I yearned for the woods, the lake, the fields. I was a knot of longing, and I was embarrassed by it. After all, I considered myself an adult, as a … I wanted to make over the world,

---

2 Long coat formerly worn by male Jews of Eastern Europe, now worn by Orthodox or Hasidic Jews.

simply turn the world on its head. Anka intuitively felt my homesickness, calmed me, made this unknown world familiar to me, sweetened my bitterness, fed me when I was hungry, even bought me shoes when my worn shoes were no longer serviceable.

Anka, twenty years old, from a respectable, well-established home, was in her element in her native city. I, barely sixteen years old, came from a home in a distant farming village, and felt myself to be a stranger here. The four years, which would normally make a great difference at our age, were erased by our close friendship. Anka, a student at the University of Warsaw, and also in Korczak's pedagogy courses, had observed the workings of his orphanage from inside. I still had two years until matriculation, but, mostly through Anka, I picked up something of Korczak's child-rearing system. Anka was ahead in both years and knowledge; I, however, had more life experience. Both of us were inspired by Korczak's achievements with the orphaned child, using his child-rearing method, and we wished with all our youthful enthusiasm to be part of it.

Anka had large, dark shining eyes, thick black curly hair, a ready smile on her gentle, pleasant face, a jewel of a heart and an unbounded belief in her calling. Make a better and more beautiful world? To that end, we must shape a better person, prepare the child to become an exemplary adult. And didn't Korczak believe that we could reform and improve life through the education of children?

I, a girl of fifteen or sixteen, under Korczak's influence and under Anka's direction, also believed in the magical power of child-rearing, and like Anka, wished to participate. I, however, had seen more of life's harshness and cruelty than she had. Since childhood, I'd seen in my village farmers beating their wives and children, had observed extreme need, and the poverty of Jews in small towns. Shall we wait until we have raised children to be good honest people? That's too long a wait! I was already captivated by this world view, and burned with impatience to reshape the world.

Anka and I had long arguments.

"Imagine how long it will take until … until we make something of all the children … meanwhile the barefoot go barefoot, the hungry will perish from hunger, the strong will beat the weak, men will flog their wives and children, and you, and all of us, will wait until we raise good, decent people?" I spoke with fiery passion. Anka remembered something, burst out laughing, joked: "Nu, let's get pails of cold water. Let's release the wild horses from the stables. Ha ha ha." Anka laughed heartily and melodiously, just like her singing, and we both dissolved in laughter. It was impossible not to join in her singing and laughter.

66 Holocaust

Sometimes we would sit alone in her room, telling each other our stories, shaking with laughter. Big-city Anka liked me to tell her stories of my village, of the farm. She especially liked the story of the bucket of water and the horses I released.

"How was it?" Tell it again," she would beg me, laughing, and I would retell the story – each time in a slightly altered version.

The story with the pail of water was like this: Two fifteen- to sixteen-year-old boys were itching for a duel, and, of course, in the presence of a fourteen-year-old young lady – me. This happened towards the end of summer, on a Shabes afternoon, in their parents' shared orchard outside the town. At first, it was a joke to see who was stronger. But the joking soon turned into a serious fight and I couldn't separate them. They were rolling on top of each other in the grass; their noses were soon spouting blood. I begged them, appealed to them, yelled, but they ignored me. So I dragged out a big pail of water and with one sweep poured it over them. They jumped up like wet cats, hot heads cooled off. I developed a whole theory based on this. As I got caught up in my story, it became newly evident to me that with words alone we can't be rid of evil – we need revolutionary acts.

The story about the horses was only one of many. Beating a wife or children was more or less a normal thing for our gentile neighbours. Among Jews, it was rare, but still occurred occasionally, though without the same viciousness. In this respect, Fayfke the wagon driver was like a gentile. He was a strong young man, had two beautiful wild horses and a colt, and an unfortunate wife. He was very gentle with his horses, rarely gave them the whip. An unusual love and gentleness with horses. Not so with wife; for a yes or a no he beat her. Thank God Fayfke was away most of the week, and couldn't beat her every day. But nobody cared, especially because like us, he lived among the gentile population. Nobody intervened, except … me. It was my task in life to break Fayfke's habit of beating his wife, not to mention his children.

Then one day, on a summery Shabes afternoon, heart-rending screams were heard from the wife and from the children. Like an arrow I shot across to the wagon driver's house, stood under the closed window, banged on the glass, and threatened that I would throw rocks at them. Had it not been Shabes, I might have broken the window. Fayfke didn't pay the slightest attention to my threats and just carried on. I went over to the stable, and with great effort, released the bolt, freeing the untethered horses and the colt. This threesome, it seemed, was quite happy with my deed, and, neighing, raced off to the peasant's vegetable garden. Hearing the neighing, Fayfke let go of his wife, ran after the horses,

Anka: To Her Eternal Memory 67

chased them until he brought them back, and then let out a stream of curses about the damage the horses had done.

Anka just loved my story, and it supported my side of our disagreement.

"So, how would you, Anka, with your fine talk, break Fayfke of his habit of beating wife and children? How would you educate him?"

"Rather we want to educate his children, we want ..."

"And meanwhile, should we let him thrash them? And meanwhile the poor ..."

"Who is saying that? You're comparing apples and oranges. You have to get to know Korczak better. Korczak demands ... Korczak maintains ..."

In one breath she laid out for me a mountain of humanitarian measures that reined in my rebelliousness and my revolutionary zeal somewhat. Korczak was electrifying, fascinating. His name alone had a magic power. There was nothing I was more jealous of than the fact that she was Korczak's student, knew him really well, was close to him, and was a regular on Krochmalna Street.

And now here she is taking me to Korczak on Krochmalna. Shabes mornings, you could come and listen to him reading aloud, to both children and adults.[3]

Anka walks ahead. I follow. We enter a large white hall. We're a bit late. The hall is full, all seats taken. At the front, at a small table stands a man of medium height, bald; a short blond beard reaches his sideburns, and he is wearing something like a housecoat. He reads aloud, clearly, with emphasis. All around are children, bigger, smaller, younger, and older. Every so often, another visitor enters – the door is open to all. Some sit; others stand, as there is a shortage of seats. All eyes are fixed on the reader. Here and there a child stirs, but in the hall it is quiet. Only the voice of the reader is heard. Suddenly a young boy bolts from his place, approaches Korczak, leans into him, and hugs him with both his little hands. Korczak, without interrupting his reading, pats his head, and disentangles himself. The boy sits himself at Korczak's side, and looks about with sad eyes. Soon, he springs from his seat and finds a spot a bit farther. Near me, a little girl is squirming on her chair, opens a notebook, and looks inside. Nobody pays attention. Whoever doesn't want to listen, doesn't, as long as one doesn't disturb – and the child knows – one mustn't disturb.

Anka whispers in my ear, "A good story, funny, no?"

---

3 Lili Berger, *Korczak: Un Homme, un symbole* (Paris: Magnard, 1990). Berger refers to a friend who is a student, and with whom she attended Korczak's lectures.

68   Holocaust

I nod discreetly, agreeing. But it's a lie; I don't hear the words, the content – I just hear the tone, the emphasis. I am all eyes; my sense of sight swallows my sense of hearing. I observe. My eyes wander over the hall, over the children who listen attentively, and my gaze returns to Korczak. I keep looking at him, hoping to recognize something of the person in my imagination. However, he is so different from what I had imagined when I read his books, or when Anka told me about his accomplishments. Such an ordinary figure; he doesn't have the appearance of a learned person, a famous author, who cared for so many children. And yet, I can't tear my eyes away from his face. Oh, what a gentle, calm face, what intelligent, kind blue eyes! Anka draws my gaze away from him, nudging my shoulder. With a look, she indicates a twelve- to thirteen-year-old boy, with a head that looks like a smoothly mowed meadow. He sits not far from us, alert, his mouth open, concentrating on the reader.

Anka whispers in my ear: "That's him."

"Who?" I whisper back.

"The one with lice, who wanted to bite me."

The boy feels my stare, turns around, sees Anka, and lowers his eyes; he remains seated, though the reading has ended. Anka approaches him, puts her arm on his shoulder in a familiar manner, asks him if he liked the story.

"Yes, a very good story" – and his face breaks out in a smile.

Korczak has now emerged from behind the table; people encircle him. Anka tugs me by the sleeve; my heart is beating harder and harder.

"Good morning, Herr Doctor, I've brought along a future pedagogue, she already teaches a few hours a day, private lessons. She has already read most of your books, she has already … she wants …"

Korczak sizes me up with his intelligent blue eyes, as though I were too young, not grown up enough for such responsibilities. I feel myself blushing. I'm tongue-tied, I can barely reply to his words.

"There is a lot to learn, you have to love children in order to work with them."

But he soon turns to Anka: "And what are you thinking of doing, what path will you choose when you complete your studies?"

"I've already chosen, Herr Doctor; I will follow in your path."

And years later, Anka, together with her daughter, went on the same path as her professor Janusz Korczak – to Treblinka.

Translated by Sam Blatt
Geshtaltn un pasirungen, Paris 1991

Thoughts on Reading "The Medem Sanatorium Book"

A sense of holiness engulfed me. My heart tightened as I began to leaf through the Medem Sanatorium Book: about five hundred oversized drawings filled with photographs created by forty participants including teachers, school activists, writers, past "sanatorists," memoirists. The famous, vibrant Medem Sanatorium rose up before me. I recalled it from one, and only one, visit. It was a summer day, and I could hardly wait for a free half-day to visit the sanatorium. I was a provincial student in the final year at the gymnasium, already a teacher in a private children's Jewish *pensionat*.

It is remarkable that in prewar Poland, among the most impoverished and oppressed Jewish population, there were institutions based on the most modern and innovative pedagogy. Each in its own way was like a rainbow in a rainy sky, bursting with the vividness of a new, authentic humanistic educational philosophy. Both the Korczak house and the Medem Sanatorium had sought to uproot fear and distrust from the poor, often neglected children, planting in their hearts joy, independence, comradeship, and trust.

Founded in 1926, the Medem Sanatorium was funded primarily by American organizations to serve as a healing institution for the children of Jewish poverty. And wonder of wonders: the healing institution quickly became one of the most avant-garde educational institutions in the country. And this could happen because it was created and existed in a period of great Jewish spiritual growth and flowering. During this period, it was part of the Tsysho[1] school system in Warsaw, which educated 3,000 children in the spirit of justice, humanitarianism, and, let us not shy away from it, in the spirit of purest socialism.

---

1 The Central Yiddish School Organization, commonly known by its acronym, TSYSHO or CYSHO, was established in Warsaw in June 1921.

70 Holocaust

The Medem Sanatorium was the creation of the Tsysho movement, becoming what it was because of the intense, committed effort of school and community workers as well the devotion and abilities of its teachers. The director, Shloyme Gilinsky,[2] understood fully that healing the body succeeds best when the soul is also healed, restoring childish joy, awakening trust, independence, and innate energy.

In the midst of this wonderland, all the children, even those taken out of "garbage cans," carried out their responsibilities under the watchful eye of the educators. During their short stay, every child developed a healthy attitude towards beautifying the children's republic. The closeness to nature, the devoted love of teachers awakened in them a love of all plants and an interest in discovering the secrets of nature. Most important, they learned about friendship: the care shown to a sick friend, the attention given by the older children to the younger ones. These qualities could only develop in an atmosphere of love and humanitarian feelings, independence and self-discipline.

In the profound Jewish poverty of prewar Poland, the Medem Sanatorium grew and blossomed from year to year. Specialists, educators, and child psychologists came from around the world to admire and learn from its achievements. In its thirteen years, several thousand children were both treated and educated at this remarkable children's institution; even the Nazi occupation could not destroy its educational practice nor discourage its teachers.

With the outbreak of war, the children were sent home; it was natural that at such a time parents would wish to have their children near them. But the Medem Sanatorium did not remain closed for long, even though the building had been vandalized, its inventory stolen. Within a few months of extraordinary effort and creativity, it was again ready to receive children. Jewish parents felt fortunate to be able to place their children into trustworthy hands. Though there was no heating during the winter, the Medem remained a bright, warm home. Under conditions of hunger and cold, pervasive uncertainty, danger threatening at every corner, the spirit of that prewar children's home came to life again. The children not only helped with all the work but also studied in the newly re-established school.

Let us acknowledge that we do not know all that happened in the Medem Sanatorium during the occupation, particularly in its final days. The catastrophic course of events is inscribed in the Memorial Book, but few witnesses of that last period have survived.

---

2 Shloyme Gilinsky (1888–1961): Under his leadership approximately 10,000 children were treated at the Medem Sanatorium between 1926 and 1939.

Thoughts on Reading "The Medem Sanatorium Book" 71

One witness of the sanitarium's last period was Salo-Henryk Fiszgrund,[3] who died a few years ago. A Bundist, he maintained a connection with both the leaders of the Bund and the Polish Socialist Party. With his fine appearance and his polished Polish accent, he could, more readily than others, move about on the Aryan side. From time to time, he was a guest at the Medem Sanatorium and always took "secrets" away with him. In the summer of 1968, while I was secretly taking notes, he described to me certain incidents and happenings in the Medem Sanatorium. I am now looking at my notes taken at that time and adding certain new facts.

Before me is a book on the subject of Janusz Korczak, written by a certain Jaworski[4] in Warsaw in 1973. After pointing out all the good qualities and accomplishments of the great pedagogue and acknowledging his martyrdom, he reminds us that Korczak was mistaken in keeping the children near him instead of sending them out and forcing them to save themselves.

Over two hundred children and staff of the Medem Sanatorium were led to their death on 20 August 1942. Two weeks earlier, on the morning of 5 August, the same number of children and staff had gone on their last walk with Korczak leading them. That summer the Nazi axe came down on all the children's homes. Just like Korczak, and like Dr. Tola Mintz,[5] the educators and teachers chose death rather than leaving the children.

The organized murder of children's collectives in Warsaw and surrounding areas, where numerous orphanages and dormitories were located, occurred in those summer months, some earlier, and some later. The German child murderers worked according to plan, keeping an eye on all the children's homes. In the summer of 1943, in Bialystok alone they removed 1,260 children from the orphanages at one time.

---

3 Salo-Henryk Fiszgrund was a member of the Bund and the Jewish Underground in the Warsaw Ghetto. He died in 1971.
4 Marek Jaworski (1937–) wrote a book entitled *Janusz Korczak*. The English edition was published by Interpress Publishers in Warsaw in 1978.
5 Dr. Tola (Tolla) Mintz was a prominent doctor working at the Medem Sanatorium in 1942. Having refused offers to help her escape during the liquidation of the Warsaw ghetto, she died together with two hundred children in the Treblinka extermination camp.

72 Holocaust

In September of the same year, in the Łódź Ghetto, which the Nazis had scheduled for later annihilation, they implemented the infamous "Shpere."[6] First sacrificed were 5,000 children from orphanages and dormitories. About 15,000 were torn from the arms of their parents, dragged out of hiding places. 20,000 child-martyrs with labels around their necks were loaded onto trucks sent to unknown destinations. To this very day we do not know what violent deaths, what terrible suffering the children of Łódź were subjected to in the "Shpere"; like the general public, we ourselves know little about the death throes suffered by these thousands of Jewish children.

More than one and a half million! When we now read in the Medem Sanatorium Book about the children's last hours in that institution, unending rows of Jewish children driven to their destruction rise up before us. They call to us, asking us not to forget them. It is never too late to memorialize them in a book of remembrance, remember them from generation to generation.

Forgetting is wiping out, erasing. The Ba'al Shem Tov said, "Remembrance leads to redemption."

Abridged and translated by Sylvia Lustgarten
In loyf fun tsayt, Paris 1988

---

6 Shpere (Sperre): An abbreviation of the German Geshpere (curfew). During a deportation during a week in September 1942, the Germans hunted down "unproductive" Jews in the Łódź Ghetto – mainly children under ten, the sick, and the old – and sent them to their death.

ARTS AND LETTERS

Bruno Schulz, Artist and Jew

In the Jewish world Bruno Schulz is little known. However, Bruno Schulz, the gifted Polish Jewish artist, deserves more than just a passing mention, both for his role as a multi-talented creator and as a Jewish martyr.

Among the Jewish authors and artists felled by Hitler's sword were those who wrote in Polish. Their fate under the Nazi regime was tragically complicated and particularly heart-rending. Completely unknown to the vast majority of Jews, they found themselves doubly confined and isolated in the ghetto due to their lack of contact with those who shared their fate. This was especially true of the younger writers who had not yet made a name for themselves. Only a few, the most talented and the most energetic, found a way to connect with the Yiddish-speaking population by involving themselves in the feverish life of the ghetto. In his famous *Złote okna* (Golden Windows), Adolf Rudnicki[1] depicted a talented Jewish Polish poet who maintained his dignity shoulder to shoulder with the ghetto rebels, while another poet wallowed ghost-like in his own misfortune. In his ghetto writings, Emanuel Ringelblum described the uniquely tragic fate of the Jewish writers who wrote in Polish. After their death, their memory and the little that remained of their literary legacy suffered an equally tragic fate. They were all killed as Jews but remained unknown in the Jewish world. Generations earlier, Maimonides had written that those murdered solely for being Jews

---

1 Pen name of Jewish writer Aron Hirszhorn (1909–1990), whose series "The Time of the Gas Chambers" (*Epoka pieców*) included *Złote okna* (Golden Windows). See Antony Polonsky and Monika Adamczyk-Garbowska, eds., *Contemporary Jewish Writing in Poland* (Lincoln: University of Nebraska Press, 2001).

76   Arts and Letters

should be regarded as martyrs. Thus, in writing about Schulz, how could I not mention at least a few of those martyrs?

For example, the talented Jewish Polish poet Władysław Szlengel[2] wrote prolifically in the Warsaw Ghetto, while throwing himself into the frenzied Jewish communal life of the ghetto. He inspired courage with his popular poem "Kontratak," and even composed announcements and verses for the children in Korczak's orphanage. Although, fortunately, a portion of Szlengel's work survived, who today knows about him or other poets like him, or about their poetry?

The sensitive poet Henryka Lazowert (Łazowertówna) earned a reputation in the Warsaw Ghetto for her moving poem "The Little Smuggler," in which she described the tragedy and heroism of Jewish children. How many of us today know about this poet and her literary impact? There were other poets, and also prose writers such as Irena Gajzler (Geisler) and Gustawa Jarecka. We could go further down the list, and not just the list of writers in the Warsaw Ghetto. A weighty illustrated volume by the Kraków poet and pedagogue Julius Feldhorn entitled *Works and Creators or General Overview of the History of Art* was published sixteen years after the war. The author had been killed, but the manuscript was rescued. Nonetheless, it had long to wait before finally seeing the light of day. Feldhorn had published a few books of poems as well as prose in Polish, in addition to being a first-rate translator. His translation of the Song of Songs from the original demonstrated how intimately familiar he was with traditional Jewish sources.[3] Who today would remember a writer and art historian like him, not to mention the many young talents who had not yet established their reputations, or those whose work disappeared without a trace?

It would be wrong to apply to Bruno Schulz what I wrote about the above-mentioned writers, even though his name was shrouded in a fog of mystery for a long time. In his book about Schulz, the Polish

---

2 For Władysław Szlengel, Henryka Lazowert (Łazowertówna), Irena Gajzler, and Gustawa Jarecka, see Samuel D. Kassow, *Who Will Write Our History?: Emanuel Ringelblum, the Warsaw Ghetto, and the Oyneg Shabes Archive* (Bloomington: Indiana University Press, 2007).

3 Feldhorn Juliusz (1901–1942). The manuscript of his popular overview of the history of art, completed in 1939, could not be published until 1956.

poet Jerzy Ficowski recounts that on two occasions prior to 1950 he had submitted essays about Schulz to Polish literary periodicals, but they were rejected. Ficowski adds that "for several years one could either say something negative about Schulz, or be silent." Only in 1957, after the Polish October,[4] was most of his surviving literary work published. It came as a revelation, although the name Bruno Schulz had already been well known prior to his death.

When Schulz was murdered in November of 1942 in the Drohobycz[5] Ghetto by a Nazi bullet, he was fifty years old and had already produced a large body of literary work, and an even greater corpus of visual art. He was recognized as an extraordinarily skilful and creative printmaker, especially for his gelatin-coated glass plate technique. His albums of prints and drawings, artistically bound by the artist himself, were widely collected. He was also a painter.

Following the publication of two books which are now famous, *The Cinnamon Shops* (*Sklepy cynamonowe*) and *The Sanatorium under the Hourglass* (*Sanatorium pod Klepsydrą*), he was compared to Kafka.[6] Perhaps that was because Schulz was the first to introduce Kafka to Polish readers through his translation of *The Trial*.[7] Yet he was unlucky as an artist and as a writer, both during his lifetime and even after his death. His attempts to publish his literary work encountered serious obstacles every step of the way. It was only thanks to the efforts of the Polish writer Sofia Nałkowska, who was captivated by some of his short stories that found their way to her, that these two books appeared during his lifetime.

---

4 Stalin's death in 1953 and Nikita Khrushchev's famous speech in February 1956 denouncing Stalin's "cult of personality" led to a series of events in Poland that culminated in the Polish October, or Polish Thaw, when Władysław Gomułka, seen as liberal, was confirmed as leader of the Polish Communist Party. See Anthony Polonsky and Leszek W. Gluchowski, "1968, Forty Years After," in *Polin: Studies in Polish Jewry*, vol. 21 (Oxford: Littman Library of Jewish Civilization, 2008).

5 The Polish spelling of the city is used throughout this essay, since throughout Schulz's lifetime, under the Polish and Nazi regimes, that was the spelling. Today, as part of Ukraine, the correct spelling is Drohobych.

6 The English translations are included in Bruno Schulz, *Collected Stories*, translated by Madeline G. Levine (Evanston, IL: Northwestern University Press, 2018).

7 A Polish translation of Franz Kafka's *The Trial* was published in 1936 with Schulz's name as translator, although the translation had actually been done by Schulz's fiancée, Józefina Szelińska. See Eugenia Prokop-Janiec, entry on Bruno Schulz in the *Yivo Encyclopedia of the Jews in Eastern Europe*, https://yivoencyclopedia.org/article.aspx/Schulz_Bruno, accessed 19 April 2022.

78 Arts and Letters

As a quiet, shy, somewhat sickly, and always fearful adolescent who was raised both in the Polish language and culture and in the Jewish tradition, Bruno Schulz began writing almost in secret. Writing was his second great passion, after drawing and painting. But he wrote only for himself, occasionally reading for friends. After the war, he was lumped together with Kafka. His alleged great literary affinity with the Jewish Czech writer sealed his fate. While these writers were fundamentally different, they did have much in common. Kafka, too, was not eager to publish. Each novella or short story had to be wrested away from him, and it is common knowledge that in his will Kafka directed that all his manuscripts be gathered and burned.

Bruno Schulz, on the other hand, in dramatically different tragic circumstances, wanted to save his creative work. Confined to the Drohobycz ghetto, forced into slave labour by the murderers, he was constantly seeking ways to hide his manuscripts, paintings, and prints. He sent one package of manuscripts out of the ghetto, and other works he hid wherever he could. These have disappeared without a trace. Were it not for Jerzy Ficowski, we would have scant information about the tragic life and struggles of the Drohobycz Jewish Polish artist. For almost two decades Ficowski relentlessly searched and rummaged wherever he could, but was only able to travel to Drohobycz when it was already too late, after it had become part of the Soviet Union. From the documents, testimonies, and other information about the Schulz family he found in every corner of the world, from letters and photographs, from little crumbs and slivers, he created a book entitled *The Regions of the Great Heresy*, taken from an expression in Schulz's novel *The Cinnamon Shops*. Ficowski recounted to me at length how difficult it was to collect the material for his book, and to what extent any traces of the Drohobycz artist had been erased, not only in his birthplace, but also in the nearby towns and vacation spas, where Schulz spent his summer holidays. In addition to biographical profiles, some letters, and a small number of short stories published in 1964, Jerzy Ficowski also collected close to fifty reproductions of drawings in India ink, graphite, and charcoal, as well as prints, among which were a few self-portraits, and illustrations to the artist's novels.

Not a single oil painting remained, but from his drawings and prints, some of which were saved in museums and private collections, we can assess the high quality of Schulz's visual art. To comprehend the essence of the artist's written work, I believe it necessary to examine his visual art. They go hand in hand. Therefore, let us examine, albeit superficially, the prints and drawings: otherworldly figures, expressed in unusual compositions, all sunken within themselves, as though the world and its shocks are to be found within them, yet they are not of this world. A kind of mysterious, magical power reigns over everything and everyone. Everything moves as if in a mysterious enchanted circle, in an incomprehensible world, but the incomprehensible, the fantastic, is built on the real, on the authentic. The bizarre figures and situations are from real life, from the artist's immediate neighbourhood, from his Jewish milieu, and in all this he himself and his authentically Jewish father have a significant place. Jewish reality in its supernatural state: Jews in prayer shawls in the synagogue, ordinary Jews in the market-place and at home – Jewish shadows, sometimes depicted as dwarfs in their powerlessness, sometimes again as shrivelled figures, medieval mystics in a state of transcendence, deep in thought, with soundless prayers on their lips.

Completely different is the world of women. They are figures with demonic powers, smiling scornfully. Their eroticism is a blend of domination and submissiveness, or, one could say, helplessness coupled with brutality, human powerlessness with brutal authority. Naïveté and severity go hand in hand. That is how he sees the world around him. His own inner world, his complicated and multi-faceted personality, stare out from his self-portraits.

When questioned about why he chose such themes, Bruno Schulz always answered that he did not choose them, they chose him. Thus, we can say about him what we often say about great artists: he was a prisoner of his art and created like one possessed. All his life – he had already begun to draw as a three-year-old child – art alone was the content and the foundation of his life. As an adult, he often complained in letters to friends that he had so little time left for his creative work. The greater part of the day was consumed by teaching. He was a drawing instructor in the Drohobycz Gymnasium.

The modest Drohobycz teacher, almost in secrecy and in great loneliness, undertook to write a kind of bible of his own. Although fantastical, it was purely authentic. Just as in his graphic art, he was inspired by his immediate neighbourhood, his own Jewish city, sometimes indirectly. His own Jewish self, his "I," caught in the web of Jewish fatalism, left a strong imprint on his creative work.

From an early age, Bruno Schulz was attached to his Jewish home. According to Ficowski, although his parents spoke Polish to the children at home, Jewish traditions were observed. When his father went to

80 Arts and Letters

synagogue on the holidays, the little Bruno was always at his side. The boy was more fascinated than the other two children with Jewish religious rituals. As a young man who was mystical by nature and already a writer, Schulz would silently blend into the Jewish crowd on Yom Kippur. An examination of his biography and his work today makes it clear that for Schulz, the Polish writer, his Jewish home was his only place of refuge.

From childhood, he was a solitary individual, and extremely sensitive. In one of his letters, he relates how his mother read him Goethe's ballads when he was eight years old, and how those first kernels which resonated in his child's heart later reappeared in his artistic world view: "Barely understanding the German language, I could grasp the content, and, shaken to the depth of my soul, I cried when my mother read to me." In the same letter, writing about art and artists, he continues: "The early pictures depict for the artist the limits of his own creation ..."

Yet the greatest source of support for the artist, for whom "the limits of his own creation" were determined so early, was his father, the Jewish shopkeeper Jacob Schulz, about whom it has been said that he was more a dreamer than a shopkeeper. It was he, the Jewish shopkeeper, who, after his death, was transported into his son's literary work.

In her book about famous authors, the Jewish Polish writer Hanna Mortkowicz-Olczakowa, daughter of the famous prewar publisher Jakób Mortkowicz, who had sacrificed so much to publish the works of Polish writers (he went bankrupt and committed suicide), also portrayed Bruno Schulz's rich and complex personality, highlighting the incomprehensible fear which often gripped him. Apparently, he was one of those great visionary artists who clearly, and with their entire beings, in their current alienation sensed the dangers which were increasingly imminent. Perhaps that is why he was always troubled, spoke quietly, and looked as though danger was lying in wait for him. More than once he was attacked by the antisemitic press, especially when his novel *The Cinnamon Shops* was published. However, Polish writers and democratic literary circles in Poland began to value his great talent. In 1938, the Polish Academy of Literature awarded him a prestigious prize for his literary work. However, this did not dispel his dejection, his disquiet or his *bodenlosigkeit*, his lack of groundedness, which he wrote about in his letters to his friends in those days. When we read his letters, which are also works of literature, Franz Kafka again comes to mind. Jerzy Ficowski and others did not notice the Jewish fatalism shared by these two artists. Perhaps that was why they did not see their many similarities, despite the fact that fundamentally their work was different. First and foremost, their work was influenced by their tragic lives. There is also something similar in their writing. When we trace the evolution of the modern novel, of contemporary prose, we turn to Schulz and Kafka as much as to James Joyce and Virginia Woolf. We find in both writers elements which, little by little, altered the course of the traditional narrative, such as their flight from the traditional storyline, their emphasis on introspection, the psychological analysis of the "I," the interior monologue, and a preoccupation with their own actions, their own *Lebensakt*, the act of living.

One should not make comparisons, and, of course, these two writers should not be labelled, as has been attempted at various times. However, when one reflects on the life and personality of Bruno Schulz, Franz Kafka inevitably comes to mind.

Kafka, raised in the German and Czech cultures, and writing in the German language, felt uprooted and alien in his non-Jewish surroundings. It is known that he tried to get closer to Jewish life, to the Jewish creative milieu, but he remained a stranger in both non-Jewish and Jewish environments. Certainly there are contrasts in the personal lives of both artists, but in those contrasts there are sometimes similarities.

For Kafka, his Jewish home was alien and oppressive. For Bruno Schulz, on the contrary, his Jewish home and his childhood, under the protection of his parents, seemed a peaceful island in a raging sea.

As a writer, Bruno Schulz, the lonely and *bodenlos* Jew, the Jew without a sense of groundedness, sought to recapture his Jewish home, his father and his childhood, which became for him a kind of mythology as well as a lush oasis in the desert. The lonely writer longed to take himself to that oasis with his artistic imagination. He had yearned to find a hiding place, at least in an artistically created world. This he succeeded in doing in his two books, *The Cinnamon Shops* and *The Sanatorium under the Hourglass*, a world in which the Jewish milieu, his father, and at times the artist himself, appear at various stages and in a variety of situations.

Of his literary work that was salvaged, two novels, or, more precisely, collections of stories, come first and foremost to mind. Although each story can live on its own, they have an essential affinity, they build a wholeness, and thus should be called a novel. To specify their subject or convey their plot would be difficult. Schulz himself, answering a literary questionnaire, said about this: "My next book will be a volume composed of four stories. The theme, as always, is insignificant and difficult

82 Arts and Letters

to summarize. The real subject matter, the ultimate raw material I find in myself without any interference of will. Even so, it has a very definite atmosphere, indicating a specific kind of content that grows out of it and is layered upon it ..."[8]

The inner imaginary condition and its mood are almost tangible. So, for example, *The Sanatorium under the Hourglass* deals with the mythological Hades, the kingdom of the dead, but resurrected as a civilized Hades. The dead father goes through various transformations and strange reincarnations, in which he continues to live. His leave-taking from the living becomes immaterial because his soul and spirit live on in everything and everyone. The artist simply crosses out the real fact of his father's death. A myth of life wipes away the reality of death, and in that myth the resurrected father turns into the spokesperson of the artist's thoughts, the expression of his feelings, the reflection of his childhood. The return to childhood stops the march of time.

The longing for one's childhood is not new in art. Seldom, however, has anyone so artistically and powerfully breathed life into this longing, and never in such a form. Escaping from his demons, Bruno Schulz created a unique artistic vision, a magical world with our own Jewish sounds, melodies, and colours, as though he intended to revitalize what was about to disappear. And this is where he diverged greatly from Kafka.

In the visual arts today, the great masters look to the primitives, to the work of primitive folk art. It is quite possible that Schulz, in his literary work, drew on old folk myths, on ancient beliefs about transformations of human life, and created a mythology based on his own biography, on his Jewish milieu, on Jewish fatalism.

Bruno Schulz was deeply rooted in the shtetl, the small Jewish town. Even with industrialization, technology, and electrification, the greyness of small-town daily life still predominates, the ordinary lives in harmony with the remarkable, the lofty with the grotesquely debased, the animated with the paralysed. How significant are the words of the father, "We want to recreate man ..."?

To recreate – a mannequin? Is man not a mannequin? Yes, there are human beings who are mannequins, in other words, automatons. Their spirit is fettered by matter. A human being must escape from those automatons, from the material world, and from soullessness, escape

---

8 Translation by Jerzy Ficowski in Jerzy Ficowski, *Regions of the Great Heresy: Bruno Schulz, A Biographical Portrait,* translated and edited by Theodosia Robertson, 146–7 (New York: W.W. Norton, 2002).

into an enchanted world, back to one's childhood, before being swallowed up and devoured by time.

Schulz wrote a story entitled "The Old-Age Pensioner."[9] A lonely person, already retired, decides to go back to school. He wants to start his education anew. Here is another version in another style, but the same return to childhood, and perhaps to a younger era of mankind.

While Kafka saw man as threatened from every direction, a prisoner in an invisible, widely cast net, Schulz saw him as lost in the march of time, which could quickly gobble him up and obliterate him. To protect himself, he created a subjective time, a psychological, unmeasurable timeframe, as in fairy tales.

People usually write about Bruno Schulz in connection with his short stories, novels, his few essays, and his notes. The truth is, they should begin with his letters. Had they all survived, they would have taken up several thick volumes.

At one time there was a respected literary genre called epistolography. Bruno Schulz revived this genre. He began his literary career with letters. He fulfilled his need to express himself in artistic language in the extensive correspondence he conducted with the pre-eminent artists and writers of his day, among them Thomas Mann. In times of great loneliness, he wrote to his close artist friends, especially to women. "I need a friend, I long for the warmth of a someone close," he wrote to the famous Polish writer Breza.[10]

His letters, however, were more than just letters.[11] In them he conducted interior monologues, dialogues with other writers, conversations with the world. Also, he polished them artistically, often composing them in a notebook first. It was a true literary workplace. He later wrote about his letters: "There was a time when I revived myself through letters. At that time they were my only literary output."

---

9 G. Hyde, "State of Arrest: The Short Stories of Bruno Schulz," in S. Eile and U. Phillips, eds., *New Perspectives in Twentieth-Century Polish Literature*, Studies in Russia and East Europe (London: Palgrave Macmillan, 1988).

10 Tadeusz Breza (1905–1970) was a novelist and essayist, as well as a diplomat in the service of the Second Polish Republic and the Polish People's Republic. During World War II he was active in the resistance movement.

11 Jaimy Gordon, "The Strange Afterlife of Bruno Schulz," *Michigan Quarterly Review* 43, no. 1 (Winter 2004).

84 Arts and Letters

In some of the few letters that survived, the lonely man emerges more clearly than in other works. The letters convey the tragedy of a Jewish writer who felt as though the ground was swaying under his feet: "I am completely sick, shaking uncontrollably, perhaps the beginning of melancholia? Biting at me from within is a despair and a sadness in which I will lose everything … perhaps I should consult a doctor? But I don't believe any doctors." That is what he wrote in a letter in early 1939. He was then working regularly in the Drohobycz Gymnasium, was active in both artistic spheres, and had completed his novel *Messiah*[12] while in his heart and soul he felt the coming catastrophe "in which I will lose everything."

To assess how much literary work was lost, it is sufficient to recall that of several thousand letters, only one hundred and ninety were later collected. The rest were destroyed by various means, as were his friends. Some letters were found after the war in houses that had been ransacked. Among them are the most important letters in which Schulz wrote about literature, art, and his own work – he was also a literary critic. In the letters to the murdered poet Debora Vogel he included outlines of *The Cinnamon Shops* and other literary projects. They tell us about work he began and work he finished. Among them was the manuscript of a novel in four parts, which was about to be printed, and the finished novel *Messiah*,[13] in which the return to his childhood was represented by the Jewish Messiah legend of the salvation and the perfection of man.

As already mentioned, Bruno Schulz tried with all his might to save his work. He had hoped that his art would physically save him. His painting greatly appealed to a Drohobycz Gestapo officer by the name of Landau, who made him his slave. He forced Schulz to paint his portrait, and to cover the walls of his spacious home with murals. In

---

12 The novel Messiah was never found, although Jerzy Ficowski made every effort to track it down. See https://culture.pl/en/interrupted-country/in-search-of-the -messiah-bruno-schulz-his-detective, accessed 28 June 2024.

13 See, for example, the description in Cynthia Ozick's novel *The Messiah of Stockholm* (New York: Alfred A. Knopf, 1987).

Bruno Schulz, Artist and Jew   85

exchange for long days of work, Bruno Schulz received enough to keep him alive, and a promise of protection. With revulsion and contempt, he completed the work he was compelled to do. Sick and broken, with the greatest of effort, he managed not to fall off the scaffolding while working on the wall and ceiling paintings. He prolonged the work to prolong his life, to survive. His German guardian, however, had shot another Jewish slave, a Jewish dentist, employed by a German officer with whom Landau had quarrelled. "You have killed my Jew, I shall kill yours," said the latter. And he kept his word.

In the Drohobycz ghetto, on a day that was called "Black Thursday," Jews were being snatched from the street and shot. Bruno Schulz immediately began returning home with a friend. Under his arm he was tightly pressing a loaf of bread. Suddenly there was confusion and running, but he was too weak to run. At the same time, the enemy of his "guardian" passed by and recognized him. He grabbed Schulz by the neck and shot two bullets into his forehead. At dawn Bruno Schulz was secretly buried in the Jewish cemetery. There the murdered Jewish artist rested for years under a mound of earth beside his parents' graves, next to the headstones which he himself had designed and placed to commemorate his parents.

The Drohobycz Jewish cemetery, I've been told, was destroyed years after the war. Houses were built in its place. Even in his grave, the great artist was not left in peace. Who knows how his remains were desecrated.

The Schulz family home still stands in Drohobycz.[14] The house where the artist was born, where he lived, and where he created was left unharmed, although without a commemorative plaque or any other trace of him, either on the house or anywhere else. In Poland, the works of the Polish Jewish artists were silenced for many years.

Everything came too late. In 1942, under the leadership of Zofia Nałkowska,[15] plans were underway on the Aryan side to rescue Bruno Schulz from the ghetto. They were too late. Similarly, the search for his manuscripts, paintings, prints, hidden in various places, was also delayed for too long. Nonetheless, the little that was saved has placed Schulz in the ranks of the great masters. His above-mentioned books

---

14 Drohobycz is now in Ukraine in the Lviv Oblast.
15 Zofia Nałkowska (1884–1954) was a Polish prose writer, dramatist, and essayist. She served as the executive member of the prestigious Polish Academy of Literature (1933–9) during the interwar period.

86   Arts and Letters

have been translated into many languages, including French, and the author is known the world over as a talented Polish writer.

It is our duty to know, and to make known, that although he wrote in Polish, the writer Bruno Schulz thought, created, suffered, and died as a Jew. As a Jew he must be remembered.

Translated by Vivian Felsen
In gang fun tsayt (Au fil des années), Paris, 1976

Postscript

The following appeared in Lili Berger's 1991 collection entitled *Geshtaltn un pasirungen* (*Vies et destins*)[16] (People and events) (Paris: 1991), 117–18.

In *Di Goldene Keyt* (no. 128) there is a review by Nathan Gross about an exhibition of drawings by Bruno Schulz. The exhibition is taking place in the Israel Museum in Jerusalem. All the pieces in the exhibition were brought there by Janusz Odrowąż-Pieniążek, the director of the Adam Mickiewicz Museum of Literature in Warsaw. He was accompanied by Wojciech Chmurzyński, the official curator of the exhibition, which consists of one hundred and fifteen drawings. In addition to the drawings, the exhibition contains approximately sixty other documents such as manuscripts, letters, first editions of his work that appeared in *Skamander*[17] and *Sygnały*,[18] and photographs with family and friends. Among the drawings are illustrations for his books, title pages to his first editions, Jewish motifs, streets, dances ... and, of course, the drawings for *The Book of Idolatry*.[19] I read this news with great joy, with many memories, and with very deep regret that, due to a lengthy illness, I was not destined to travel to Israel for the exhibition.

For almost a decade, a few friends and I had tried to track down where we could find out something about Bruno Schulz's legacy. We were searching at a time when a heavy silence had descended over Schulz's work, and we gave up. However, just before I left Poland, I met the Polish poet Jerzy Ficowski at the Polish Writers Union. He told me

---

16 Translated in my entry about Lili Berger in the last section entitled *Selected Works*. https://jwa.org/encyclopedia/article/berger-lili, accessed 7 June 2024.

17 *Skamander: Miesięcznik poetycki* was a Polish literary magazine edited and published by Władysław Zawistowski in 110 issues between 1920 and 1939 in Warsaw.

18 *Sygnały Magazyn* (Signals magazine) was a Polish cultural and social magazine published from 1933 to 1939 in Lwów (Lemberg, today Lviv, Ukraine).

19 English translation published by Interpress Publishers, Warsaw, 1980.

Bruno Schulz, Artist and Jew   87

about his own painstaking search during which he had literally turned the world upside down to locate drawings, letters, photographs, and anything else he could possibly find. His relentless searching enabled him to collect a variety of materials out of which he constructed a valuable monograph that he sent to me in Paris almost twenty years ago. At the time, I knew that the poet Jerzy Ficowski's search was still ongoing. I am so happy that it has finally been crowned with success.

The exhibition is also a sign that something has changed in Poland since I left the country.

Translated by Vivian Felsen
In gang fun tsayt (*Au fil des années*), Paris, 1976

Vasily Grossman: The History of a Book or the Path to Jewish Identity

The history of literature, as told in various ancient chronicles, informs us that in all times great literary treasures have gone missing, perished in a variety of ways. Over hundreds of years, manuscripts and whole collections of books have been lost forever because of wars, revolutions, natural disasters, and migration. It is well known that in antiquity, primarily in Greco-Roman times, there were renowned collections that housed the writing of generations, such as the collections of ancient Rome and the even greater one in Alexandria. Little remains of them.

Today we know that Sophocles wrote over a hundred dramatic works. Only seven have come down to us. Euripides, Aristophanes, and Aeschylus had similar losses. The famed Greek poetess Sappho left us only a few poems and a few fragments of writing.

People's fanaticism, both religious and political, caused yet further damage through war, upheaval, massacres, and other calamities. The medieval church and the Inquisition, wherever it extended its power, condemned and burned manuscripts and books, or threw them into the cellars of cathedrals and churches. As a result, almost nothing is left of what was written by the Italian thinker Giordano Bruno, who was burnt at the stake in Rome in 1600 by decree of the Inquisition. To this day, in the great old cathedral of Palma, the capital of one of the Balearic Islands, there are stacks of Jewish holy books, stashed away by the Spanish Inquisition when it compelled the local Jews to convert, burning Marranos at the stake in the central square, a place I have visited more than a few times.

During the early Italian Renaissance, the great humanists Petrarch, Boccaccio, and others would make their way inside certain cathedrals and churches to search out condemned books and especially manuscripts. However, they would usually find stacks of ruined and torn pages. It was difficult to bring these banned, handwritten pages back to

Vasily Grossman: The History of a Book or the Path to Jewish Identity   89

life. Now, in our time, when man is conquering the cosmos, we have an instance just over twenty years ago of a manuscript (and not the only one) captured and condemned to death. Approximately two years ago it made its way to us, as if awakened from the dead by a miracle.[1]

We are speaking about the now famous book *Life and Fate*, by the Jewish Russian author Vasily Grossman. Two copies of the manuscript escaped arrest by the KGB via clandestine means and came to Switzerland, where the Russian text saw the light of day. A few months ago in Paris, the French translation appeared and it caused a literary sensation.

Vasily Grossman was widely known in the land of his birth into the 1950s. His reputation was made mainly during the World War II, when he was a correspondent at the front accompanying the Soviet army from Stalingrad to Berlin. His war correspondence, reportage, and essays were mostly printed in *Znamya*, but were featured in many other papers as well. After the war, they appeared in several publications and finally in a volume of 500 pages. After the defeat of Hitler, he was the first person to enter the destroyed Treblinka concentration camp. Based on what he himself witnessed and information from the sole survivor, Yankl Wiernik, and from the local farmers, Grossman described the full horror of the death camps.[2] The terrifying descriptions published in *Znamya* appeared in book form in French translation by November 1945. To this day I remember the shock I felt reading that thin volume *The Hell of Treblinka*. Shortly after, I had the chance to read *Stalingrad as I Saw It* in book form (in a largely adequate translation), and just these two works, read almost forty years ago, have remained in my mind as terrifying depictions.

It is relevant to mention that Vasily Grossman was a member of the Jewish Anti-Fascist Committee in Moscow and that immediately after the war as well as during the war, along with Ilya Ehrenburg,[3] he

---

1 The manuscript of *Life and Fate* was taken by the KGB some time shortly after October 1960. It was smuggled to the West in the 1970s and appeared in a French translation in 1980.

2 V. Grossman and Y. Wiernik, *Treblinka* (Tsentral farband fun poylishe yidn in Argentina, 1946) (Buenos Aires: Unión Central Israelita Polaca en la Argentina, 1946).

3 Ilya Ehrenburg (1891–1967). Writer, journalist, and poet who wrote primarily in Russian. Lived for a time in Paris but returned to Russia in 1940 when the Germans occupied Paris. During the war years, he was one of the Soviet Union's most prominent journalists. Ehrenburg's memoir *People, Years, Life* was serialized in the Yiddish Communist daily *Di Naye Prese*'s weekend supplement of 18–19 September 1965. On the page preceding it is a review of Berger's own story collection published that year. The clipping is found in Berger's archive in the Medem Library in Paris.

90 Arts and Letters

collected a massive amount of material about the destruction of the Jews and wrote "The Black Book," which was destroyed on Stalin's orders. (A hidden copy made its way years later to Jerusalem and appeared in Russian and eventually in a Yiddish translation.)[4]

The destruction of "The Black Book" in Moscow was the Soviet regime's first rebuke to Grossman as a Jew. And when I say "as a Jew," this is because before the war Vasily Grossman was remote from Jews and Jewish problems. The descendant of several generations of assimilated Jews, he had no Jewish upbringing whatsoever in his secular home. After the war, when he began to have an emotional breakdown, he looked for traces of his lost family in the city where he was born and could not find a single family member in three generations who spoke Yiddish.

There is little biographical information about Vasily Grossman. We don't know, for example, what became of his rich archive. The curtain of silence that descended on him from the time he wrote his great epic *Life and Fate* has made it difficult to gather Grossman's biographic and bibliographic information. The blanks were filled in, thanks to diligent research by Simon Markish, the older son of the murdered poet Peretz Markish.[5] His edifying book entitled *The Grossman Case*[6] came out in French (translated from the Russian) at almost at the same time as the publication in French of *Life and Fate*; it is from Markish that I drew most of the biographic particulars.

Vasily Grossman was born in 1905 in Berdichev. Jewish Berdichev also contained a small class of assimilated professional intelligentsia. Grossman's father was an engineer; his mother was a professor of French. In

---

4 The Spielberg Digital Yiddish Library contains a version of sixty-six pages credited to Ehrenburg. It was published in Moscow in April 1944 by the publishing house Der Emes. It appears to be "a short monograph in Yiddish under the title *Merder fun felker: Materialn vegn di retsikhes fun di Daytshishe farkhaper in di tsaytvaylik okupirte Sovetishe rayonen* (Murderers of peoples: Material about the murders by the German occupiers in the temporarily occupied Soviet territories); a second volume under the same title appeared, also in Yiddish, in September 1944." *YIVO*, s.v. "Black Book." The Shoah Resource Centre of Yad Vashem indicates that a Yiddish version of the completed book was not published until 1984. https://www.yadvashem.org/holocaust/resource-center/lexicon/b.html.

5 Peretz Markish (1895–1952) was one of the most important Soviet Yiddish writers and the only one to receive the Order of Lenin (1939). Markish headed the Yiddish section of the Soviet Writers Union and was a member of the Jewish Anti-Fascist Committee (JAC). He was arrested as part of a liquidation campaign aimed at JAC members and the undermining of Jewish culture. He was executed in secret in August 1952.

6 Simon Markish, *Le Cas Grossman* (Paris: Julliard, 1983).

Vasily Grossman: The History of a Book or the Path to Jewish Identity   91

the novel *Life and Fate*, the mother writes in a letter from the ghetto to her physicist son, the protagonist Shtrum, that she never saw herself as a Jew. Shtrum, it is easy to surmise, is the personification of Grossman himself, and Shtrum's mother, his own assimilated mother.

Grossman established his bona fides as a writer through Maxim Gorky. Characteristically, when Grossman shows how the Soviet regime degrades people, how the government grinds them up in the wheels of state, he recalls with bitter irony Gorky's well-known saying: "How marvellous is Man! How proud the word rings – Man!" Until the war, Grossman was a loyal Soviet writer. It is noteworthy, that at that time, he did not touch on Jewish problems in his writing, nor did he introduce Jewish characters despite coming from Berdichev, a very Jewish town. Antisemitism? If he was not personally touched by it, one can easily suppose that such a sensitive writer might somewhere have felt the pestilent air of antisemitism. Nonetheless, like his assimilated protagonist Shtrum, he believed that it was a remnant of tsarist times that would gradually vanish.

What then led Vasily Grossman to such a violent inner crisis that he had to introduce Jewish characters into his novel? Was it to expose antisemitism? Was it to memorialize, alongside the Jewish victims of Hitler's genocide, the victims of the Soviet camps? Was it to initiate a veritable duel with Soviet power and, last but not least, to become the first dissident of Soviet literature, as would happen?

Simon Markish, in the above-mentioned book, writes that it was above all the annihilation of the Jewish people by the Nazis that had a deep impact on Grossman. There is no doubt of this. But at the same time that he was getting closer to his Jewish roots, Vasily Grossman, a committed Communist, was becoming an outspoken opponent of the Communist government. His thorough analysis revealed, as no one before him, the great evil of the Soviet regime's totalitarian apparatus. I believe it is this that gave rise, properly speaking, to his wartime and postwar period. It was during the war that all the deformities and all the festering wounds on the body of an enslaved people, the indifference to human suffering and human need, emerged so strikingly. During the war Vasily Grossman wasn't sitting in his study or even in a factory office as an engineer, as in his youth; he travelled with the army through cities and towns, through villages, and on roads, and came into close contact with real people. True, he portrayed the heroism of the Soviet army, the self-sacrifice of a nation, but at the same time he felt the great disgrace of the Stalinist regime that had permitted Hitler's soldiers to get as far as the Volga to the point of encircling Stalingrad. He depicts in his novel the confusion and disorientation of Stalin right

92   Arts and Letters

after the assault by Hitler, whom he had trusted and to whom he had sent, just a few days before the outbreak of war, long trains loaded with rubber, and military and technological materiel.

Probably it was not an easy matter to turn one's back on a fine ideal that should have become a reality. It took years after the war: things were stirring in the aftermath of the victory over Hitler (and even during the war) and there arose a dark nationalism, a Great Russia chauvinism, accompanied by a growing antisemitism in which the then renowned writer Grossman saw a great crippling deformity on the body of socialism. It was a dismal horror show. It was in this atmosphere of growing terror and Jew-hating, which he compares to the Black Hundreds that Grossman, the then renowned writer, set himself the goal of composing a great epic.

The first part of the projected work appeared in 1952 under the title *For a Just Cause*.[7]

Stalin was still alive. One can imagine that the writer had to tread lightly using a protective inner censor when he depicted the negative side of the October Revolution. At the outset, the book was reviewed in a positive light by the critics. It was, after all, by Vasily Grossman, who sings the praises of heroism. He was at the peak of his writerly reputation. But soon after, there arose a torrent of accusations.

Vasily Grossman retreated to his solitude and worked away at the epic he was conceiving. Did he, like his protagonist Shtrum, constantly anticipate an arrest to come in the night? It's possible, but that didn't force the pen from his hand. In the meantime, Stalin died. The screws were loosened. The dread receded in part. Not everyone could still the inner censor, but Vasily Grossman, as we see in his work, got free of it. He worked for ten years without interruption, and in working on the novel, he was altered as a writer. Both artistically and philosophically Jewish, he was now a different person. In 1960 a monumental novel was ready: it was independent of the book *For a Just Cause*, although some of the same characters appear in that first published book. The new work is a novel that stands alone. The author took the manuscript to the chief editor of *Znamya*, where a lot of Grossman's work had been printed before coming out in book form.[8] He handed it in and waited a long while for a response until he began to expect the arrival of the KGB.

---

7 The work did not appear in English until 2019. "For this first publication in English, Robert and Elizabeth Chandler have revised the Russian editions of *For a Just Cause* with material from Grossman's politically riskier manuscript versions and given the book his preferred title: *Stalingrad*." https://www.theguardian.com /books/2019/jun/07/stalingrad-vasily-grossman-review, accessed 25 June 2021.

8 Vadim Kozhevnikov was then chief editor of *Znamya*.

Vasily Grossman: The History of a Book or the Path to Jewish Identity   93

One fine early morning, there was a knock at Grossman's door. Two high-ranking persons from the KGB showed him an authorization for a revision, took away all the copies of his completed work, and even the carbon paper and the ribbon of his typewriter, because even these could be used to make a copy. They also confiscated a large stack of paper, little note papers, and some individual fragments.

How did the matter come before the KGB? Simple – the chief editor of *Znamya*, reading over the thick manuscript, became very frightened. Could he just give the manuscript back to the author and be done with it? In order to take precautions, for whatever reasons, he gave it to two of his more important editors to read and as a group of three they decided to hand the manuscript over to the central committee of the party, who would do their part. This is how all the copies of the manuscript fell into the hands of the KGB. Vasily Grossman did not remain idle. He made his way to the leadership of the party. After reading the manuscript, Suslov,[9] the party's chief ideologue, received him and offered him a curt "consolation" that such a book might be published in perhaps two to three hundred years. Returning the manuscript was out of the question.

Vasily Grossman lived another few years as an impoverished outcast. Though sickly, he managed to write the book *Everything Flows* and in 1964 at the age of 59, he died. Before his death, he had sent the manuscript of his last book abroad. It appeared in Italy, France, and England. As for the confiscated manuscript, he recited Kaddish for it.

How did the two copies of the confiscated manuscripts reach us? There are two conjectures: one copy might have been hidden by a friend of Grossman's. But two copies appeared that were not identical, and that Grossman had not yet corrected. A second conjecture is one that stands to reason: the two copies originated in the Lubyanka Prison.[10]

Life and Fate is a great undertaking of a novel in which the author immerses himself in the farthest reaches of Soviet society and its regime.

---

9 Mikhail Suslov (1902–1982). The chief ideologue of the Khrushchev and Brezhnev years.

10 Robert Chandler explains in his introduction to *Life and Fate* that Grossman left one copy of his manuscript with Semyon Lipkin, a writer and poet who was a close confidant of Grossman's and another with Lyolya Dominikina, a friend from his student days. He did not tell Lipkin about the copy given to Dominikina. It was Lipkin who got the manuscript to writer Vladimir Voinovich, who in 1970 smuggled it to the West. Vasily Grossman, *Life and Fate* (New York: New York Review Books, 2006). See Vladimir Voinovich, "The Life and Fate of Vasily Grossman," *Index on Censorship* 14, no. 5 (1985): 9–10. https://journals.sagepub.com/doi/10.1080/03064228108533305, accessed on 25 June 2024.

94 Arts and Letters

He looks into all its hidden recesses and carries out a careful analysis that is at once political, sociological, and economic, but is above all an analysis of human relationships. It is an epic made up of three linked parts and spread over 800 large-format pages. Here Grossman demonstrates both his great talent to construct an epic novel and his vast learning, his great knowledge of various domains.

The novel is expansive, epic, sweeping. It is an enormous fresco, painted in vivid colours by a great master. The action takes place across practically the entire country, both where the war is raging and in the vast hinterlands. It extends even to the far north, where the Soviet camps are scattered, and is also set partly in Germany, in its death camps. The period is mainly the war years, with the emphasis on the battle in and around Stalingrad. Dozens and dozens of characters are portrayed for us. Some are historic figures, but for the most part they are fictional creations with their outward appearance, personality, and exploits, their thoughts and feelings, their dreams and hopes, their fanatical beliefs and their great disappointments. They are simple soldiers, officers, and generals, the well-educated, the simple folk, Soviet Communists and German Nazis. It is clear that Vasily Grossman was influenced by Tolstoy; he describes his characters in all their particulars, so that even their appearance is vivid to us. In the construction and the composition of the novel there is also something of the Tolstoyan.

One could say that the Shaposhnikov family is the axis of the novel around which the action turns. There is the mother, the chemist Alexandrovna Vladimirovna; her three daughters, one of whom dies in the bombings; a son, who finds himself in a Soviet camp; a grandson, who dies after being brought from the front seriously injured; and a second grandchild, who is worried over by the refined Alexandra Vladimirovna. Included in the family are also the educated Jew, physicist Victor Pavlovitch Shtrum, who is the husband of the oldest daughter, Lyudmila Nikolaevna, and their young daughter Nadya.

Other members of the family are the former husband of Lyudmila, one Abarchuk, and the former husband of the younger daughter, Yevgenia. The former is in a Soviet camp, the second is in Lubyanka Prison. Events unwind within and outside of the Shaposhnikov family, the action occurring on many different levels.

On rereading this epic novel, I asked myself who is the main protagonist? Is it the Jewish scientist Viktor Pavlovich Shtrum? We can guess that Vasily Grossman, who in all his writing had never introduced a Jewish character or taken account of any Jewish problems, did, during his Jewish crisis, deliberately introduce in a primary role a Jewish figure

Vasily Grossman: The History of a Book or the Path to Jewish Identity   95

with whom he identified. But the hero could also be the suffering nation or the war itself.

The book opens on a Nazi prisoner of war camp in Germany. Before the war, the camp was reserved for German political prisoners; the author notes, "National Socialism had created a new type of political criminal: criminals who had not committed a crime. Many of the prisoners had been sent here merely for telling political anecdotes or for criticizing the Hitler regime in conversation with friends. The charge against them was not that they actually had distributed political leaflets or joined underground parties, but that one day they might."[11]

These words are an allusion to the inmates of the Soviet camps. And often the author shows us situations, set in Hitler's Germany, that can easily be located in the Soviet reality.

Among the prisoners of war in the German camp is an old Bolshevik, who languished in tsarist prisons and knew Lenin. The Obersturmbahnfuhrer Liss lurks around such prisoners, hoping in a sly way to extract intelligence from them. He carries on a long discussion with Mostovskoy, the Russian Communist, trying to convince him that there is no difference between the two regimes: Lenin created a party of a new character and Hitler created one as well. Liss would rather have been an academic occupied with history or philosophy but the party appointed him to another position. Would Mostovskoy turn it down if the party assigned him a similar job? Doesn't he know that it was not only Hitler who arrested German communists, but that in Soviet Russia too communists were arrested and murdered?

Vasily Grossman introduces these parallels on more than one occasion. How did it happen that two such different world views should lead to similar systems of rule? To similar actions? In Germany, the basis was Nazism, which led to National Socialism. Meanwhile, in Russia the basis was class and from the outset it led to class socialism, which little by little transformed into a national socialism.

This answer is not the answer of a character in the book but of the author himself. From time to time the narration of the novel breaks off. The animated dialogues come to a halt and the author digresses, revealing his own thoughts on matters Jewish, philosophical, and historic.

And while we are on the subject of digression, when the narration breaks off and the author emerges on his own, it is to remind us of the historical overview of antisemitism, concluding that totalitarian rule by the state leads directly to state sponsored antisemitism. It was hoped

---

11 Grossman, *Life and Fate*, 21.

96   Arts and Letters

and anticipated, especially by the author, that the war against the Nazis, the victory of Stalingrad, on which the victory over Nazi Germany depended, would bring freedom and would eradicate antisemitism. But history is full of surprises. Stalingrad was the great triumph of the nation, but it was also Stalin's triumph. Opposing fates were decided in Stalingrad: the liberation of nations, the defeat of Hitler, and the victory of Stalin. Accompanying these were extremes of nationalism and antisemitism:

> What was at stake was the fate of the Kalmyks and Crimean Tatars, the Balkars and Chechens, who were to be deported to Siberia and Kazakhstan, who were to lose the right to remember their history or teach their own children to speak their mother tongue.

> What was at stake was the fate of the actors Mikhoels and Zuskin,[12] the writers Bergelson, Markish, Fefer, Kvitko, and Nusinov, whose execution was to precede the sinister trial of Professor Vovsi[13] and the Jewish doctors. What was at stake was the fate of the Jews saved by the Red Army: on the tenth anniversary of the victory Stalin was to raise over their heads the very sword of annihilation he had wrested from the hands of Hitler.[14]

Soviet antisemitism and genocide take up a large part of the novel. Grossman shows us the Nazi genocide carried out against European Jewry by taking us across Jewish cities and towns in Ukraine and White Russia, where the Nazis led out whole populations of Jews, shot them and

---

12 Solomon Mikhoels was the director of the Moscow State Jewish Theatre. He and Benjamin Zuskin were members of the Jewish Anti-Fascist Committee, as were writers Bergelson, Markish, and Fefer. Mikhoels was killed in a staged accident several years before the Yiddish writers were rounded up and executed in 1952. https://www.tabletmag.com/sections/community/articles/night-of-the-murdered-poets, accessed 8 November 2021.

13 Miron Vovsi, a doctor who had treated leaders at Kremlin hospital and had a clinic at Botkin hospital, was an accused in the "Doctors' Plot." http://www.cyberussr.com/rus/vrach-ubijca-e.html, accessed 5 November 2021.

14 Grossman, *Life and Fate*, 646–7.

Vasily Grossman: The History of a Book or the Path to Jewish Identity   97

threw the dead along with the wounded into pits prepared beforehand. Before our eyes, the gas chambers and the crematoria that he depicts rise up. Grossman's book adds a major new chapter to the literature on the genocide of European Jews. As well, Vasily Grossman describes as genocide the annihilation in Soviet Russia of millions of peasants and their families, including children and the old. He also gives us the massive extermination of the old communists and ordinary people that Stalin sent as slaves to a slow death in the labour camps. Between Treblinka and Kolyma,[15] there is a common thread, he assures us.

Did everyone understand this? Did any try to distance themselves, to protest? No, is his answer. Not merely out of fear or stupid indifference, but also on account of the hypnotic power of a former ideal. The author takes us into a Soviet camp and shows us the previously mentioned Abarchuk, who finds himself there with his Communist mentor. He finds his former teacher Magar, in a small room there on the point of death. Across from the living lies a corpse. Magar gathers all his strength to explain to Abarchuk the great mistake that he, Magar, and others like him have made. He sees it as his obligation, before dying, to tell his former pupil the truth. But Abarchuk becomes despondent: "Stop! ... What you're saying is all lies. You're raving."[16]

And what of the Shaposhnikov family, around whom the events unfold? At the centre are Lyudmila Shaposhnikov and her husband, the previously mentioned Jewish physicist Victor Pavlovich Shtrum, Lyudmila's younger sister Yevgenia, and her husband. Dramatic events play out around both families.

The Jewish physicist Strum makes an important scientific discovery. At first his colleagues at the scientific institute are full of praise for him. It doesn't take long before they deride and belittle his discovery, casting aspersions on its Judaic spirit and disparaging Albert Einstein. Inspired by a young representative of the Central Committee who has no scientific background, the institute demands a renunciation of the discovery.

Shtrum refuses to back down. He stays at home and expects to be arrested. His wife hardly understands him. Moreover, deep in his heart is an open wound: his mother has perished in the ghetto. In a

---

15 The Kolyma region under Stalin was where numerous labour camps were located.
16 Grossman, *Life and Fate*, 193.

98 Arts and Letters

letter to him, her only son, Dr. Anna Semyonova Shtrum writes: "I never used to feel I was a Jew ... but now during these terrible days, my heart has become filled with a maternal tenderness towards the Jewish people ..."[17]

Viktor Pavlovich Shtrum has all at once, precisely like his mother, begun to sense that he is a Jew. A persecuted Jew. Persecuted by his own non-Jewish colleagues. However, one call to him from Stalin (because the "Father of the Nations" has become aware that they're interested in atomic physics abroad) is enough to restore him to his laboratory and to make those who had accused him of wrongdoing into sycophants.

The experiences and actions of the head of the Shaposhnikov family, the noble Alexandra Vladimirovna and her granddaughter, the sixteen- to seventeen-year-old daughter of the Shtrums, are a separate story. The girl, Nadya, rebels against injustice, laughs off everything around her with youthful derision, and speaks out against privilege, when "in cold and hungry Moscow the institute is an oasis of well-being," although there too a hierarchy rules.

The novel is a series of stories within a larger history and the stories are woven together artfully and organically. The numerous problems link together. One of the issues, which is connected to all the others is the unbounded power of the centralized government that crushes the individual.

In sum, it is a monumental novel detailing a tremendous array of problems, a diversity of characters, events, and situations. It may not be an exaggeration for the Jewish Russian immigrant in Paris Professor Efim Etkind[18] to describe *Life and Fate* in his foreword as the greatest novel of our century and its author as one of the greatest of this century's novelists.

Translated by Judy Nisenholt
Oyf di khvalyes fun goyrl, Paris 1986

---

17 Grossman, *Life and Fate*, 86–7.
18 Efim Etkind (1918–1990), an eminent Leningrad literary scholar, wrote the foreword to the French edition of *Life and Fate*.

Reyzl Zhikhlinski: On Her Poetry

It is my honour and my pleasure to present to the Parisian Jewish audience our guest, the poet Reyzl Zhikhlinski.[1] This is a happy undertaking because it is always a pleasure to present an esteemed artist, especially when that artist is a close friend, as is our guest. But the task is not an easy one because it's hard to say all there is to say about Reyzl Zhikhlinski in a limited time. To supplement the opening speakers' remarks, the author has asked to leave her time not only to read her poems, but also to interpret them, and she will certainly do that better than any speaker.

So, before I introduce the author and her work, I would like, first of all, to share with you the effect that reading Reyzl Zhikhlinski's poetry has on me. A distinguished author once said to me that poetry is just like wine: you don't have to drink the whole bottle to know whether the wine is good or not. And even good wine should be drunk in sips. This is how he advised me to approach poems. If not, it's exactly as if you had gotten drunk and missed out on the wine's essential flavour.

So now, as often happens, I have done the exact opposite of what the distinguished writer advised, and I have read over Reyzl's six books of poetry in one sitting. The truth is I had sampled their fine essence in the first poems, but the further one reads, the wider are the territories and the horizons that open up, albeit the poems are short and the poet in general does reveal to us some of the particulars of her life. It is just as if one has looked into clear water reflecting back one's surroundings; the more you look into it, the more you notice, and the more you read, the more associations, feelings, and ideas arise.

---

1 Berger gave this talk at a public celebration of Zhikhlinski's sixth collection of poems, *November Sun*, published in 1976.

100   Arts and Letters

In her poems, Reyzl Zhikhlinski seldom writes in the first person. She rarely tells us directly about her mood, about her own sadness or joy. But depicting a circumstance or sketching a picture, Reyzl Zhikhlinski creates literary images with a frugality of words, just as an experienced artist with an economy of brushwork creates the flecks and lines from which a fine picture or portrait emerges. The author concentrates her power within a few lines, creating, in spare language, a situation of complexity, a mood, a charged atmosphere, and deeply felt experiences. These all flow spontaneously, as if improvised. Her longest poems comprise little more than twenty lines, but each line is a melody where a tune is building; she sings out the pain and the sadness, the longing and the deep melancholy of the lost, lonely individual. Through this outcry over another's grief and heavy heart, we sense the author's spirit.

This was how Reyzl was from her very beginnings.

There are writers and other artists who do not reveal themselves all at once. They are the ones who come to their callings on a zigzagging path. If you want to grasp their creative work, you have to go into each phase separately. Reyzl Zhikhlinski is among those creative artists who appear with their poetic personality fully formed; it takes a mere word for a verse to become stronger, perhaps also more concise. Her poetic maturity is continuous because, although she was then only a young girl, she achieved her poetic sense authentically with her own melody, her own poetic resonance and tone. She was and she remains the true original, not only among women poets but among Yiddish poets in general.

The small-town girl from Gombin attracted the notice of such creative figures as Melech Ravitch, who published her first poems, Moyshe Broderzon, Noah Prylucki, Zalmen Reyzen, and similar literary mavens. It is no wonder that even at the time of her youthful engagement with poetry, Reyzl was worthy of having distinguished mentors. When her first poems appeared in book form in 1936, it was no other than Itsik Manger and the renowned painter Yankl Adler who ushered her into the halls of Yiddish poetry. Manger wrote the introduction and Adler illustrated the cover. Comparing her first book to her five later books, it is easy to confirm a uniformity of quality that was there from the outset, originating from a special character that is, one can say, unique to Reyzl Zhikhlinski.

Every true poet comes with something original or tries to find her own voice for her own song – and song in poetry also means lament. Even when a poet sings with the choir, writing from within a community of poets, she must also have her own voice, her own poetic vocabulary or instrument on which she plays her own melody.

Reyzl Zhikhlinski doesn't sing in any choir. She is in her own league entirely. She hits the notes, writes her poetry on her own intimate lyrical instrument and is so original that it is difficult to compare her to anyone. There is no point in specifying under whose influence she came, as is often done in analysing an artist. She is the master of the poetic miniature. Among her poems are some that consist of four or five or even three lines. Here's an example of such a poem:

When you are silent
I hear you.
When you speak
I hear only my own stammering.

This poem, so spare in words, so rich in content, reminds me of a sketch Picasso drew before my very eyes. During an interview with him,[2] he took my notebook from my hand and with two strokes of his pencil drew his famous dove that whispered tidings of peace to us.

And here is a second concise poem:
From the depths of seas ...
so comes the poem
with word and sound
when lit through by a flash
comes the thought.[3]

In these few spare words we have the birth of a poem. Her poems stem from deep in the heart. They trickle and flow and burst spontaneously from the depths of her soul. Are they perhaps stormy and turbulent? No, quite the contrary, they are very quiet and gentle, with the subtle delicacy of a spring flower and the freshness of morning dew; at the same time, they exude a quiet and compelling melancholy.

It's worthwhile to stop to take a look at Reyzl's subject matter. Aside from the fate of the Jewish people, which is expressed in the particularly moving Holocaust poems, the poet writes mainly of the fate of simple people when they are sunk in the not easily fathomed depths of their

---

2 Berger refers to this 1949 encounter with Picasso at the World Congress of Partisans for Peace in her essay "Picasso der shturmer in der kunst," in *In gang fun tsayt* (Paris, 1976).

3 Zhiklinski's poem in its original published form includes six lines of verse between the first and second lines that Berger quotes here.

102   Arts and Letters

grey everyday lives. With the poet's eye or with the artist's camera, she captures pictures of daily life, and she does this with the greatest simplicity. Simplicity is her profound originality. In just a few phrases, she brings out the sorrow and melancholy of the lonely wife, the pain and the heavy heart of the person gone astray, of the poor black man sleeping in the street, or the image of the beggar begging in the place he calls home. Here and there motifs from the Tanakh unwind through primordial images that are interwoven with the sad, suppressed rumble of the universe – because from time to time, with Reyzl Zhikhlinski, the wind does not blow gently; it rumbles. The snow does not gleam like silver; rather it sparkles with intense coldness. In a word, it is a world of human moods. And what does the poet carry in her heart? Victor Hugo said that the poet is an entire world that is inhabited by one person, and that the surrounding life is given its artistic and poetic fulfilment by the poet.

Yes, in Reyzl's poetic world, there is, as mentioned, not a little Jewish sorrow, solitude, human loneliness, and alienation in place and time. Here and there, however, are meditations, philosophical contemplations, and poetic reflections. At times the wolf in Reyzl is transfigured. There is a kind of intellectual calm that eases the torment and soothes the melancholy.

And when I say the word *intellectual*, I want to add a reservation. In recent years people in the larger non-Jewish world have spoken and written about intellectual poetry the way one speaks about intellectual painting, which they sometimes rip the soul out of. In truth, it is absurd to try to distinguish between art of the emotion and of the intellect. Authentic art, whatever branch it comes from, is an emanation, an outpouring of all the peculiarities of the human spirit. The true artist is affected by all aspects of his nature and his imagination. All stimuli, both the emotive and the intellectual, prompt his creativity. We may speak of philosophical contemplation and intellectual thoughtfulness, but Reyzl Zhikhlinski's poetry is, at the same time and perhaps above all, drawn from a profound emotionality: a wide gamut of feeling.

In sum, Zhikhlinski's poetry is exceptionally original, absorbing, and refreshing. She has brought to our Yiddish poetry a new form, a new tone, a new sound and coloration.

We must remember that Reyzl Zhikhlinski also writes stories. In the just-published book "The November Sun," there are seven tales, and it is noteworthy that they adopt the same short form as her poems. The content is concentrated and a theme is sometimes exposed within a half-page. Again there are the same images captured in a white heat from the greyness of daily life. And over these stories sweeps a poetic breath: the storyteller did not leave the poet behind.

It is worthwhile also to remember the poet's approach to her creative work, her great sense of responsibility to creative language, to the Yiddish word. And there is her persistence and her devotion to ensuring the accuracy of the published book.

Among all the troubles that Jewish writers face at the publication of a book, we must include the bother of typographical errors. There is hardly a Yiddish book without typographical mistakes. I informed Reyzl that at this particular Paris printer it would be impossible to avoid typographical errors. She responded, "No! In my book there will be no mistakes!" And she saw to it. The proofreaders at the press had a lot going on. Reyzl fought it out for a long time, carrying on a bitter dispute. The poet returned the proofs dozens of times till there was not one misprint. It is likely that it was the first book to emerge from that printing house without a single mistake.

To close, I would like to return to the poet's beginnings: in the spring of 1967, I was returning from the United States, where, by the way, I had met Reyzl a number of times. I stopped for several days in Montreal and spent an unforgettable evening with Melech Ravitch and his wife, Rokhl. Telling me about his encounters with specific Yiddish writers, among others, Ravitch recounted how he had, in 1928 or 1929, received Reyzl Zhikhlinski in his Warsaw office. On a cold winter day a young girl from the provinces came in with a quick step. She was wrapped in a heavy winter coat covered in wet snowflakes and had on a pair of muddy galoshes. And even though she was just a young novice, totally green in literary circles, he could tell from their conversation, and infer from her responses, that this young girl from the provinces would stick with her poetry and, whether by virtue of her talent or by force of her strong will, would go far.

And Melech Ravitch was not mistaken.

Translated by Judy Nisenholt
In loyf fun tsayt, Paris 1988

A Visit to Chana Orloff[1]

If the Jewish public knows little about Jewish visual artists, it knows even less about Jewish women artists. Yet there are many talented female painters, graphic artists, and sculptors, among them artists in whom other nations would take great pride. If an epic novel were to be written about the life of a Jewish artist, how much more sweeping and dramatic would be such a novel about a Jewish woman artist. Just imagine a book about the tragic life of the painter Esther Carp, whose days ended prematurely in a psychiatric institution, or about Chana Kowalska, who managed to continue drawing in a concentration camp. And I am not even starting at the very top of the list.

The difficult lives of many visual artists have inspired great writers in the non-Jewish world. In every other national literature, artists are the subject of a large number of books, not only monographs and essays, but also novels and literary biographies. I am referring here not only to novels about famous artists such as Rembrandt, Goya, Toulouse-Lautrec, or van Gogh, but also to books about lesser-known artists and contemporary artists. Yet we had Maurycy Gottlieb, Naum Aronson, Chaim Soutine, and Kisling, to name but a few. What does the Jewish public know about these great Jewish masters or about such tragic figures as the women I have already mentioned? How many Jewish writers chose to address this subject? Even the Yiddish press devotes little space to Jewish artists, and still less to Jewish women artists.

---

1 For more information on Chana Orloff (1888–1968), also known as Chana Orlov, see Paula J. Birnbaum, *Women Artists in Interwar France: Framing Femininities* (Farnham: Ashgate/Routledge, 2011); Paula J. Birnbaum, *Sculpting a Life: Chana Orloff between Paris and Tel Aviv* (Waltham, MA: Brandeis University Press, 2023).

The truth is that Chana Orloff is an exception. Although, as she confided to me, she has experienced her share of adversity, Chana Orloff has had the good fortune to have two homelands in which her art has resonated profoundly. She is known in both France, especially in the arts community, and Israel, and in other countries as well. Her work has been prominently displayed in museums and major exhibitions. One of her exhibitions in Israel, entitled "50 Years of Sculpture," travelled throughout the country.

Chana Orloff has had a long artistic career. She experienced the divine creative spark early in life. At the same time came years of wandering. At the age of fifteen, she emigrated with her parents from a Ukrainian town to Palestine. There, in the land of her ancestors, she took her first artistic steps. Her great desire to study and perfect her art brought her to Paris at the age of twenty-three. Although she settled in the "City of Art," she remained connected by every fibre of her being to the Land of Israel, and later the State of Israel.

People had told me a great deal about Chana Orloff. The first was my older friend Chana Kowalska, who took every opportunity to stir my curiosity about the plastic arts. Although Kowalska wrote (and lectured) primarily about ancient art, about Egyptian art in particular, she was still very much attuned to contemporary trends and living artists, especially Jewish artists. A few days before her arrest, we took a long walk through the streets of the Jewish quarter of Paris after a meeting connected to our work in the French Resistance. She wanted to tell me about the various Jewish artists about whom she had written, and promised to take me to meet them. Chana Kowalska could not keep her promise to introduce me to Chana Orloff. Her life ended in the ovens of Auschwitz.

Years went by. Then, by coincidence, while living in Warsaw, I received two photographs of Chana Orloff's sculptures, both on the theme of motherhood. The first was of a young mother, her face radiating kindness and love, a small child on her lap. She gazes at her child with eyes full of hope. The second mother was a full-bodied woman with a child at her breast. This massive nude lies outstretched like mother earth, bursting with fertility, creating life and nurturing life. The two photographs brought back memories, and I vowed to visit Chana Orloff at the earliest opportunity. When the day of our appointment, pre-arranged by telephone, finally

106   Arts and Letters

arrived, I had the sensation that Chana Kowalska's shadow was accompanying me.

~

The small side street named after the artist Seurat was inhabited almost entirely by artists. The modest single houses lining both sides of the street resembled large boxes planted in the ground. Not far from the residence and studio occupied by Chaim Soutine during his last years was Chana Orloff's one-storey house.

Recently I had been told that she had become very hard of hearing. To spare me any disappointment, Mané-Katz found it necessary to inform me "that she is no longer the woman I once knew." Hence what a pleasant surprise it was to for me to come face to face with a sturdy woman, elderly, yes, but still erect, with an energetic and cheerful face, and a good-natured smile. Her aged face exuded warmth and energy. I soon began comparing her appearance with the Israeli women, more precisely, the pioneers of yesteryear, whom she had sculpted in her atelier. She herself came to the door, and, with a warm welcome, led me into a hall where many of her sculptures were on display – entire worlds frozen in bronze, in stone, and in wood. Frozen, however, is the wrong word, because Chana Orloff's images and compositions quiver with life, with ideas and emotions, clearly conveying the impression that the inanimate materials – metal, stone, and wood – had been infused with the breath of life.

Because the two pieces of sculpture which I knew from photographic reproductions were in bronze and plaster, I was not expecting to find so many pieces carved from blocks of wood. However, I soon learned that this artist had always worked either in stone or wood, and especially in wood, because she did not like to take the easy way. In the modelling process, changes can be made easily. Clay can be removed, added, and reworked. Solid materials like wood or stone, on the other hand, demand a great deal of concentration, precision, and physical exertion, with the result that the sculptor develops a strong feeling for form, an acute awareness of planes, and skill in construction.

Chana Orloff interrupted her explanation to remind me that I had confessed to her upon my arrival that unfortunately, apart from two photographic reproductions, I was completely unfamiliar with her work. Therefore, she wanted me first to see it for myself. I looked around in amazement, unable to tear my eyes away. Which was more marvellous, the ease and youth of the Amazon on her horse, sculpted in wood, or the ferocity of the wild beast cast in bronze, a helpless bird in its claws? The gentle nobility and innocence of the Madonna, or the tender passion of the lover? The coupling of elegant simplicity with symbolism in some of her work, or the grace of the dancer? What I found most striking was that in Chana Orloff's work the female body is almost always a mass of softness. Even in the most graceful movement or gesture there is a certain monumental quality because for her the mystery of femininity and motherhood lay nestled inside this massiveness. Yet, looking at *The Amazon*, and especially at *The Dancer*, I was also struck by the lightness, flexibility, and playfulness the artist was able to elicit from the hard material through the use of spiralling lines.

Each piece of sculpture is compelling in its uniqueness and captures one's attention at first glance. A proprietary and intimate bond is immediately established between the work of art and the viewer. It is almost a truism that the more we look at a painting or sculpture, the more we are able to see what escaped us at first glance. Yet it seems to me that here a connection is established at first sight. Chana Orloff's sculptures possess that magical power to immediately engage the viewer.

Her range of subject matter is broad and diverse – human beings and their thoughts, their creativity, and hard physical labour, women and children, motherhood, animals and birds, human relationships and behaviour – all expressed in the posture and appearance of animals. The bronze monster, mouth open, nostrils quivering, one eye squinting, the other open wide and alert, actually has human features. In the Rodin Museum there is a wounded lion. From the depths of his being through his open mouth escapes a terrifying cry of pain. Rodin modelled the lion realistically yet we experience the agonizing cry as human suffering. Chana Orloff's animals are not sculpted realistically, yet they starkly portray our reality: the cruelty of human beings. These allegorical beasts, their limbs twisted, claws extended, and teeth sinking into the bodies of their enemies, are horrifying. The fury spewing from their open mouths recalls the banal evil of Picasso's ox in *Guernica*, even though there is no similarity between these two artists. So much is expressed in the wild beast standing upright like a man – eyes closed and jaws open, it stares blindly at the innocent bird it holds by the throat, about to devour its prey.

A special place in Chana Orloff's studio is occupied by portraits of famous personalities – mostly Jewish writers and artists. Here, cast in

108 Arts and Letters

bronze, are Edmond Fleg, Chaim Nachman Bialik, Peretz Hirschbein, Chana Robina, and Lumilla Pitoeff. Spirituality, dignity, intellect, and creativity radiate from their faces. Chana Orloff brings out the individuality of the model posing for her, while at the same time approaching the image architecturally as a material structure. Thus, for example, she sculpted Bialik in bronze in an extremely solid construction, as though chiselled from a block of stone: a powerfully massive image, with an energetic face, sharp features, a profound and penetrating look, the forehead of a man who is still thinking, who knows much and desires to know more.

I was very interested in seeing her studio. From experience I have learned that artists have their own individual attitude to their studios, their own idiosyncrasies. Some, like Chagall, protect their workplace from the eyes of visitors. His studio in his villa in Vence is completely separate from his house. Other artists enjoy receiving visitors in their workplace. I always found that the atmosphere in the studios of Arthur Kolnik, Alfred Aberdam, Michel Adlen, and Pacanowska, for example, resembled an art gallery or rather a miniature museum. Aberdam, who at the end of his life produced large paintings in sombre grey tones, received me in his dark paint-stained smock, brush in hand. After I had climbed up the crooked outdoor staircase leading to his "exotic" atelier, he deliberately continued painting uninterrupted to give me the opportunity to observe his creative process. Occasionally Benn would engage in animated conversation while he worked. On one occasion, while he was drawing a portrait of my son, I tried to move away so as not to disturb him. "Sit down," he told me, "we'll keep talking." Eyes on his model or his easel, charcoal moving across the paper, he told his usual gripping stories. By contrast, arriving at the atelier of Mané-Katz, I felt as though I was in a museum of antiques, both Jewish and non-Jewish. Few of his own paintings were to be seen on his walls. If a canvas happened to be on the easel, it was covered. "Can I see your latest paintings?" I asked him. "You'll see them eventually. This is not your last time here." Unfortunately, it did turn out to be my last time. He preferred to show his antiques, to recount how he had obtained them, and, of course, to regale his visitor with endless anecdotes, rather than to reveal the secret of how his canvases were created.

Chana Orloff opened wide the doors of her atelier. I could look, explore, and investigate her creative secrets to my heart's content. With her unassuming warmth, she allowed me first to view everything on my own, and then answered my questions. Soon we were conversing as easily as people who had known each other for years.

A Visit to Chana Orloff   109

In the large exhibition room were sculptures that combined the figurative with the abstract. In the workroom my attention was drawn to two large plaster sculptures, both of women, waiting to be cast into bronze. A sturdy young woman with a basket on her shoulders, looking proud and self-assured, stood erect as if to show that her burden could not bend her. The second, the embodiment of a pioneer with a scythe in her hand, posed as though she were listening to the blessing over the fruit of the earth.

"Israeli women?" I asked rhetorically.

"Yes, you guessed it. Here I want to show Jewish rebirth through agricultural work, Jewish people at work in their own land. I, too, was there at the beginning, so this is a part of me."

My eyes rested on various elements of the workshop, the raw material: wood, clay, and plaster of Paris. In one corner of the atelier was a carpenter's workbench with all the requisite tools.

"Do you have anyone to help you? Doesn't it take strength to carve wood?" I inquired.

"It is not so much a matter of strength as training and skill," she replied. "It is not true that women cannot use such tools. Women are as adept as men in handling them."

After that I refrained from asking her whether it was physically difficult for someone over 70 years of age. Opposite me was a woman who exuded creative energy, an artist who, particularly in recent years, had the desire to create her forms in wood. Hard of hearing, she listened to the music of the saw, and the cutting and carving of wood. She demonstrated and explained how each woodworking tool had its own sound, its unique melody.

As we made our way back through the large room filled with statues, I once again examined the masterworks. For the artist each work represented a different event in her life. Chana Orloff told me what she had endured during the Hitler occupation, how much valuable time she had lost. When the German fascists came to this studio to arrest her and could not find her, they took revenge on her work. One hundred and ten statues in her house were lost, most destroyed by the Germans in their madness. Others were stolen. Not a single one was ever found.

"You see," she said pointing to the wild beast choking the innocent bird, "after the war I channelled all my emotions into this sculpture, all

110   Arts and Letters

my hatred for the suffering they had caused us. This work took me a long time. It consumed my whole being."

It must be said that Chana Orloff had poured her heart and soul into each of her sculptures. As she herself explained, she was totally committed to her creative work. Sometimes commitment is understood in the popular sense of adherence to an established system or a certain doctrine. But there is an essential inner commitment that every true artist possesses.

When I asked the artist whether the symbolism evident in several of her sculptures is her favourite form of expression, she nodded and smiled. "Yes, I have an affinity for symbolism, but I don't restrict myself to any one mode of expression, I don't tie myself to a concept. I don't like to follow what's in vogue. Modern art and fashion are two different things. What is most important is that artists look at the world and see everything with their own eyes.

My attention turned to birds, forged in metal, that symbolized the pilots in the Israeli War of Independence, as well as a movingly symbolic work dedicated to the fallen Israeli soldiers. As if to save me from a probable error, Chana Orloff volunteered: "I have already been asked if this is abstract art. I will tell you something. Just recently I discovered that certain abstract artists consider me one of them."

"What do you think of it?"

"Abstraction? It's not new in art. The abstract can also be found in nature. In most cases painting or sculpting abstractly is possible until people reach a certain age. They are still searching, not yet knowing what they want. Old age has its advantages. At my age one knows exactly what one wants. And let me tell you one more thing. It is extremely important for an artist not to copy oneself. To repeat oneself is a misfortune for a sculptor or painter."

"Have you ever painted?"

Chana Orloff led me by the hand into her spacious reception room where a few paintings and prints hung on the walls.

"These paintings are from a long time ago. Sometimes I feel like going back to it, but there isn't enough time left. At one time we had to know it all. A Jewish artist had to be able to do everything."

We sat down at the table where she offered me some refreshments. A conversation ensued about Jewish artists and Jewish art. I told her that most of the Jewish artists I had had the opportunity to interview were very dubious as to whether there was in fact something that could be called "Jewish art."

"We don't have a long tradition in the visual arts for reasons I'm sure are familiar to you," Chana Orloff said. "But it is not true that we don't

A Visit to Chana Orloff 111

have our own art. I can personally state that when I look at a painting or a piece of sculpture, I am almost never wrong when I make up my mind as to whether or not a painting or sculpture is by a Jewish artist."

"Have you never been mistaken?"

"I said 'almost.' In any case, we have many of our own, and I can recognize them."

It was no longer necessary for me to ask her how she viewed her own art. I felt it in everything she had said. I also felt it when she told me about her exhibitions in Israel, about her many visits there, about her longing to live there. "I am torn between France and Israel. France will not hold this against me. The real France, the France we love, detests liars."

Chana Orloff also detested lies and self-deception. She was exactly like her art: authentic, honest, principled, and compassionate.

Translated by Vivian Felsen
In gang fun tsayt (Au fils des années) Paris 1976

Czajka: The Painful Path to Self-Discovery

(A memoir in place of flowers on a grave)

More than once have I been called upon to write about the fate of alienated Polish Jewish writers during the dark times of our Jewish people. Alas, we tend to write about those who are no longer with us.

Recently, it came to my attention by chance in the press that the Polish Yiddish writer Czajka had died in Warsaw. At the same time, a slim volume of poetry titled "Mourning Songs of the Ghetto" fell into my hands. The author was Izabela Gelbard, and in parentheses, Lieutenant Czajka. On the front page was a photo of a beautiful, vibrant woman in an officer's uniform with the inscription "Lieutenant Czajka." This book had been published simultaneously in several languages in 1946. When I saw the dedication dated 1964, I felt great heartache; it took me back to a wintery evening about six years ago, six long years ago.

I had heard a lot about Czajka, an almost legendary figure. Who in Poland had not heard of her? Coming from an assimilated family, rooted in Polish culture, she was far from Jewish life. Prior to the war, she had been one of the most popular women in Polish literary and artistic circles. In earlier times she would certainly have presided over a salon. An educated woman, with great knowledge of languages, literature, and especially the plastic arts, she was also gifted with great humour, an inner sparkling intelligence, dynamism and beauty. What more does one need! It was said of Bella that she could turn night into day. There were as many stories about her love affairs as there had been about George Sand, although, at that time, she was not yet a writer, nor did she ever achieve the heights of the great French author. Yet it was a life well lived. Then came the war, and the Nazis took away her right to live. They reminded her that she was a Jewish woman.

Izabela Gelbard lived through all seven circles of hell in the Warsaw Ghetto, followed by great torment on the Aryan side. In the constant shadow of death, fleeing thousands of life-threatening dangers, she had written the poems which appeared in 1946, and which lie before me now. In her introduction, she wrote that she had never considered herself a poet. Fortunately, her life was spared, her poetry saved, and at the end of the war she enlisted in the Polish army, where she became known as Lieutenant Czajka. With her new name she entered the world of literature, and became best known for two volumes of prose, *I Was Rescued by a Blacksmith* and *I Fly into the World*.

Before I became acquainted with her writing and with her personally, I came to know the proud, self-confident sound of her voice. I recall an incident that occurred when the eighty-year-old mother of Henryk Berlewi[1] was exhibiting her paintings in Warsaw. The artist son of the debuting painter ended his brief introduction with the proclamation "Long live Poland!" In a warm, resonant voice, Czajka had added "Long live the people of Poland." She was full of passion and enthusiasm for the new Poland. So great was her enthusiasm that one might have thought there was something she had once again forgotten.

But let us turn to another, later, event – to an evening about six years ago at Czajka's. When one was invited to Czajka's two-room apartment, a veritable miniature museum, conversations went on for hours and hours. What caught my eye more than the paintings by great artists was an "objet d'art" which stood by her bedside: a huge pot-bellied crystal vase with a large swastika on it. "What is this?" I asked, stunned, taken aback. She replied: "My vengeance for all my suffering and humiliations."

I learned from her that the Nazi Governor-General Frank had commissioned the vase to be manufactured in a Polish glassworks. It had adorned his rooms in the Wavell Palace in Kraków. But he could not bring it to the German fatherland, as he had planned. Izabela was delighted to acquire the vase, which she used as a chamber pot. This was her revenge!

This was not the only story I heard at that time. In particular, carved into my memory, remaining there like a stone in my heart, was another episode: Czajka had given me her book of poems, inscribed with a dedication to me, and asked if I would perhaps consider translating it. I

---

1 Henryk Berlewi (1894–1967). Artist, graphic designer, art critic, and theorist.

114   Arts and Letters

demurred, saying that I did not translate poetry – to do so one had to be a poet. Rudnicki's work I had translated because it was prose. Czajka became despondent and her age began to show itself more noticeably. She implored, "If you can translate prose well, you can also translate poetry. Try. If you took it on, it would go quickly."

"You seem intent on having this book appear in Yiddish as soon as possible."

"Yes, you would really be able to make use of this little book. Would you read it over?"

Suddenly, I saw before me an elderly Jewish woman, a Polish writer, yet a Jew, who carried deep within herself a hidden wound. Was it that she was already sensing the bitter winds approaching? Or was it that her star had already begun to fade? I did read her book of poetry at that time, but made no effort to translate any part of it.

Some years later, I met her on the way to the Polish Literary Association. She asked me to take her arm as we approached the crosswalk. I could see that her eyesight had worsened and that her appearance had changed. Her features had become distinctly Jewish. I think, like me, she was avoiding any mention of the request she had made long ago. I was uncomfortable. Not only had I not translated any of her Ghetto poems, but I had also never mentioned these poems anywhere my essays.

Now I have read these poems more thoughtfully and attentively than I had the first time. Yes, they are lacking in poetic sophistication in composition and in rhythm. In her brief introduction Czajka had written that she did not consider these poems to be a poetic achievement. They were written, not with ink, but with blood and tears, as reflected in one poem: "Give me the ancient harp – so that I might pluck its strings."

Furiously she strummed on the strings of the Jewish calamity, and did this while wandering, while hiding, while starving, in the very shadow of thousands of deaths. It is poetry of great pathos, modelled perhaps, consciously or unconsciously, on the Greek tragic poets. Yet the spirit infused by Izabela Gelbard was that of the Book of Lamentations and the Book of Job. In her sometimes unpolished verse, she cried out the suffering and pain of millions, and mourned the destruction of her nearest and dearest: Korczak[2] and Roman Kramsztyk,[3] as well

---

2 Janusz Korczak (1878/9–1942). Physician, educator, and writer. See also Berger's essay in this collection; *YIVO*, s.v. "Korczak, Janusz."
3 Roman Kramsztyk (1885–1942). Polish painter and illustrator. *YIVO*, s.v. "Kramsztyk, Roman," accessed June 2021.

Czajka: The Painful Path to Self-Discovery   115

as random people whom she had raised to the highest pinnacle in the hour of annihilation.

We find among her works a poem on Rubinsztajn,[4] the famous street singer of the Warsaw Ghetto, that jokester and mocker of the German murderers. This highly educated woman who drew from all the world's cultural sources, considered it her duty, as did thousands of anonymous folk poets, to preserve in simple verses what she had seen. Indeed, she wrote that a poem is not written by a hand, but rises in red flames from the fiery ashes so that the shame of humanity shall burn for centuries. She accuses all who looked on with indifference, and curses the indifferent world. I strongly doubt whether Poland today would allow the publication of lines such as these:

No one helped us, the unfortunate
No one stretched out a hand.

I do not know how Izabela Gelbard, Czajka, felt in the last two or three years about the new tragedy which had swooped down on the tiny remnant of Polish Jews. When I now think about her, it seems that, as in the past, she again felt herself bound to the Jewish people, and from her anguished heart burst bitter words condemning the new oppressors. It was this assimilated, estranged Izabela Gelbard who in her poem of December 1943 made a vow to her Jewish grandfather:

Aimlessly, wandering in forests, in ditches
The net is widening
Zeyde, I swear to you I will prevail
And take revenge, holy revenge
For all the unknown graves all
To you I swear, Zeyde
I hear your blood in my veins.
Paris, April, 1970

Translation by Sylvia Lustgarten
In gang fun tsayt, Paris 1976

---

4 Rubenstein (Rubinsztajn) a popular figure in the Warsaw ghetto in 1941–2, used humour and biting mockery as a way to express the anger and hatred Jews felt towards the Nazis and the ghetto police. https://fcit.coedu.usf.edu/holocaust/gallery/p098.htm, accessed 1 June 2024.

Ber Mark, The Man and the Author: On the Twenty-fifth Anniversary of His Death

I was destined, a mere two decades ago, to work closely alongside Ber Mark,[1] at the journal *Yidishe shriftn* [Jewish writing][2] and to share common concerns at the publishing house, Yidish Bukh [Yiddish book].[3]

---

1 Along with their joint political affinities and membership in the Communist Party of Poland (KPP), Mark and Berger shared a calling to bring about Polish Jewish repatriation. Berger left Paris to return to Warsaw in 1949; Mark went from Moscow to Łódź, then Warsaw, in 1946. For both, advocacy of postwar Jewish Polish reconstruction was a fervent mission. They summoned their respective readerships, the surviving remnants, to a reconstituted Poland where Yiddish secular culture would thrive. Mark toed the internationalist party line, all the while appealing to Jews not to abandon their ancestors' graves: "[We] Polish Jews in Moscow, in the Urals, in Central Asia ... are those who should breathe life into martyrs' ashes" ("Mir kumen tsurik," *Dos naye lebn* (The New Life) 10 (1946). Cited in Joanna Nalewajko- Kulikov, "Profiles: Three Colours: Grey. Bernard Mark's Portrait Sketch," *Holocaust Studies and Materials* 2: 205–26, 216. Khayim Leyb Fuks, "Ber Mark." *Yiddish Leksikon*, https://yleksikon .blogspot.com/search?q=ber+mark, accessed 14 February 2021.
2 The monthly *Yidishe shriftn*: *Tsaytshrift far literatur, teater un kultur* (Jewish writings: A periodical for literature, theatre and culture) (1946–68) was published in postwar Łódź and Warsaw. Mark was at the helm; Berger was on the editorial board in the 1950s and 1960s. *Yidishe shriftn* merged with *Folks-shtime* (People's Voice) (1945–91) and became *Dos Yidishe vort* (The Yiddish word), a bilingual Yiddish-Polish periodical (1992–2003), to which Berger contributed and where her works inspired many critical reviews. Leonard Prager, "Literary Journals: Yiddish Literary Journals," *YIVO Encyclopedia of Jews in Eastern Europe*, 26 August 2010, https://yivoencyclopedia.org /article.aspx/Literary_Journals/Yiddish_Literary_Journals, accessed 12 March 2021.
3 Berger's *Eseyen un skitsn, Fun haynt un nekhtn*, and *Nokhn mabl* were published under this imprint in the 1960s. Her colleague and friend Dovid Sfard was its director. Yidish Bukh was housed at the storied Tłomackie 13 in Warsaw during the war.

Ber Mark, The Man and the Author 117

I had, thanks entirely to him, full access to all the materials kept at the Jewish Historical Institute and very frequently enjoyed collegial conversations in his office. I should not neglect to mention here that Mark, in internal critiques at Yidish Bukh, would entirely dismantle the appraisal by a cowardly reviewer who would ask whether a certain book dare appear in Socialist Poland. I am not the only one whom he helped navigate a threatening critical wave. In sum, I have had ample opportunity to recognize both the man of integrity and the prolific writer. With great curiosity and wonder, I have closely observed his wide-ranging and imaginative life's work over the years and, at the same time, noted his very difficult and bitter struggles, his inner discord about which few people knew.

Indeed, for many years he was a privately conflicted person in so-called Socialist Poland.[4] And just as his tall, erect figure, his solidly built physique, disguised a serious illness which gradually dimmed the light in his eyes, so too did his energetic, pleasant face, his ebullient sense of humour and playful wit, conceal the psychological turmoil and spiritual wounds which had accumulated most prominently in his later years.

Ber Mark was born in 1908 in the city of Łomża, widely known for its *yeshivas*; he died prematurely at the age of fifty-eight. He was born into a Zionist home; his father Tsvi Hersh Mark was an adherent of, and activist in, the Mizrahi movement.[5] He gave both his sons a substantial Jewish education and, simultaneously, a secular one. When Ber Mark began his studies in 1927 at the University of Warsaw he had already absorbed many of the ancient Jewish sources, connected as they were to modern Jewish intellectual and spiritual trends. Communism, that brilliant humanist principle, was hammered home and subsequently resonated in his consciousness. Like many of his generation of informed

---

4 Soviet Communism co-opted Socialism by way of obfuscation: "... politics in Soviet occupied Europe were designed to be opaque." Anne Applebaum, *Iron Curtain: The Crushing of Eastern Europe: 1944–1956* (New York: Doubleday, 2012), 67. Gomułka himself noted the "communist party's elimination of the Polish socialists" (221). The role of the Socialist prime minister in Poland was "distinctly limited, if not entirely fictitious" (222). Hence the "so-called" descriptor Berger ascribes to Socialism in those years.

5 Abbreviation for Merkaz Ruhani (spiritual centre), a religious Zionist movement, founded in Vilnius in 1902 by Y.Y. Reines. It defended a world view situated at the intersection of nationalism and orthodoxy. Ze'ev Jawitz, chief ideologue of its first proclamation, sought "to recast Halakhic Judaism in a way congenial to Palestinian settlement," and to the "culturalist's" position and its "modernist nuances." Bernard Avishai, *The Tragedy of Zionism: Revolution and Democracy in the Land of Israel* (New York: Farrar, Straus and Giroux, 1985), 95.

118   Arts and Letters

young Jews, he believed that this inspired ideal would also engender the deliverance of the Jewish people. So, later, when Mark, a Jewish historian with a warm Jewish heart, came face to face with an ideological and political force which gradually and progressively erased and uprooted everything he held dear, his inner struggles deepened. Yet neither the state of his psyche nor his illness, which spread in stages, could stand in the way of his prodigious creativity or the pursuit of his wide-ranging interests and activities.

Professor Ber Mark was a titan of creativity in its varied domains: he was a social and cultural activist as well as a talented lecturer and public speaker. Until 1949 he was editor-in- chief of the first Yiddish newspaper in postwar Poland, *Dos naye lebn* [The new life].[6] Until the end of his life he headed the Jewish Historical Institute.[7] He was a proficient researcher and chronicler, ardent essayist and columnist, and a deeply thoughtful literary critic. In a word, he was a creative force in many and varied domains. Already gravely ill, he took on new research and writing projects. He had always written with great alacrity as if he were holding an enchanted pen, as I once remarked to him at his home. In the fog of impaired vision, he was still able to write articles and feverishly to prepare his last book, *Megiles Oyshvits* [The scrolls of Auschwitz],[8] for which he had assembled a considerable body of authentic documents.

---

6 Mark debuted in *Dos naye lebn* in its early version (1919–31), published in Białystok. It had a subsequent iteration in 1945 in Łódź and Warsaw. Mark seized the reins upon his return from the Soviet Union in 1946. Editorships were fluid in those years, the borders between publications porous. *Dos naye lebn* exhibited much content overlap with *Shriftn*, until its demise in 1951. Both publications were organs of the Fareyn fun Yidishe literatn un zhurnalistn in Poyln (Association of Jewish Writers and Journalists in Poland), active 1916–39. Under Mark's chairmanship the association was revived (1945–8) to become a cultural hub for literary and performance art. A member of the PPR, the Polish Worker's Party and the Communist faction of the Central Committee of Polish Jews, Mark impossibly defended the political independence of the Fareyn. Nathan Cohen, "The Renewed Association of Yiddish Writers and Journalists in Poland, 1945–48," *The Mendele Review: Yiddish Literature and Language* (A companion to Mendele) 9, no. 4 (sequential no. 156) (15 March 2005), https://sztetl.org.pl/en/towns/w/18-warsaw/101-organizations-and-social-institutions/76616-association-jewish-writers-and-journalists-warsaw, Newly corrected accessed 12 June 2021. See Prager and Historical Jewish Presses in footnote 2 for source material on *Dos naye lebn* as well.
7 Mark was the institute's director from 1949 until his death in 1966. Under his tenure, the JHI/ZIH became a state institution which issued the scholarly publications *Bleter far geshikhte* (Pages of history) and *Biuletyn* (Bulletin).
8 Tel Aviv: Yisroel Bukh, 1977.

He remained a frequent public lecturer: on the commemorative occasion of the seventieth birthday of the martyred writer Peretz Markish, Mark, almost completely blind, regaled his audience in a fully packed theatre with a detailed and spirited talk about the life and work of the murdered poet.[9] Guiding him from the podium, I asked him with wonderment how he was able to accurately recall so many details, episodes, and dates. He answered, "The memory now does the work of the eyes." Indeed, he always had rare and extraordinary powers of recollection, which served him well until his very last days. As he lay in bed, by this time in complete and utter darkness, he dictated to his wife, the historian Esther Mark, various fragments of this, his last book [noted above], partially written in his own hand, which only she was able to decipher after his death. Incidentally, she put in order items from the archive which he kept for this monumental work about Jewish annihilation and heroism in Auschwitz. She researched and interpreted evidence and recovered names for the Auschwitz prisoners who authored the buried documents. It was Esther, the experienced historian, who saw this research mission to its conclusion. Then she concerned herself with translations, but all of these were merely episodes in Mark's tempestuous, actively creative, and tragic life.

Although his own life span was cut short, Ber Mark represented an expansive epoch of Jewish ascent and decline, of dramatic and cataclysmic events in which he participated. He lived through, and survived, the Holocaust to become among its first historians.

While in the Soviet Union during the war, Mark was a member of the Jewish Anti-Fascist Committee.[10] He unremittingly kept track of the murderous German fury, primarily the extermination of the Jews in

---

9 Insurgent and Expressionist poet. His avant-garde battle cry was "Rear the head like the middle finger." With Uri Tsvi Greenberg, he was founding member of Di Khalyastre (The gang) (1919–24) and editor of the journal of the same name (Warsaw, 1922; Paris, 1924). He went on to contribute to *Albatros* and *Literarishe bleter*. In late career, he was among a cohort of twelve Yiddish poets executed by Stalin on 12 August 1952. Their commemoration by Yiddishists everywhere is known as the "Night of the Murdered Poets."

10 Partly owing to ideological commitments, partly to curry favour with the regime, Yiddish writers founded the Jewish Anti-Fascist Committee (1941–8). Mark was among its recruits, writing "correspondences" for the JAC organ, *Eynikeyt* (Unity). The JAC was headed by Shlomo Mikhoels, director of GOSET, the Moscow State Jewish Theatre, and poet Itsik Feffer, its chief apparatchik. Mark found himself among Yiddish literati who were thoughtful critics of capitalist privilege. His colleagues grew progressively resolved to protect all acts of Yiddish expression, their political attachment to the motherland a secondary consideration. Accordingly

120 Arts and Letters

Poland. During the Warsaw Ghetto Uprising he did not rest. Day and night, he assumed the mission of memorializing the destruction of the Jews and their resistance to it through the courage of the partisans. As early as 1944, his Polish pamphlet about the Warsaw Ghetto Uprising was published in the Soviet Union. The book *Der oyfshtand in Varshever geto* [The uprising in the Warsaw Ghetto], among the first studies of its kind in Yiddish, was also to appear in 1947, in Moscow, from the publishing house, Emes [Truth]. Indeed, in the most difficult circumstances, Mark researched and gathered materials and testimonies[11] with great urgency, exposing for all the world the annihilation of the Jews. However, it was the unfortunate lot of these efforts that, from the beginning, Mark did all this work in Moscow, where he had to comply with local Muscovite policies.

From the moment he returned to Poland in 1946, he, once again, and with all his strength, undertook the task of writing about Holocaust themes; his book *Khurves dertseyln* [Ruins recount][12] was written in blood. Here he revealed both the atmosphere and the mood of the captives of the Warsaw Ghetto and presented the uprising not only as the resistance of individuals, but also the resistance of the diminished remnants of Warsaw's Jews.

He persisted relentlessly in his research of events in the ghettos and camps. He published books about the execution of the Yiddish writers and the erasure of their works, and about the uprising in the Białystok

---

the committee evolved from a Sovietizing propaganda apparatus into what critics deemed a counter-revolutionary vehicle for Yiddish culture. Ultimately, the Stalinist regime, under Zhdanov, saw the ruthless disestablishment of Jewish and Yiddish institutions, schools, and theatres. Gennady Estraikh, *In Harness: Yiddish Writers' Romance with Communism* (Syracuse: Syracuse University Press, 2005). Boris Groys, "From Internationalism to Cosmopolitanism Artists of Jewish Descent in the Stalin Era,"in *Russian Jewish Artists in a Century of Change, 1890–1990*, edited by Susan Tumarkin Goodman, 81–8 (New York and Munich: Prestel, 1995). Michael Stanislawsky, "The Jews and Russian Culture and Politics," in Tumarkin Goodman, 16–27.

11 See details of Mark's effort to preserve these records in *Dokumentn un materyaln vegn oyfshtand in Varshever geto* (Documents and materials about the Warsaw Ghetto Uprising) (Warsaw: Yidish Bukh, 1953).

12 Warsaw, 1945. Mark draws here from the notes of Shmuel Vinter, who documented the Warsaw Ghetto Uprising while in a bunker at 34 Swietojerska Street. Mark restored these documents, placed them in the archive at ZIH, noting that "encoding and deciphering these notes ... played as great a role as did Ringelblum's diaries in preserving the memory of ghetto resistance." Yitskhok Kharlash, "Shmuel Vinter," *Yiddish Lexicon*, https://yleksikon.blogspot.com/search?q=shmuel+Vinter, accessed 12 July 2021.

Ghetto.[13] He also added to his canon of works in Polish, but their political fallout would shadow him like a spectre. Yet, countless times, he returned to the subject of the Warsaw Ghetto Uprising from different perspectives. About these, the Polish censors were far from restrained. In 1963, just three years before his death, there appeared a new volume, also with newly discovered documents under the same rubric, *Der oyfshtand in Varshever geto.*[14]

In 1957, after the famous "Polish October," when the bolts were loosened,[15] Mark seized the opportunity to travel to Israel and actively participate in the Congress for Jewish Studies in Jerusalem. During a public appearance, he had the courage to openly declare that the grievances against him were justified.[16] What is more, he asked forgiveness in the

---

13 *Di umgekumene shrayber fun di* getos *un lagern un zeyere verk* (The murdered writers of the ghettos and camps and their work) (Warsaw: Yidish Bukh, 1954); *Der oyfshtand in Bialistoker geto* (The uprising in the Białystok Ghetto] (Warsaw: ZIH, 1950; 2nd ed. Buenos Aires: Ikuf, 1953).

14 2nd ed. Warsaw: Yidish Bukh, 1963 (see body of this text for details of the first edition).

15 The workers' strike (Polish United Workers Party) and uprising to protest untenable conditions in Poznań in June of 1956 kicked off the historic October insurrection. Under the reformist guidance of Władysław Gomułka, the Polish October strike saw a "loosening" (Berger's terminology) of the Soviet grip, referred to by commentators as a liberalizing "thaw." Berger includes the opening of borders to free travel in this newly found latitude. The ensuing decentralization resulted in some measure of autonomy for Poland. The new regime, however, came to engender, for some, the very domination they sought to disarm. Glenn E. Curtis, ed., *Poland: A Country Study* (Washington, DC: GPO for the Library of Congress, 1992), http://countrystudies. us/poland/17.htm, accessed 6 September 2020. George Sakwa, "The 'Polish October': A Re-appraisal through Historiography," *Polish Review* 23, no. 3 (1978): 62–78, *JSTOR*, www.jstor.org/stable/25777588, accessed 6 June 2021.

16 Mark attended the World Congress of Jewish Studies in Jerusalem to lecture on the role of the Jewish proletariat in the 1905 Russian revolution. Mark's apology in the press to which Berger refers may be attributed to an incident in 1955 that provoked considerable ill will: In a letter to the Polish Ministry of Foreign Affairs Mark declined collaboration with Yad Vashem as an "institution of reactionary character," which was called into being "for sabotage purposes" (cited in N-K, 220). Mark admitted later that it was a "misunderstanding" and that he was "misled" (Y. Rimun, in *Keneder odler* [Canadian eagle] in Montreal, 12 March 1957; cited in Fuks, "Ber Mark"). For most of his career Mark expressed support for Palestine, and later, Israel. Yet his relationship to Israel, finally, was a conflicted one. The above-noted Fareyn, under Mark's tutelage, sent an independent congratulatory message to the State of Israel in May 1948, which was subsequently "redacted" by the Central Committee of Polish Jewry, also under Mark's chairmanship, to recommend that Jewish activity be based solely on Marxist ideology. Yet Mark flouted the Stalinist policy

press. But there were more than a few grievances of a contrasting sort, both prior and subsequent to his trip, expressed by his close friends in Poland. [17] This was especially the case as he returned from Israel, singularly buoyed and inspired.

In his all-too-short life, Ber Mark was the author of thirty-nine varied books, both historical and literary-critical; he published a few hundred essays and sketches in periodicals and in scholarly publications on vastly different themes. In 1954, twelve years before Mark's death, the title "Professor" was conferred on him. During this time, Ber Mark worked as if he were possessed, prodigiously researching and writing some of his most important pieces. Alongside the subject of the Holocaust, Mark, as a Jewish historian with a zealous Jewish heart, conceived of setting down, based upon the latest documents, the history of Poland's Jews from their earliest days. Unfortunately, only the first hefty volume, concerned with Jewish life up until the end of the fifteenth century, was published. [18]

---

which discouraged cooperation with scholars outside of the Soviet Union and its protectorates. When in Israel, Mark worked to strengthen ties between the Jewish Historical Institute and the National Library of Israel and helped establish connections with ORT, The Joint (Distribution Committee), and the World Jewish Congress. Berger's own perspective on Israel was less nuanced: "One certainty ... emerges from her work written after her disillusionment with the new Poland: the centrality of the State of Israel in Jewish life" (Vivian Felsen, "Lili Berger," in *Jewish Women: A Comprehensive Historical Encyclopedia*, 31 December 1999, Jewish Women's Archive, https://jwa.org/encyclopedia/article/berger-lili, accessed 18 May 2020.

17 A simple and schematic version of these grievances in Israel and Poland respectively: not Jewish enough, or too Jewish. Berger is doubtless reflecting on Mark's vilification over the course of his career for countless real or putative offences, largely emanating from his duties as a *publitsist* (political columnist). Communists of different stripes castigated him for bourgeois affronts to the cause. In the interwar years, the editorial staff at the *Folks-tsaytung* (People's Paper, an organ of the Bund, reviled him for expressing anti-Bundist sympathies. Some of his postwar detractors held that Mark made numerous historical mistakes in his many publications on the Warsaw Ghetto Uprising, most egregiously his attributing greater contribution to the Polish Resistance fighters than they merited. He was denigrated as a "scholar in service of a regime," or a "regime historian." In 1943 *Eynikeyt*'s editor, Shakhno Epshteyn, fired Mark for what he perceived to be Mark's "nationalistic tendencies," such as listing the surnames of only the Jewish fallen soldiers. Such Jewish self-concern was seen as inimical to the spirit of Soviet internationalism (N-K, 205, 220, 213). See also Estraikh, *In Harness*; Fuks, "Ber Mark"; and Prager, "Literary Journals."

18 *Geshikhte fun Yidn in Poyln: Bizn sof fun XV yorhundert* (History of the Jews in Poland: Until the end of the fifteenth century) (Warsaw: Yidish Bukh, 1957).

Ber Mark, The Man and the Author 123

In the intervening years, Mark worked assiduously, thoroughly researching the collected documents on Auschwitz and the Jewish resistance in this, the largest death camp. He began to write this monumental work when he was seriously ill. His wife Esther, as previously mentioned, prepared it for posthumous publication.

Until his last breath, Professor Ber Mark called to the world's attention both the annihilation of the Jews and their heroism at the very threshold of death.

In a tribute such as this it is impossible to express the full extent of his accomplishments and his scholarly works, many of which have been translated into English, French, German, Spanish, Portuguese, among others. For all of his achievements may his memory eternally remain with the Jewish people.

Translated by Linda/Leye Lipsky
Ekhos fun a vaytn nekhtn, Tel Aviv 1993

Moyshe Shulshteyn: On the Tenth Anniversary of His Death[1]

How the years fly! A full decade has elapsed since Moyshe Shulshteyn was wrenched from our lives, yet it seems to me that not too long ago he was here among us.

When a writer would pass away, it was Moyshe Shulshteyn's custom to deliver a eulogy in the form of a testimonial article. In his book *Geshtaltn far mayne oygn* [Figures before my eyes], he both mourns and celebrates no fewer than fifteen departed or violently murdered fellow writers. After the death of Itsik Manger he wrote a eulogy entitled "A Bright Star, Illuminating Our Roof, Has Been Extinguished."[2] These very words are heartbreaking today because they apply with equal force to Moyshe himself, as ten years ago a comparably luminous star watching over us was snuffed out. And just like his family, so our time-honoured Yiddish literature is bereft again, and his friends are left to mourn anew the loss of a devoted companion.

---

1 See Berger's original, longer essay from which this essay is adapted: "Moyshe Shulshteyn," written in January 1982, shortly after his death in 1981. In *Oyf di khvalyes fun goyrl: Noveln, dertseylungen, literarishe eseyen* (On the waves of destiny: Short stories, tales and literary essays) (Paris: IMPO, 1986), 173–86. Berger notes here both biographical details and childhood perceptions elided in this tenth *yortsayt* essay: his birthplace Korev, the din of his father's sewing machine, the oil lamp's insufficient light. She cites his poetry more extensively in the original essay. Berger notes his prominence in Parisian Yiddish literary circles, all the while implementing a *kheshbn hanefesh*, a spiritual self-assessment.

2 *Geshtaltn far mayne oygn: Eseyen, portretn, dermonungen* (Figures before my eyes: Essays, portraits, remembrances) (Paris: Bukh-komisye baym fareyniktn sotsyaln fond in Pariz, 1971). "A shtern af undzer dakh hot zikh farloshn (vegn Itsik Manger)" (see translation in the text above), 79–96. In this essay Shulshteyn elaborates: "A shtern af undzer oremen [poor] dakh hot zikh do farloshn," as if in anticipation of the poverty of our lives without Manger.

Moyshe Shulshteyn: On the Tenth Anniversary of His Death 125

He was taken from us suddenly, and too soon. Not four hours before his death we were engaged in a genial conversation about his new book, a historical verse drama, which he had me look over as he needed to submit it promptly for publication.[3] His new creative projects and ambitions were as plentiful as pomegranate seeds. He simply welled up with inspiration.

For more than a half-century Moyshe Shulshteyn portrayed in his poetry Jewish life, Jewish destiny. He sings of man, indeed of the totality of humanity and creation. He was born into poverty, his home a basement apartment. From childhood on, he was forced to eke out his paltry subsistence by the labour of his bare hands. Yet at the tender age of fourteen or fifteen he walked around with pockets stuffed full of pieces of paper on which he had jotted down his first verses. At that time he received a poet's *smikhe* [rabbinical ordination] for his proficiency in writing from Yitskhok Meyer Vaysenberg,[4] who published Shulshteyn's juvenile poems in his journal *Hofening* [Hope].[5] "The boy has talent," Vaysenberg observed to Shulshteyn's "protector."[6] At this tender age, and in a time of great penury, Moyshe Shulshteyn answered his poetic calling and gradually rose higher and higher on his poetic trajectory, a path of wide-ranging creativity. This poet was also a cogent

---

3 Berger is referring here to the piece of historical theatre originally published as *Yehuda Hamakebi: A dramatishe poeme in zibn bilder* (Judah the Maccabee: A dramatic poem in seven tableaux), which appears in Shulshteyn's collection *A leyter tsu der zun: Lider un poemes* (A ladder to the sun: Poems and longer poems], (Paris: Oyfsnay, 1954), 93–237. I cannot trace the second edition, prepared on his deathbed, to which Berger alludes here, and again at the end of this essay.

4 Prose writer and editor, Vaysenberg leapt onto the literary scene with his novella *A shtetl*, published serially in 1906, in the Warsaw paper *Der veg*. Translated and edited by Ruth Wisse in *A Shtetl and Other Yiddish Novellas* (New York: Behrman House, 1973), 23–78, it was hailed by Peretz and others for its astute naturalistic depiction of the ill effects of the 1905 revolution. See Shulshteyn's reverential eulogy subtitled "Mayn ershter literarisher rebe" (My first literary master and teacher), in *Geshtaltn*, 9–16. Here Shulshteyn recalls Vaysenberg's mentorship with great delight.

5 Extant 1926–32, Vaysenberg at the helm. Printed in Warsaw, this literary journal is known variously as *Unzer Hofenung/Inzer Hofening* (Our hope). Berger writes "Hofening" in keeping with what Shulshteyn names Vaysenberg's "passionate institution" of "Polish" over "Litvak" phonetical spelling, the journal's title a crucible of this effort. https://www.nli.org.il/en/newspapers/?a=q&r=1&results=1&txq=unzer%20hofenung, National Library of Israel, Historical Jewish Presses, accessed 23 August 2021.

6 An unnamed neighbour from his apartment courtyard, a Hasidic young man, uncommonly well-versed in literature, noted this in the aforementioned essay. He made the initial contact with Vaysenberg, submitting a sample of Shulshteyn's adolescent poetry. *Geshtaltn*, 11.

126   Arts and Letters

prose writer, a colourful narrator, a perceptive essayist, and an accomplished translator of foreign language poetry, which he had masterfully decanted from one vessel to another, recasting it into Yiddish poetic form.

Moyshe Shulshteyn wrote his carefully wrought poetry as naturally as one draws breath. This can be seen clearly in his poem, "I sing, I sing, as I breathe, I breathe as I sing."[7] In sum, his poetry was his lifeblood. And this was the case in every circumstance. Even when he was confined to "La Santé" prison[8] during the occupation and didn't have the means to write, as he explained to me, he used a small pin to scratch out verses in Yiddish letters on the broad margins of old newspapers.

Very often I think of my friend Moyshe and our first meeting: our acquaintanceship began in 1937.[9] We were both "green," newcomers, two lost souls in the big Parisian metropolis. "How do you propose to support yourself?" I asked. "I haven't had the time to consider this question; first of all, I think about how I might be able to get down to writing." There, in short, I had his answer. Indeed, Moyshe always thought about how to get down to writing before he thought about a roof over his head and his meagre livelihood.

He was still wet behind the ears when he set out for the wider world. Yet Moyshe had always had the keen artistic curiosity of a true humanist, deeply concerned about his fellow man and what truly defines the

---

7 "Ikh zing," in *Der orem fun libshaft* (The Arm of Affection; Le bras d'amour) (Paris: A Komitet, 1977), 16–17.

8 See the cycle of thirteen poems. "La Santé" in *A boym tsvishn di khurves: Lider un poemes* (A tree among the ruins: Poems and longer poems) (Paris: Oyfsnay, 1947), 135–49. The poem "La Santé" considers incarceration, its indignities, and what lurks ominously on the other side of the wall (138). Built in 1867 at 42 Rue de la Santé, it was a notoriously brutal prison, second only to the Bastille in enforcing cruel directives. Deemed a *lieu de mémoire* (site of memory), it figured largely in French gangster movies and popular songs. "Beset in recent times by horrific conditions, it has become a *cause célèbre* for politicians hoping to curry favour with a progressive electorate": https://www.theguardian.com/world/2000/jan/21/paulwebster, accessed 12 November 2021, and https://www.theguardian.com/world/2014/dec/07/la-sante -prison-paris-visitors-welcome, accessed 18 May 2021.

9 Berger and Shulshteyn enjoyed a collegial relationship, their political and literary interests coinciding in the early years of emigration to Paris from Warsaw, she in 1936, he in 1937. While Berger went back to Poland (1949–1968), then back to Paris (1968–96), Shulshteyn never left Paris. They appeared in the same journals and thematic anthologies. For astute appreciations of Shulshteyn's work see articles by Rivke Kope, Melech Ravitch, Nakhmen Mayzl, among others. See *YL* and http://passages. yiddish.paris/ecrivains-yiddish-en-france, accessed August 2021.

Moyshe Shulshteyn: On the Tenth Anniversary of His Death   127

essence of a man, the essence of a Jew. He contemplated, observed, and researched everything in his purview. From the start of his journey, his artist's gaze captured all the teeming details of his new reality, both present and past, which beckoned to him coyly and found their way irresistibly into his writing. While taking root in this foreign soil was a merciless ordeal, especially for one so sensitive, he did grow fond of this world, far from his home. Simply put, he received love because he loved mankind. All the strings of his vulnerable heart were inextricably connected to the vital, pulsating life from which he drew his inspiration. Although he still saw himself as grounded by deeply entrenched roots to his ancestral home, at the same time he penned his poetry about the fate of Jewish life in the new world, and with it, celebrated the "old-new"[10] home, Israel, to which he offered much affection.

With singular poetic skill he immortalized the Holocaust and the execution of Yiddish writers and artists by the Stalinist regime.[11] The poems "Kh'hob gezen a barg" [I saw a mountain], "Di lyalke in Oyshvitz" [The doll in Auschwitz], "Baym pinkes fun Lublin" [Reading the chronicles of Lublin], and also "Blumen fun badoyer" [Flowers of regret] will forever remain as sacred monuments.[12]

---

10 This oxymoronic descriptor is a reference to Theodore Herzl's autobiographical novel *Altneuland,* a prophetic, literary turn on the Jewish state. Shulshteyn was a devout Labour Zionist throughout his life, even when such allegiance butted up against his other contending ideological commitments.

11 See his review of the anthology of Soviet Yiddish writers "*A shpigl af a shteyn* – a shteyn far a denkmol" (*A mirror on a stone* – A stone as a monument), in *A ring in a ring: Zamlung fun eseyen, fartseykhenungen, reportazshn* (A link within a link: An anthology of essays, sketches and journalistic reportage) (Paris, 1975), 134–8. See the poems "Balade vegn dem toyt fun Peretz Markish" and "Di fidl fun Dovid Bergelson" in *Blumen fun badoyer: Lider un poemes* (Flowers of regret: Poems and longer poems) (Paris: Di Goldene Pave, 1959), 15–16 and 26–8. Indeed this volume is dedicated to the "Jewish writers and artists of the Soviet Union executed on 12August 1952 and to those who met an unknown fate."

12 "Kh'hob gezen a barg," in *A boym tsvishn khurves,* 170–2. An excerpt appears on the wall of the US Holocaust Memorial Museum in Washington, DC. "Blumen fun badoyer" is the opening poem of the volume *Blumen fun badoyer,* 11. *Baym pinkes fun Lublin: Dramatisher khizoyen in a kupe ash* (Reading the chronicle of Lublin: A Dramatic Vision in a Heap of Ashes) (Paris: Imprimerie A. Schipper. 1966). "Di lyalke in Oyshvits" is a possible conflation: in the section on Shulshteyn's translations from Polish poetry, Stanislav Vigodski's poem "A meydele mit a lyalke" (A girl with a doll) notes the location and the date at the bottom of the page: "Auschwitz, 1943": *Der orem fun libshaft,* 275.

128   Arts and Letters

In his last few years, Moyshe Shulshteyn was remarkably active. At the same time that he wrote his memoirs, he also busied himself with other projects. His last book, *Dort vu mayn vig iz geshtanen* [There where my cradle stood],[13] was published posthumously, thanks to the extraordinary efforts of his wife, Milke Shulshteyn. Moyshe considered this volume to be the debt he owed his family and the other shtetl compatriots who perished; the book was a fitting monument. At the same time, he reworked and revised the dramatic-historical epic poem, *Yehuda Hamakebi* [noted above], which was to be adapted for the stage. He also undertook a translation into French of a selection of poems,[14] a large number of which had already been translated. What is more, I was witness to how Moyshe, after the translation proper was over, would go back to it, and temper it with his signature artistic authenticity.

Over the years since Moyshe Shulshteyn's death, we have sensed the monumental loss, the gaping void which he has left in his wake. We miss him more than ever! Oh, how we feel Moyshe's absence! The only consolation is his legacy, contained in eighteen volumes, which will remain with us as an eternal spiritual treasure of the Jewish people.

On the occasion of this commemorative anniversary a slim volume of selected poetry has just been published: *Sod un kavone* [Secret and intention].[15]

1992
Translated by Linda/Leye Lipsky
Ekhos fun a vaytn nekhtn, Tel Aviv 1993

---

13 Paris: A Komitet, 1982.

14 There is no evidence that this effort came to fruition but Shulshteyn did publish translations going the other way, the works of Victor Hugo and Guillaume Apollinaire among them. See the section "Fun der frantsoyzisher poesye" (From French poetry) in *In der orem fun libshaft*, 279–89.

15 Paris: 1991. Both these terms figure prominently in Kabbalistic lore, as the intentional prayer with which one arrives at the esoteric, recondite meaning of Lurianic mysticism. See Jean Baumgarten, "Yiddish Ethical Texts and the Diffusion of the Kabbalah in the 17th and 18th Centuries," *Bulletin du Centre de recherche français à Jérusalem* (online), 18 (2007), http://journals.openedition.org/bcrfj/223 ©, accessed 20 September 2022.

FABLES, SHORT STORIES, AND HISTORIC FICTION

All Because of the Wife or
The First Quarrel

After God had created Adam He was uneasy: Here was a creature in His own image! Who knew what such a creature could think of! Could not this Adam, in time, desire to become His equal and want to rule over heaven and earth as if he himself were a god?

God almost became regretful that from the dust of the earth He had formed a human being. But what was done was done. In the wink of an eye He, the Almighty, came up with a plan: He would provide for Adam so that he'll want for nothing but He would do everything to keep him in a state of ignorance, and frighten him with such frightening threats that he would not even dare to sample the taste of knowledge. Ah, then there would be nothing to fear! In his ignorance Adam would be obedient and submissive.

Pleased with his bright idea, God stroked his long, broad beard and no longer regretted that He had created Adam. How would His world look without a human being? Who would serve Him, who would praise Him and bow before Him? Who else could be commanded this way, and who could carry out orders like an Adam?

And God began to care for Adam in a fatherly manner. He settled him in a beautiful garden which He had planted for his sake in Eden and warned him that he may eat of all the fruits of all the trees but not of the trees in the centre of the garden. Should he, perish the thought, taste of the fruits of these two trees, he would die; may that hour never come. And the trick succeeded.

When Adam heard these words, he was terrified. To die right now! Such a delightful garden! A joy to live here, and suddenly, such danger because of some nice little apple, he would, perish the thought, leave this world. No, he would not go near; he wouldn't even take a whiff.

And Adam stayed away from the trees in the centre of the garden.

132   Fables, Short Stories, and Historic Fiction

God was pleased with His Adam and continued to show him great kindness. He saw that it was sad for a human to be alone. Is anything harder to bear than loneliness? God assembled all the beasts of the earth and all the birds of the heavens that Adam might choose from among them a partner according to his liking. But Adam, puffed up with an inflated sense of himself, boasted that none of these creatures was good enough for him. Was he just anybody? Was he like some beast or animal? Did God not create him in His own image, like a self-portrait? God, the Creator, realized that Adam was a bit impertinent but after all he was Adam, created in His image, and He relented. He immediately put Adam into a deep sleep, cut a rib from his body, crafted from it Eve, and said to Adam: "Here you have your equal; see, with Me you have true democracy, you can choose whatever you want.

Adam blinked, shrugged his shoulders as if to say what kind of democracy is this where you have to take whatever is shoved under your nose. You can choose! As if there were something to choose from. But nevertheless he was content; she was, after all, a creature in his and in God's likeness. And he named his partner WOMAN, that she should know she was taken from man, belonged to him, and must obey him.

But this woman, like all women, likes to stick her nose into everything, to chat a little here, to hear a bit of news there, to embellish and retell. So Eve began rushing around the Garden of Eden, making new friends and acquaintances, what else? Should she hang onto Adam's coattail, the oaf? May her enemies have only one husband and one shirt! A husband, just like a bureaucrat, dull, grey, without the least hint of poetry. She, Eve, would not be a "sit at home." She would go out in search of company.

And as she was looking for friends, Eve met the snake. The snake was still a respectable walking creature then, not yet crawling on its belly. Devilishly clever was this snake with a full grasp of all the ins and outs of God's crafty tricks. So it slyly inquired of the lady of the garden about the two trees at the very centre. Eve was unable to keep a secret. She thought to herself that there was nothing to hide, and in great detail she revealed everything to the snake.

The snake burst into laughter, and then quietly whispered into the ear of the lady of the garden that God was leading Adam and Eve around by the nose. Eve almost burst with indignation. So that's what's going on! Who did God think He was? Were they His town fools? A person needed to know what was good and what was evil.

Her womanly curiosity spurred her on. She dashed at full speed to the tree in the centre of the garden, picked an apple, and swallowed every last bite. Oh, what an apple, what sublime taste; it melted in her

All Because of the Wife or The First Quarrel   133

mouth. Now, her eyes were beginning to open, and God forbid it should harm her.

Again, she dashed off at breakneck speed to Adam and began to persuade him: "Oh Adam, my darling, try, it's the true taste of the Garden of Eden. I swear on my life that it won't harm you; God forbid you should die because of it. You will only discover the meaning of good and evil.

And Adam continued sitting under a fig tree. Sullen, blinking his eyes, he was too frightened to take the fruit into his mouth. He watched as Eve greedily swallowed each bite; his mouth watered, but he didn't dare taste it. His cowardice was more than Eve could bear. She ridiculed him, letting loose a barrage of insults as women will in such situations: "You big ox, you fool, you good for nothing; God pulled the wool over your eyes, and you let Him do it. Adam dear, be a man, taste the apple; you'll get the real Jewish flavour and you'll be as enlightened as I was. Sweetheart, listen to your wife.

And Adam obeyed, partly because his pride would not allow him to have his wife regard him a coward, and partly out of curiosity. So he took the apple and ate it. And the first thing Adam and Eve were aware of was that they were naked, naked as the emperor in Andersen's fairy tale. And they were not only ashamed, they were frightened. Who knew what God could do to a naked person? In the meantime there was nothing to do but hide.

But God had observed it all (such was His nature to stroll around in the shade of the trees, hiding and observing the human being); He played the fool, as if He knew nothing), and began to question Adam who was so frightened that he turned deathly pale, because he was by nature a bit of a coward. He didn't think long and blamed his wife for everything, and began stammering: Lord, my Lord, You have given me a wife and that wife has given me the fruit of the tree; I did her will as I do Your will.

Upset as she was at Adam's cowardice, she nonetheless did as he did, and put all the blame on the snake.

God didn't even trouble Himself with the snake; surely, it, too, would also find someone else to blame for the mischief it had instigated. God thought and thought and came to the conclusion that if someone blames another they both deserve to be found guilty. And God sentenced them all to the punishment we all know.

From that time on, there was no longer a Garden of Eden in the world.

Oh, how Adam and Eve longed for the Garden of Eden! And this longing they bequeathed to their children and grandchildren forever.

Translated by Frieda Johles Forman and Sylvia Lustgarten
Ekhos fun a vaytn nekhtn, Tel Aviv 1993

The Rebbetzin's Sense of Justice

He was small, skinny, timid, eyes always downcast. She the opposite, big, full-bodied, a Jewish Cossack who tolerated no injustice. A big talker! These were my teachers, Reb Fishel and his wife, Khaye.

Behind his back they called him "Fisheleh hunchback," although he was not a hunchback, merely bent over. And her they called Big Khaye. We, the seven-year-old pupils, called Big Khaye "Rebbetzin."

How two such opposites were brought together only God in heaven knows. In our shtetl there was a story told that when Fisheleh saw his betrothed for the first time, under the bridal canopy, he almost fainted from fear. Opinion had it that this first scare pursued him all his life, not because Big Khaye was a miserable or wretched wife, quite the opposite. She had a good heart and could bear no injustice. She protected her husband like a mother hen protects her chicks, as if, without her, Fisheleh Hunchback would, God forbid, have drowned in the waves of life like a leaky ship in the ocean.

So what then? From their first moment together the contrast between the dreamy otherworldly Fisheleh and his down-to-earth Big Khaye terrified him.

It often happened that the absent-minded Rebbe forgot where he put things, and most often this misfortune happened with his eyeglasses.

Here we sat, the whole gang of pupils, around the long, scratched table, waiting for the signal to begin, while the Rebbe wandered about, searching, sighing, and eyeing us with suspicion. Finally he mutters "No one saw the glasses? My glasses? Which one of you … didn't see? How …?" "We didn't see," the children answered in chorus. Helplessness and sadness were etched on the Rebbe's face, but we pranksters didn't pay much attention. You couldn't say we disliked the Rebbe and wanted revenge; we simply enjoyed these moments.

Whoever had anything in his pocket pulled it out, and away we went: a button for a string, a string for a glass, a peppermint for a macaroon. We settled all the old accounts: whoever was owed a pinch, a jab, a quick punch in the nose – this was an opportunity to repay our debts. The victim took the gift with a quiet groan, with resignation, or hit back immediately. So, without the captain's oversight, the gang around the table, quietly waved their hands about, whispered, and would have continued happily who knows how long, were it not for the Rebbetzin. In the kitchen, separated from the classroom by a folding screen, Big Khaye sensed that something was not right. Instantly she appeared before the unruly gang and with her thunderous voice shouted, "Quiet here immediately!" As though by a magic wand, all transactions, accounts, and tricks stopped. Three rows of urchins around the table were silenced, not so much out of fear, but because of the Rebbetzin's authority. It didn't occur to any of us that we could disobey Big Khaye.

Then the Rebbetzin went into the second act. She approached the table, where the rabbi's chair stood, sized us up with a severe searching glance, lifted one prayer book after another, and then, turning to face the Rebbe, stuck her hand into the pocket of his robe and pulled out his eyeglasses. Once she had even pulled out a lost pointer from the Rebbe's pants pocket. The Rebbe, standing like a lost lamb, like a strapped school child, looked even smaller and thinner. The Rebbetzin then faced him with these words: "Here are your glasses, clumsy, dummy. First have your glasses ready, and then seat the scamps at the table."

In addition to the women's work, of which the Rebbetzin had more than enough, she also kept an eye on the whole classroom, and on each pupil. She knew who was a blockhead and who had a quick mind, who was capable of sitting a whole day like a block of wood, who was up to nasty tricks, who brought fine food for lunch, and who, unfortunately, chewed a dry piece of bread.

More than anything she sought justice and righteousness; most important for her was righteousness. Even in figuring out the school fees, not the Rebbe, but the Rebbetzin, decided. "You say that Reb Fishel let you down? What does he know?" she answered the haggling woman with a question, and continued. "Why should you demand that Khana Dvora the widow pay the same school fee as you? You have a breadwinner, may he live to one hundred and twenty. Is it not fair that you should pay the entire school fee and Khana Dvora half? What do you think – has he become the decision maker? It is not his business for whom to lower fees and for whom not. His business is to teach the

136 Fables, Short Stories, and Historic Fiction

children!" And it remained not as the Rebbe had agreed, but as the Rebbetzin had judged.

In only one aspect of the school did Big Khaye not interfere: the pedagogical side, in the teaching method. Perhaps because Reb Fishel had a reputation in town as a God-fearing, honourable Jew, or perhaps because she respected him as a Torah scholar while she was a simple, unlearned woman, Big Khaye gave no suggestions regarding her husband's pedagogy and methodology. And Reb Fishel had a brilliant teaching method: he put the greatest emphasis on the individual child. The whole group was arranged sitting on the floor against the wall, and the Rebbe called each one to the table, and kept each little prodigy until he was certain that he had knocked some learning into his head.

Only once a day, the Rebbe seated all the children around the long table and taught them as a group, repeating the lesson in unison. This was indeed the Rebbe's most difficult task. We, his pupils, knew the Rebbe's weaknesses, his helplessness when he had to deal with us all together. "Why are you looking out the window?" "And you there, why are you staring like a clumsy fool?" "And you, why are you squirming like a worm?"

"Yankeleh always has a drippy nose."

"Rebbe, Shloimeleh pinched me."

"Dovidl made fun of me. Dov v id dle m-m-made fun of m me," stuttered Faivel Sepliak.

From words, the Rebbe moved to action. He didn't have a strap at hand, the reason being that it was against his pedagogic philosophy. But he had two thin, bony hands and, whether he wanted to or not, he had to use them at times. He slowly shuffled over to the guilty ones, to one he gave a tweak on the ear, to a second he gave a light slap, to a third a whack; then the Rebbe returned to his place with a pained look, as though use of corporal punishment was a hard experience for him. Even Dovidl, the mischief-maker – a nickname the Rebbetzin gave him – used to say that the rabbi's smack really didn't hurt.

I don't know, because his punishing hand never fell on me. I was the only girl among the entire group of boys. It is very possible that the Rebbe, Reb Fishel, was a gentleman, or wouldn't want his hand to touch a female, because actually I deserved it. The Rebbe used to say that I was worse than a boy. Oy, you will say, how does a girl get into a boys' classroom? About this I only know this answer: it was arranged between my mother – peace be with her – and Big Khaye; and when the Rebbetzin agreed, the Rebbe had to agree. For me it was generally good: I was a girl and never received my earned punishments.

The Rebbetzin's Sense of Justice   137

But the Rebbe's punishment would have been useless were it not for the Rebbetzin. She always knew, from behind the folding screen, that something was going on in the classroom. She appeared in full majesty to quickly make order.

"What? Again? You are as pale as a corpse." She looked at her foolish husband.

"They drive me out of my mind," the Rebbe responded with a tearful voice.

"Well, woe to him who allows himself to be driven out of his mind. And from such unruly types. Is it worth raising a hand to them? You have to yell, such a look give them that they will feel it in their belly." After this lecture that she gave the Rebbe, the Rebbetzin turned to us, gave a look that actually cut through to the belly, and ordered: "Silence, do you hear?" Is there any question that we listened?

In addition to her inborn abilities to control people in times of upset, the Rebbetzin had many more talents. She showed great womanly skills in baking macaroons and *fefferlakh* (gingerbread cookies), which the students purchased, some for one groschen, and some for two or three groschen. Faivel got them for free.

In the heders of our shtetl, there was a tradition for which a rebbe's wife was responsible: she baked macaroons and *fefferlakh* that melted in your mouth, and looked like little yellow geese with red eyes. But none could compare to our Rebbetzin's macaroons and *fefferlakh* that melted into all your limbs; Big Khaye outdid them all.

But mostly our Rebbetzin had a reputation with us for her sense of justice. First, she didn't see it as fair that the littlest pupils should be stuck in school from early morning till evening. Every day, at a certain hour, she sent us outside for a bit, and kept an eye on us through the little kitchen window. "Let's go! Be on your way, air yourselves out!" she ordered, opening the door wide. She didn't have to ask long. But the Rebbe occasionally protested.

"You're already chasing them out? I haven't accomplished the day's work; I need more time."

"It's okay, tomorrow is also God's day."

"You are breaking up my classroom; you are destroying the, the ... you don't let me ..." whined the Rebbe with his weak, crying voice.

"Destroyed? Destroyed? And where is your justice? To keep children locked in the whole day, in such a heat?"

"We are still, heaven forbid, not Gentiles. Jewish children sit in school a whole day. Are you raging against heaven? And what in heaven has been ..." The Rebbe gathered his courage.

138   Fables, Short Stories, and Historic Fiction

"When God almighty sends us such a beautiful day, with such a bright sun, He wants his children to enjoy it."

"You are a woman and ..." The Rebbe could not contain himself, yet he was not bold enough to speak his mind.

"And if a woman, so what? Just look at him, my big shot!" And the Rebbetzin gave him such a look that the Rebbe was immediately silenced.

On such a heavenly day, we used to stay outdoors longer than usual. When the Rebbetzin considered that we had had our fill of air and sun, she again opened the door wide, and ordered, "Into the classroom."

The object of the Rebbetzin's greatest concern was Faivel Sepliak. Faivel was the young son of Hanah Dvora the washerwoman, a widow. He was called Sepliak because he had been nursed a long time. Therefore, he started school late and was the eldest among us. It seems something was wrong in his head. When he spoke, his entire face moved, as did his hands. No one knew exactly what was wrong with him. We all had an affection for Faivel. Maybe the Rebbetzin's concern affected us. Nevertheless, it was difficult to keep ourselves from laughing. Big Khaye forbade us from making fun of him, so sometimes we would choke with laughter, covering our mouths with both hands and giggling. We had to be very careful not to call him by his nickname. If the Rebbetzin caught someone calling Faivel "Sepliak" or mimicking his way of speaking, he got such a gift that he would be careful not to repeat it again. Faivel was given special privileges in the classroom. Like all the children, he brought lunch to school, but his lunch was dry dark bread.

Yoyne, the butcher's son, shared his warm lunch. Shakhne the butcher was more of a cattle dealer than a butcher. People used to say about him that he was a schemer, an "operator."

It seems that the butcher's youngest son, Yoyne, didn't take after the father. He was a round chubby boy with thick red cheeks and clumsy hands. He carried himself like a leaden bird.

"A blockhead, nothing goes in; go do something about it," the Rebbe complained.

"A child shouldn't stuff so much into himself. He must have a hole in his stomach, or an endless intestine," the Rebbetzin explained.

Yoyne used to bring a red linen bag full of all the best foods for lunch. Big Khaye gathered the warm lunches together in the morning, and put them on the high cupboard so that the children shouldn't "peck like hens at their lunches." At noon, each child received his lunch. Big Khaye was never mistaken; with closed eyes she knew what belonged to whom. Faivel Sepliak usually chewed a dry crust of bread; occasionally he had a piece of sugar which the Rebbetzin had given him. Suddenly he was restored by a piece of stuffed chicken neck that came into his meagre portion, or a roasted chicken liver. Faivel asked no questions – only his eyes shone and his mouth swallowed.

Everyone in the group of rascals knew from where Faivel's good luck came. We were happy that Faivel Sepliak also had some pleasure in life. Only one, Yoyne, sat sulking, chewed, and looked at Faivel angrily.

Once at lunch, Faivel enjoyed a big yellow pear, chewing with obvious delight and relishing each juicy bite, maybe for the first time. His entire face ate. Every feature was at work. Often when he spoke, his eyes silently wept, but now they sparkled with glee. Yoyne also chewed a pear, looking angrily at Faivel. Suddenly he shoved his hand into the red bag and blurted out: "There were two pears, two, now there is one."

"One is not enough for you?" the Rebbetzin spoke out from behind the folding screen. "That's why you are a blockhead; you stuff too much into yourself."

"One is not enough for you," the children repeated the Rebbetzin's words, and took revenge on Yoyne, who was not liked by the pupils.

The next day Yoyne's mother appeared. A short woman, heavy-set, her big belly preceding her. She rolled into the school, angry, and, without a "Good morning," went straight behind the folding screen, where the Rebbetzin, with a master hand, was preparing the macaroons and *fefferlakh*. The Rebbe paled. Yoyne, learning at the table, turned his head away. Our unruly gang, seated against the wall, began stuffing into our pockets little buttons, pieces of string, small stones; we perked up our ears. We children knew that something would play itself out here, as soon as we heard this dialogue:

"Tell me, my dear Khaye, if it's true, what my Yoyne tells."

"What, for instance, does your Yoyne tell?"

"He says that you give half his lunch to Sepliak."

"Your Yoyne exaggerates. A half, no, but something yes."

"So tell me, my dear Khaye, is it right to take from my child's mouth and give it to another? Is it fair?"

"So tell me, my dear Bryne, is it fair that your Yoyne should eat so much that it actually gives him a stuffed head? And a poor orphan should waste away?"

"Khaye, what are you thinking, Khaye? You think there are no rules in this world?"

"What I myself think? I think that there should be a little justice in the world. Meanwhile you stuff your Yoyne. Because of this, nothing goes into his head, his stomach is always so stuffed that he moves like

140   Fables, Short Stories, and Historic Fiction

a leaden bird ... and ... and, don't take offence, he fouls the air. One shouldn't overstuff a child this way and a poor orphan should ..."

"What are you saying, Khaye? It is not yet a lawless world. We'll see about that, Khaye, we'll see ..."

The butcher's wife was not finished. She was probably afraid that with Big Khaye none of her arguments would do. Pushing her belly forward, she left the school in a burning rage, and repeated "We'll see yet! We'll see ..."

The Rebbe, pale, frightened, arose from his bench, took a few steps to the folding screen, and sighed. "You will ... you will yet, God forbid, bring a tragedy with your mouth, with your ways, with ... with ... Horrors, such a tongue."

"You're already frightened? By whom? By Bryne, the butcher's wife? Just look how pale you have become."

"She is basically right."

"How is she right? Is this how you judge? Is this the way you have God in your heart? Where is your justice?'

"Justice, justice. Even in a rabbinical court she will ... she will perhaps be found to be right."

"So let her take me to court! Am I afraid? Let her. I will prove to the rabbi that it is not according to law and not according to justice that one should eat to the bursting point and another should starve. Is it right that Bryndle's young son should stuff himself and an orphan shouldn't have enough to eat? There must still be a bit of justice!" the Rebbetzin announced with such conviction and resolve that the Rebbe went silently back to his place. It seems he understood that Big Khaye was prepared to stand not only before the law, before the rabbis, but even before God Himself in order to demand that there should be some justice in the world.

Translated by Ronnee Jaeger
Fun haynt un nekhtn, Warsaw 1965

With Tevye the Dairyman in the Underground

I'd completely forgotten that I had hidden something with Sonyitchka, the Bessarabian. It had also gone out of my head that Sonyitchka had a brother; other worries and troubles were tormenting me. First, I had to convince myself that no one was following me. Second, I couldn't remember the exact address of the only house where I could sleep for a night. I'd been there only once, long ago. It could be the second or the third or fourth house in the alley.

The day stretched on and on, without end. I walked and I walked from one Paris street to another, without a goal, without a purpose. Sometimes, I'd get on a bus, ride for several stops and get off, get on another, going God knows where. It was better to avoid the Metro, where I might be detained and searched. I just wandered about, forsaken. Here and there, I stopped at store windows feigning interest in the antiques on display, all the time, throwing sidelong glances at every passerby. Everyone looked suspicious to me.

I dragged myself to the Tuileries Garden, sank onto the first bench. Leaning back, I caught my breath, and sat for a while. As if from under the ground, a personage appeared. He greeted me with a hearty "Good morning," a foolish, friendly smile, and tried to start a conversation. Had I not seen this creature before? Could he be one of those who "pull the thread"? No, they wouldn't be careless enough to draw attention to themselves. His shiny hairdo, fresh from the barber, was just too conspicuous. I'd been looking around carefully and had not noticed anyone suspicious following me. Still, I got up and with seeming nonchalance made my way to the exit. He did not follow me.

The autumn day was coming to an end and my strength with it. Should I risk taking the Metro? If they were still looking for me, I could escape more easily. After a few stations I got off again. If they were using me as a "thread," that "thread" would surely have been torn by

142 Fables, Short Stories, and Historic Fiction

now, after my convoluted wandering around the city. I was now a walking automaton. Images of struggling comrades swirled in my feverish imagination: dear ones Aviva, Anka, Sara, Solyek, Lyonek, and Hershel. Where were they now? Why them and not me? How did I escape the diabolical net? Thoughts of their torture kept jolting me. Would they be able to hold out? What could they do to hold out? An electric current coursed through my body as did a bitter stubbornness.

Sunk in these thoughts, exhausted and drained, a sudden, strong push almost knocked me over. Before me I saw a dishevelled, heavy-set market woman carrying a large basket. A hail of invectives spilled from her mouth. "Where are your eyes? You're taking up the whole sidewalk; you almost knocked my basket over. You should have to work, like me, not make eyes at the guys. I bet you're waiting for a German soldier!"

That cold shower brought me to my senses. I began to make tracks. Only at the end of the street, did I dare to look around. Where was I? Saint Denis, swarming with street vendors and street girls. From here it wasn't too far to Sonyitchka's, the Bessarabian woman's place. My feet were refusing to carry me, but I had no choice. If I didn't hurry I'd fall asleep walking.

All at once, the autumn dusk deepened and the grey twilight was quickly swallowed by the black night. Such nights – sinister, unkind – imprison the homeless and the hunted in an iron vise.

My memory strained almost to bursting. Was it the second or the third house? Probably the fourth floor! On one door, a mark indicated a tin sign had been removed; I just had to keep looking and if I saw someone on the stairs I would have to hide quickly.

The sign on the third floor stopped me. How many knocks? Last time it was three. The door opened silently, without the slightest creak, and shut instantly as I slid in. A pale, frightened Sonyitchka stared at me, opening her mouth as if to scream, mute as if I came from the other world. We entered the front hall in silence, and she began to question me.

"You – you were arrested! They told me that your whole group fell into ..."

"Not me, by chance, pure chance, I wasn't there."

"I'm afraid they left you alive intentionally, to be a 'thread' they could follow to trap the others."

"If that's what they were doing, they've certainly lost sight of me by now. I've been dragging myself around Paris for two days."

"You shouldn't have come here! I'm very sorry ..., they warned me. Today I have to ..."

With Tevye the Dairyman in the Underground 143

"Just for tonight. The contact has already told me that there's a place for me to stay. Tomorrow morning I'm gone."

"You have to leave. They've forbidden me ... it has to be 'clean,' but I can't throw you out like I did Tevye. Him I threw out."

Like lightning, a memory came to me; without reproach I asked her: "You threw out my 'Tevye'?"

Bewildered, Sonyitchka turned to me: "Yours? Oh my God! Who could have imagined that? I was sure that Tevye was Rokhl's. Who knew?"

"My 'Tevye' is Rokhl's? You don't remember?"

Sonyitchka began to console me: "Don't take it to heart. Rokhl took him to her house. Forget it, he isn't worth your ..."

"What are you chattering about? Who? What isn't worth?"

"Tevye. You. Even now all he has on his mind are girls, every few months, another one."

Only then did I remember that Tevye was her brother's name and I began to clear up the confusion. "You don't remember? I hid a book with you, 'Tevye the Dairyman'? The only book I saved from my entire library, also through a coincidence."

Sonyitchka clutched at her head. How could she have forgotten! She was certain that the house was "clean." She, with Aryan documents in her bag, had hidden a Yiddish book in her oven. In the heat of the moment, she was ready to pull "'Tevye the Dairyman" out of the oven and destroy it, but after one look at me she took pity. After all, I had blistered feet and an empty stomach. She began preparing a meal for me, even though I was a greater danger to the "clean" house than the hidden "Tevye." She agreed to postpone the execution to the following morning.

At the crack of dawn, we were both on our feet. First, we pulled out the hidden "Tevye the Dairyman" from under a pile of wood in the pot-bellied oven. "Tevye" had not suffered at all since the spring when I had led "him" into crime. At that time Sonyitchka's apartment was not yet involved in a double conspiracy. It was lucky that she, Sonyitchka, had a poor memory; who knows what a horrible end the rescued "Tevye" would have met when she made the room "clean."

She offered me the privilege of choosing the sentence: either burning "Tevye" in her bread oven or tearing it into tiny pieces and flushing them down the toilet. I was already rested and sated. Today, I thought,

144 Fables, Short Stories, and Historic Fiction

my days of wandering would be ending. I had already memorized the new address. Why not try to rescue "Tevye" again? Whatever would happen to me would also happen to "him."

Sonyitchka wrung her hands, reproached this reckless choice, and spoke sense to me. Despite her words, she gave me a special double-bottomed shopping basket and sent along some small kitchen utensils for my new household and a bit of food. I carefully packed "Tevye" and put all the gifts inside the basket and placed my handbag with the Aryan papers on the top. I took off by train to the suburb Meudon, where Zola had once established his friendly literary nest.

An old, crumbling, two-storeyed house reminiscent of the times when Zola had strolled in the area, in the early mornings. Perhaps even at that time it had not been in the bloom of youth, nor, at first sight, was the landlady, a widow, a tall, large-boned woman, with a bent back and a lined, wrinkled face. But her eyes!! Real diamonds. The window-eyes of the house were dark, sad; the landlady's eyes were bright, lively, smiling, caressing and winking impishly as if to represent the motionless mouth, which asked no questions nor sought to learn who you were.

I came to like the landlady and to dislike the house, with its rotted walls, which shook eerily at night, frightening as if angry spirits had settled there. But most disturbing was the neighbour below.

We were three neighbours: one upstairs, one downstairs, with me in the middle. I wasn't worried about the one above me, a poor unskilled labourer with a houseful of little ones making a racket, thumping all day long, making my ceiling groan. At the downstairs neighbour's it was quiet as the grave: not a peep, not a rustle, neither by day nor by night. The worst was that he kept watching me, not, God forbid, wantonly, provocatively, but somehow mysteriously. I definitely sensed that he had been keeping his eyes on me ever since I'd moved in a few days earlier. Whenever I went out or returned I had to pass by his low window which was covered with an old, thick curtain; I could tell that he was looking at me through the curtain. When I ran into him, his sidelong glance turned in my direction. That character did not please me at all. Besides, he had the milky-white face of a German and a blond head of hair; he had been living here for only a few weeks, also a bad sign.

Lately, "they" had settled their people here and there. To spy. I could have asked her what kind of person he was; I'd been told the landlady could be trusted, but I thought better not to ask questions. Daytime was only half the problem; at night, loneliness and fear bit into my bones. If only I could have been with someone. How much longer will I be sentenced to that "quarantine"? How much time would it take for me to be sure that I was not being spied upon.

With Tevye the Dairyman in the Underground 145

It didn't take long. Without warning, a subtenant was placed with me.

"For three or four days only. You could have returned to 'work' already, but we had nowhere to put him."

"He can stay longer, as far as I'm concerned, but there's something about the downstairs tenant that bothers me."

"We trust the landlady," the contact assured me. "These will be pleasant days for you."

It certainly became pleasant, so cheerful that the roof almost flew off and my head just about exploded. My tenant, who had at first seemed shy, quickly made himself at home in my cheerless apartment. He began to assert himself, thrash about noisily disturbing everything. My guest was all of fourteen months old. His Jewish parents had been interned in the Drancy concentration camp and the knights of the "Master Race" were making every effort to track down their young son. But my fourteen-month-old tenant didn't concern himself with all that. He played havoc with all my arrangements. Bad enough in the daytime, but at night!

Rooms there were two, but only one bed, which was pushed to the centre of the small second room because the walls sweated from the cold. That did not prevent my guest from tossing and turning; even in his sleep he did not rest.

Finally, he fell asleep, and, I his bedmate, exhausted from a whole day looking after him, also fell asleep. Suddenly the house shook. My sleeping companion, tossing about like an athlete, fell to the floor with a resounding crash. The crash alone would probably not have stirred up the whole house but his screaming, as one possessed, was something to behold!

Instant banging, through the ceiling from the neighbour above. The one below was "discreet," playing dead. Was that not a bad sign?

After that stormy night came an uneasy, troubling day. What to do? Now everyone knew that I was hiding a child, a little rascal at that, who doesn't let them sleep.

To make things even worse, this fourteen-month-old character had caught a cold, probably already had it when they'd brought him to me. He was hoarse, and not only from yelling. Who knew what could happen until he was settled somewhere in a village, with a "nurse." What might the one from downstairs pull off?

I had to, I must, look for help. First, I pushed the bed back to the wall. and barricaded him with a few chairs. After his sleepless night, the little scamp fell fast asleep in the afternoon. I took off to see the landlady who was in the garden of her new little house. In a conspiratorial manner I

146   Fables, Short Stories, and Historic Fiction

began to lay out my predicament: a sister in the hospital; her husband, the child's father, a war invalid; the child sick with a cold; the screams, the neighbours.

She interrupted me: "Too bad!" I shouldn't take it to heart. She already knew about the commotions of last night. The upstairs neighbour had complained. She had put him in his place, calmed him down; he had children himself, he should understand. Now I should just take some leftover coals and reheat them. She was going right now to the pharmacy to buy a cold plaster; she'll tell me exactly how to put it on his chest for ten minutes, at bedtime.

In the evening, I carried out the operation, not only following the landlady's instructions exactly but also those that appeared in the long prescription. Hardly five minutes had passed before the boy began to shriek. I quickly unwrapped the towel and removed the plaster. His delicate body was red as fire. Now my patient had something to screech about, and he did not stint. No longer was there any banging, not from upstairs, not from downstairs; however, other neighbours might come running, they could, they will.

What didn't I do to quiet the little screamer? All my pedagogical methods failed. So, go and tell him about the occupation, the Germans, the great danger. But how long could he scream? He exhausted himself and finally fell asleep, his mouth open. I, too, was thoroughly depleted, even more so than after the most terrifying actions against the enemy. But a place to lie down, and sleep, I no longer had. My "tenant" had fallen asleep right in the middle, across the breadth of our bed. Not to disturb him, I covered him and again barricaded the bed with chairs. Thoroughly worn out, I went into the front room and fell onto the one remaining chair. How to get through the night? If I only had an interesting book. Then, I reminded myself of "Tevye," which I had not yet managed to hide in a more secure place.

I pulled "Tevye" from beneath the double bottom of the basket and sat myself down to read by a shaded table lamp. I began at the first page. How long I read I cannot remember. Tevye interrupted my reading. I barely recognized him as he stood before me, alone, without his horse, without the whip, not a bit like a milkman on a back road. He was also dressed differently, in a jacket like one worn by a friend of mine in the resistance, his beard short and modern. Not the same Tevye, and yet the same. Tevye's same fine eyes. Am I dreaming? Tevye or not Tevye? Tevye recognized that I was having doubts and he began to help me.

"Daughter, don't you recognize Tevye? Where is your head? Why should Tevye make himself known to you? Tevye the Milkman is no more. He has packed himself off deep, deep into the Boiberik forest;

With Tevye the Dairyman in the Underground   147

but I'm still of use, I'm not sitting on my hands. So, so, daughter, Tevye has finally lived to see new times. In the past, when we got too big in people's eyes, they threw us out. Today, in a sophisticated world, the German has found other methods. Why are you shaking your head? Am I offending the honour of the scholarly world? Oh dear, you're crying. That's not so nice, daughter! Surely, a bitter time for the Jews; we lie buried nine cubits deep in the earth. As it says in the Scriptures, 'a plague upon a plague and on that plague an abscess.' But while he still has breath, a Jew must not lose faith. Why is all this coming to us, you may ask? Go ask your questions of the Ruler of the Universe. But then again, that is why we are Jews. As it says in the Scriptures, 'If you are a soldier, smell the gunpowder!' Oh, the world! It saddens me that it does not come to our defence. So is the saying 'what God gives with a spoon, folks give with a pail.' Oh, oh, daughter, you're lowering your head too much, not so nice. (You really don't lack for troubles.) Getting back to our discussion, in what way should you be more favoured by God than all our other brethren, children of Israel? Feh, it's not nice to wring your hands! First, have faith; second, spite your enemies.

Then, just to spite them, the little devil fell out of bed – just to spite them – I will ...

I lifted my sleepy head from my hands spread on the table. A shiver ran through my body. I looked around in fear. No one was there. Was I dreaming that someone was knocking at the door? The more reality pushed out the dream, the greater my fear became. It was not possible to hide the child anywhere!

The knocking persisted. A quiet, rhythmic knocking as if by a prearranged code. On tiptoe I neared the door, put my ear to it and heard, "The water, don't be afraid, I'm one of yours. The water is spilling over ..."

The clear, familiar accent of the French words calmed and gave me courage. I opened the door. My downstairs neighbour quietly slipped in, apologizing and stammering, again saying that the water was dripping down his walls. He followed me into the small kitchen and we both saw water coming from the half open tap and spilling out of the shallow sink. How could it have happened? All because of that little scamp.

Before I could reach out with my hand, the man from downstairs turned off the tap, grabbed a rag from under the sink and energetically wiped and wiped, wiping up all the water, as if he had been hired to do so. Afterwards, looking at me with sympathy, but hesitating, asked: "You're not sleeping? Reading so late? The night is almost over."

148   Fables, Short Stories, and Historic Fiction

The man from below cast his eyes on the book which I had managed
to close, and with a modest smile asked what I was reading so late.
Without waiting for an answer, he opened the cover, and in a Lithuanian Yiddish quietly asked: 'Oh, "Tevye the Milkman"! Maybe you
could lend it to me?'"
I lent it to him.

Translated by Frieda Johles Forman and Sylvia Lustgarten
Fun vayt un fun noent, Paris 1978

Animals and Humans

The wolf shall dwell with the lamb,
The leopard lie down with the kid;
The calf, the beast of prey, and the fatling together,
With a little boy to herd them.

Isaiah 11:6[1]

"Can you come for a visit this evening? Come over. We'll have a talk and you'll meet my friends." I was so glad to receive her invitation; I had long wanted to get closer to Maria.[2] I'd heard about her: a zoologist, she had written several books and had helped Jews during the occupation. I was pleased to have met her while on my vacation, even more pleased to be invited to her home. There I would meet new people, and Maria Wigda's friends were not just anybody.

I began preparing for my visit in the afternoon. I have a rule, no exceptions, that on vacations I shed all my city clothes and jewellery.

---

1 https://www.sefaria.org/Isaiah.11.6?ven=Tanakh:_The_Holy_Scriptures,_published _by_JPS&vhe=Miqra_according_to_the_Masorah&lang=bi, accessed 1 June 2024.

2 The Maria Wigda character bears some resemblance to the real life Antonina Żabińska, who, along with her zoologist husband, Jan, was recognized as Righteous Among the Nations. During the German occupation Jan Zabinski, director of the Warsaw Zoo and his wife Antonina hid Jews in their home on the grounds of the zoo and in some of the empty animal quarters. Żabińska was a great lover of animals and a writer of books about animals for children. In 1968 she published her memoir *People and Animals*. *Animals and Humans* was penned by Berger in 1961 at Obory, a writer's retreat outside of Warsaw operated by the Polish Writers Union. This was a vacation spot she was known to frequent. Żabińska's memoir formed the basis for a book written by Diane Ackerman, *The Zookeeper's Wife: A War Story*, which was subsequently made into a feature film.

150   Fables, Short Stories, and Historic Fiction

However, visiting Maria Wigda and meeting new people was another matter altogether; who knew what sort of "big shots" would be there?

I gave up my rest hour and soon after lunch I was off to the hairdresser, a waste of three hours. Afterwards, I examined my vacation wardrobe several times and began to regret that I hadn't brought a decent evening dress. How could I go on such a visit and meet new people in a travelling suit, or in slacks? No choice, I slipped on a light summery dress and got going. As if in spite, the day was cool and windy, the sky slate grey, and a fine, steady rain began to fall. Luckily, I had a large kerchief with me.

At the door, I took off my kerchief, fixed my tousled hairdo as well as I could, wiped the raindrops from my face, looked in the mirror, and powdered my nose. Who knew whom I would meet there? I waited awhile, caught my breath, and knocked.

The door opened, and just as I stepped over the threshold, a tawny dog, the size of a calf, jumped on me with his two front paws. At first glance, I thought I was in the wrong place. I wanted to scream but fear struck me dumb. Seeing how pale I'd become, Maria Wigda began to scold the dog. The canine creature dropped his tail as if ashamed.

"Bernard was greeting you; his way of showing you his friendship."

"Bernard? The dog?" I stammered, still frightened.

"If people have names of animals, why shouldn't animals have names of people, especially since Bernard behaves so humanely? So, let me have your coat, sit down, sit down."

I sat and had hardly caught my breath, when Bernard submissively lay himself down at my feet, as if he wanted to make up for scaring me. Maria Wigda, a tall, blond, robust woman of fifty-nine, wearing large, black-framed glasses, sat herself across from me, and smiled as though nothing had happened.

"I thought the rain would detain you, not at all vacation weather … but I see you're not afraid of it."

"I'm much more afraid of dogs than of rain. But it looks like your friends are afraid of the rain; they haven't come."

"Haven't come? Here are my friends." She pointed all around her.

I looked around and saw, lying in a corner, another tawny dog the size of a calf. He seemed to be dozing. In another corner snuggled two sleeping blue-grey pigeons. On the couch a grey cat was comfortably stretched out, two suckling kittens hanging on her stomach. I turned my gaze from corner to corner and recalled how I had fussed with my hairdo and fine attire.

"You don't like my friends?" Maria Wigda asked with a knowing smile.

Animals and Humans 151

"I don't know who I expected to meet at your home; I didn't think you would take them along on your vacation," I confessed, pointing around at them with my hand.

"Would it be right to go on holidays and leave them behind, abandoned? And Nike was due to give birth. Did she ever have a difficult delivery. Two were stillborn, and she suffered so much; without my help she would not have survived. She kept looking at me, pleading with me to help her; rarely have I seen such conduct. Nike is good and as bright as the day ..."

"Nike? A cat with the name of a goddess?"

"Yes, indeed, the name of the Greek goddess ... Nike is highly moral, with exceptional ethical principles, she wouldn't harm a weaker creature; on the contrary, she would fiercely defend it. If you could see how she acts in all kinds of situations, whereas people ... a superior ethic!"

"And the dogs? No danger leaving them with those resident cats?"

"What are you talking about? Bernard and Astra would never harm anyone, except when it's necessary to defend someone. You have no idea how able they are." Maria Wigda became lost in thought as though searching for arguments to convince me, and she continued: "People have a false impression of animals. They do them a great injustice, they vilify them, and they project all their own evil tendencies and ugly deeds onto them. 'A bitchy person'! Not true, not true, I tell you, I have a lot of experience both with people and with animals, and I know what I'm talking about."

In the meantime, Bernard had forgotten that I hadn't so gladly accepted his friendship and once again began to show me affection. As though encouraged by his mistress's words, he got up and, placing his long snout on my lap, began to sniff me. I drew back involuntarily, revealing to Maria Wigda my coolness towards the canine species.

"I'm afraid of such a wolfish snout. With such dogs the Nazis ..."

"The Nazis made of dogs what they were themselves. A pity, a pity you didn't see my "offspring" in the zoo. My little son used to play with a baby leopard, with a small tiger; I raised the young wild animals, making gentle creatures of them. As for our domestic animals, it goes without saying. I could tell you many things ..."

"You mean to say that from a wild animal ...?"

"I think you can turn a person into a wild animal – are there only a few two-footed wild animals roaming the earth? We have the wrong image. Animals are good, loyal creatures, so loyal! My Astra" – she pointed to the corner – "has shown such astonishing loyalty. Today she's eighteen years old, such an old age, a rare old age, deaf in one ear, her heart weakened, but still a good, faithful heart. I can still rely on her; she'll

152 Fables, Short Stories, and Historic Fiction

never let me down. You can't imagine such loyalty. I tell you, a person has only two great friends: a mother and a dog – a mother who never fails you, or a dog who understands you like a mother."

Hearing these comparisons, I probably scowled because Maria Wigda began to lecture me and present evidence: "Don't make such a face, don't grimace; we are not offending a mother's honour! I tell you, a dog is a great friend to people, understanding and intuitive ... Just listen: At the time of the occupation, Jews and members of the Resistance would come to me; Astra never barked at them. Although she did not know them, she did not bark. If she sniffed someone to be guarded against, especially one who spoke German, she would let loose with might and main, instantly alerting us; an amazing display in those years."

I was so afraid that the whole evening would be spent only on canine matters that I grabbed on to Maria's last words and asked: "And how did it go with Rachel Goldshteyn?"

"With Rachel? Do you know her?"

"No, but I know ... And you went to see her in Paris."

"Astra rescued her." She pointed to the dozing dog. "She was young then, agile, not even two years old, the same as Bernard is now."

It seemed we had interrupted Astra's nap. No longer wanting to lie in the corner, she got up with slow, relaxed movements. Stretching her old head, she turned her loyal dog's eyes to me as if she wanted to win my confidence in the canine species. Then, with uncertain steps, she came close to me, looking me in the eye pleadingly. I began to overcome my antipathy to this species, stretched out my hand and stroked her head. Astra took a few more tiny steps and faced me meekly, sadness and gratitude showing in her teary eyes.

"Became sentimental in her old age," Maria Wigda interpreted the dog's behaviour. "She's heavy hearted, and as soon as she's shown the slightest kindness, she looks for empathy and begins to complain."

"What about?"

"About her old age. She tolerates her old age poorly, weakness lies heavily on her spirit. She cannot make peace with aging: her heart is still young, her body reduced to nothing. Who doesn't need a little warmth, a friendly outstretched hand in such circumstances? I don't have enough time for her and she needs someone all the time. Old age doesn't tolerate loneliness and Astra tolerates neither ... Aye, old age ..."

Maria Wigda broke off, wrinkled her forehead somewhat strangely, as though she were carrying on a great debate with herself. Apparently, she is one of those people who need to share their own thoughts and doubts with themselves.

Animals and Humans 153

"A strange chaos in nature, incomprehensible: why one creature is given a long life and another such a short one. So many injustices in nature itself. If it were true that God created everything around us, then God would be without a trace of justice. But the worst is that we can't comprehend the causes; we grope in the dark, blindly. See here: the elephant, the crocodile live for hundreds of years, and my Astra is already old, has already had a foot in the grave for a long time. At fourteen, a dog is already old, worn out at an age when many small, weak creatures are in their youth and reproduce until old age, and live longer than such strong creatures like the horse and the ox. And the human being, the crown of God's creation ... The crocodile, the carp lay eggs for two hundred years and even longer; or take the parrot, the crow, they live long while other similar birds have quite a short life.

"But I tell you, the greatest wrong befell the human being. What an absurdity! The human, a bizarre contradiction, incomprehensible, without a bit of fairness or sense. The organism at fifty or sixty years is at its most developed. I now know what I want, I would conquer worlds. Look at my face; in about ten years I'll be like my poor Astra, and in my head, more thoughts and plans are being born all the time. Such nonsense in nature, a weird contradiction: the brain, the heart, and the face ..."

I became heavy-hearted hearing Maria Wigda's reflections, but Astra was not disturbed by her mistress's pessimistic philosophical exposition. On the contrary, she became livelier, bolder, moved closer to me, very close; stretching her neck she asked for a pat, and licked one of my hands, then the other. I instinctively took away my hand.

"Enough, Astra, leave us to our conversation! To your place!"

With one ear Astra caught her mistress's command, moved away from me to her place and she lay down, resigned.

I felt guilty that because of me she had to return to her corner; she had sought human warmth and I hadn't even given her a pat. I wanted to redeem myself for my hard-heartedness, at least to compliment her ...

"A smart dog, she understands everything ..."

"Smarter in many respects than people. A dog understands people's needs but people don't understand a dog's wordless speech. But what is there to say when people don't understand one another, though they speak the same language? I'd rather deal with Astra than with certain ... You wouldn't believe me if I told you about her accomplishments in those years."

"I will believe you, tell me," I said to her half in earnest, half in jest.

154   Fables, Short Stories, and Historic Fiction

"Aha, you'd have to sit with me all night, and I still wouldn't have told you everything. Every day a remarkable event ..., and if not for Astra ..."

I felt Maria Wigda was prepared to sit with me the whole night; to tell the truth, I too was tempted, but I now had reason to fear that my major interest might drown in a sea of talk about the world of dogs. And so I persisted and asked again: "And Goldberg? How was that?"

"It happened this way: I lived in a country house then, far from the city. It was a cold morning, a wet snow had fallen; nonetheless, I opened the door and let Astra out, as usual, to get some air. It had been a disturbing night, echoes of shooting were heard in the distance. At such a time, people were afraid to stick their heads out. Astra was in a more fortunate position, less exposed to danger. She would go out and live it up, to her heart's content. This time, she was back in a short while, scratching at the door as if she had to tell me about something important. Pulling the hem of my dress with her snout, she dragged me out the door. I allowed myself to be led, following Astra until she stopped at the fence and growled. On the other side were thick bushes. I looked through the pickets and saw nothing. I was then more near-sighted than I am today; the years make you far-sighted ... In short, I noticed nothing. But since Astra did not move, I stopped and looked. Suddenly, a voice of sorts, as if coming from under the ground: 'Have mercy, let me hide somewhere.' Nearby, two planks were broken off. I sent Astra out to the road to stand watch, and if there was anything, she'd let us know. A woman crawled out of hiding through that same opening and followed me like a shadow. I tell you, a terrifying picture. She had escaped when they drove them out of the town and she wandered through the forest all night; she saw someone on the road in the distance and hid in the bushes. Just looking at her, I was seized by fear. How can I describe that tangle of rags, dead eyes looking out, a terrifying face.

Maria Wigda remained silent, her mouth open, as if fear of the past had now robbed her of speech. Her gaze hung on the old dog, lying stretched out, as if she reminded her of happier events. She regained her speech: "Believe me, she guarded her the whole time. During the day, when she was in the kitchen, Astra would watch over her. As soon as she sniffed someone on the road that she didn't like, especially a German, she let loose loudly, and an alarm went off. By her barking I knew who was approaching the house and whether I should send the woman back to the cellar. Sometimes I let her stay in the kitchen at night; it was freezing cold in the cellar. Just imagine, Astra would lie at her feet at night, never moving away, her ears pointed and alert ...

A pause.

Animals and Humans 155

A dark cloud spread over Maria Wigda's face, a memory had suddenly come to her: "A bank employee lived less than a kilometre from my house. Oh, if that one knew what was going on in my house! A handsome, blond young man, without a spark of humanity. How many unfortunates he denounced! There, a man, and Astra, a dog. Believe me, Astra seethed visibly whenever she saw him at times; she held him responsible. I tell you, we have a false conception about animals and people. You may believe me, I have a lot of experience; people can be worse towards one another than animals. And look here, at my housemates."

Once again, I began looking around the spacious room. Astra was asleep, the old dog's heart beating rhythmically beneath her fur coat; in the other corner the two doves rested quietly. We had apparently disturbed their sleep; they looked as if they were still dozing. On the sofa the mother cat was spread out in all her majesty, the kittens warming themselves at her stomach. At the foot of the sofa stood the young tawny dog, the size of a calf, who looked about with intelligent dog eyes, as if drawing joy from the matriarchal picture. Maria Wigda followed me with her bespectacled eyes and, smiling, said: "So, what do you say now? Am I not right?"

Translated by Frieda Johles Forman and Sylvia Lustgarten
Fun haynt un nekhtn, Warsaw 1965

The Jew Who Came Late

The door opened slowly and a man's grey head appeared. A pair of inquiring eyes looked into the office as if to check first that there were no unnecessary witnesses about.

"Come in! Come on in!" a clerk's voice was heard to repeat.[1]

The older man came into the room, closed the door behind him, stood a while looking around, and, as if ascertaining that no other people were there, made his way to the office desk with hesitant steps.

"I'm Grynsztajn," he said in Polish. "Henryk Grynsztajn."

"Grynsztajn?" the clerk inquired, as if hearing the name for the first time.

"Yes, Grynsztajn from Katowice ..."

"Grynsztajn from Katowice?" the clerk asked again.

"Didn't you get my letter?"

"A letter? Oh yes, there was a letter from Katowice," the clerk began to recollect. "Did you write that letter? It was a good few weeks ago. You forget names, I mean unfamiliar names," the clerk added. "There was no return address, why didn't you specify your address?"

"I thought that you would understand why from my letter. Today I'm not called ... my name isn't ... how should I say this? I'm not Grynsztajn anymore, there is no such name anymore, my name was wiped away, it died along with ... But I'm alive, only under another name. I thought

---

1 Berger does not name the organization to which the Jewish man is applying. The Joint Distribution Committee's activities in Poland were curtailed when the Communist government expelled foreign aid agencies from Poland in 1949, but resumed in December 1957. Around 1960, the point at which this story is set, the JDC operated in Poland in collaborative but tense relations with Poland's officially recognized Jewish aid organization, the Socio-Cultural Association of Jews in Poland, TSKZ.

The Jew Who Came Late 157

you would guess from my letter how things are. I wanted to let you in on my situation a bit beforehand."

"What name do you go by these days?"

"Sokołowski, Henryk Sokołowski: this is what I've been called since 1942, and so it has to stay that way."

The older man sat down in the chair that the clerk pointed to. He pulled himself closer to the desk, laid one hand down on it, and supported his drooping head with the other, just like an old bent branch that can't stay straight and has to be held up by a little stick. His pale, emaciated face, which earlier bore no resemblance to a Jewish face, now changed. His mouth was more sunken; the lips were clenched as if they wanted to hold on to a secret. His rheumy grey eyes were lit with a strange fire. Sitting with his bent head propped up, he looked older, and now you could easily recognize in him an old, broken Jew. He sat there both comfortably at home but also sort of embarrassed, hesitant and saying nothing, as if with his clarification, he had told all there was to know and had nothing further to add.

"Why didn't you provide your address and your current name in the letter?"

"Well, that's just the thing, that's why I had to come here myself. I didn't want to complicate my situation, in my old age, with my health declining ..."

"Complicate things? How?"

"I figured you would understand from my letter. That's why I told you a bit about my circumstances."

The clerk opened up the drawer in his desk, took out a file of correspondence, found the letter and quickly read it over.

"Yes, yes, I recall ... I haven't forgotten what you wrote about," he replied. "It's a matter of support for you. I don't think it will be difficult; assistance for older people is the kind of support available from our institution, but we need to know something about you. You need to give us your address, your name, provide a few other particulars. We are a bureaucracy, you must understand. An institution has policies. We have to keep track of who gets assistance, where the person lives, who he is, where he comes from. On the basis of your letter I couldn't arrange anything. It wasn't clear; it isn't clear even now. There must be clarity. This is a bureaucracy; it demands clarity."

"Clarity," the Jew repeated softly with an ironic smile playing on his lips. "So, that means I need to make my entire history clear to you. It's a long story, very long, bringing clarity into it isn't a simple matter. It's a dark history, and here you want me to throw light on it."

158   Fables, Short Stories, and Historic Fiction

He stopped abruptly, letting out a long sigh, then pulled his hands away from his head, and straightened out a bit. Then he bent over again, hunched as if wanting to crawl inside himself. Quietly he stated:

"I am from Kraków, the only survivor of my entire family, all of them perished. Every single one. I was the only one left. I don't even have any acquaintances. I ran away from a ... at the end of the summer of 1942, made it to Katowice. I didn't look like a Jew, so that saved me. Now I've already gone grey, well, white. Then, I had light blond hair, I was forty-seven years old then and I had been through ... you probably know what it was like. Yes, people know what happened, but they don't know what each separate person went through: ghetto, work camps, back to the ghetto, deportation and ..."

A knock on the door interrupted his speaking. Once the clerk had quickly dealt with the new inquiry, the man said:

"Why should I tell you all this? It will take too much time. In short, by a miracle, I was saved, made it to Katowice and stayed; no one knew me there. My appearance, my Polish accent didn't give me away. I got work in my trade as a bookbinder. I had papers under the name Sokołowski, the bookbinder Sokołowski, pure Aryan, Polish Catholic ..."

"And after the war?"

"I told you. No one was left from my family. Not one living relative. Acquaintances, not a trace."

"I understand. But what isn't clear to me ..."

"What still isn't clear to you? What happened after?"

"Forgive me for questioning you so much. But your situation is not very typical. I mean to say ..."

"Yes, not very typical," he sighed.

"Don't take offence, but as I understand it, you continued to remain in hiding after the war, so ..."

"I stayed a Sokołowski, Henryk Sokołowski, understand that how you will."

"It would be interesting to know ..."

"You want to know why I am turning to Jews only now, when I'm in need? For money?" – the Jew interrupted him in a quiet melancholy tone.

"No not that. Forgive me. You don't have to be so suspicious of people about such things. I want to ask how you found out about our institution since you aren't involved with Jewish people."

"Not involved with Jews ..." The man repeated these words shaking his head. "How can you know what a person is involved with on the inside, with what a person ... what is going on in a person's heart.

The Jew Who Came Late   159

It's really my situation that brought me to you. You have to understand, a few years ago I had to stop working after a long illness. After that I got a pension. As you know, it's hard to make do and as you get older all the aches and pains start up; it's always something else. It's hard when you're old, and when you're alone, it's even harder, much harder."

"It would have been easier for you to be among Jews. I don't understand why. Why is it necessary now for you to hide?"

"Why? Why? It isn't so easy to answer all these whys. Since the Germans began to slaughter Jews, I've kept asking why and I can't find even one answer to a single why. It's hard for me to say why now. That's how it was left. Those times turned everything upside down."

"Those times ended a while back. Now there's no reason; now you can be what you are."

"Today is bound to yesterday; it is not easy to separate them. Do you know what it means to be utterly alone in the world? To be old and completely alone?"

"I understand, but that is why you should have returned to your own, I mean to be among Jews, you simply needed to ..."

"I should have, but today it's already too late. Before, I didn't understand, I was mixed up, I was terrified, like a hunted animal afraid to come out of the hole it's hiding in. The years ran on, and now it's too late."

"Why too late?"

The old man again rested his head in both hands, his eyes boring into the table. He sighed once more and continued as if speaking to himself:

"Since the summer of 1942 I am done with being a Jew, done with Grynsztajn. For eighteen years I have lived in a city among people, at work as Henryk Sokołowski, eighteen years among my neighbours as ... as a Pole of the Catholic faith, and suddenly go become something else to them, and a Jew at that! No, not easy, pretty hard; it's already too late. How do I persuade you?

He raised his head and turned it towards the man across from him.

"It's just as if I were to pull on my former skin, the skin of my youth. It wouldn't be bad, if you could go back to being young, who wouldn't want to? But age holds on to a person, shapes him more every day, changes his face, his hair. You can't escape from ... the years. You want to be young and you can't; it's too late. You can't go back to the years of your youth. To return to my very self, to what I was. It seems to me to be too late, I mean, for me, that is, too late for me, while for others ..."

160 Fables, Short Stories, and Historic Fiction

The man did not finish his sentence. He lowered his head as if catching himself in telling more than he had wanted. His sickly face was now ashen, the ironic smile at the corners of his mouth had disappeared. His shoulders trembled slightly and he now looked like a persecuted and resigned Jew, drained of all strength and unable to go on.

The clerk from the aid organization felt a bit uncomfortable, not knowing whether to console the Jew or to reproach him for his conduct, so he simply pulled a file from his drawer, asked him to fill it out and to provide an address where the assistance could be sent.

"Now I want to ask a question," the old man said, not boldly, after filling out the form.

"Go ahead."

"Can you send the money not as a Jewish organization? You know what I mean, so people can't tell."

"For what reason? the clerk questioned somewhat gruffly. "There has to be a return address; we can't do it any other way."

"There could be another address on it, what's the harm in that?"

"And what's the harm to you, if it's the right address?"

"I've explained it to you and you don't understand me. Why won't you put yourself in my shoes? You can see that I am sixty-five years old and completely on my own, not a single relative, no one at all. A person has to knock at a door, go to a neighbour – You can't live without people. And all of a sudden, I will become someone else. I know how they'll look at me; I have no more strength, it's too late for me ..."

"You're a strange fellow. Who's in hiding these days? You're an exception. You're making problems for yourself."

He gave back the file, stood up from his chair, buttoned his coat, made a motion to leave and stood standing in front of the desk as if he still had something to say.

"It will be taken care of. I'll make every effort to see that it is dealt with quickly," the clerk assured him.

He gave his grey head a shake and made a move to go, but remained standing where he was. His watery eyes looked even more watery. With one hand in his pocket and with his fedora in the other hand, he looked to the window, as if considering the rain that was coming down outside.

"Do you have something else to add?"

"Once again I want to request ... not to forget about the return address. I beg you, I need calm ... a weak heart, you understand."

"I've already promised you. You are an odd man; you have to trust people: us, other people, you can't ... a person has to have some trust."

The Jew Who Came Late   161

"You're right, it's a very fortunate thing, being able to trust. You have to have trust. It's a good thing ... but I ..."

"No one will hurt you. Relax, you can rest easy."

As if the words calmed him this time, he quietly made his thanks several times. Nodding his white head, he said goodbye and, with a series of tiny steps, left the room, mumbling to himself, *"Too late for me, too late, sadly too late."*

Translated by Judy Nisenholt
Fun haynt un nekhtn, Warsaw 1965

The Last Night

Heavy shadows of night envelop the small, shabby room. The little lamp on the writing table, covered in a dark shade, casts only a pale glow. The black paper blind pulled down over the window looks like a mourner's mantle on a casket. A dense, palpable gloom mingled with apprehension fills the tiny space. Melancholy and angst entwine, turning about in the air in confused zigzags, climbing the walls with the shadows. They fill up every cramped corner, raising alarms, screaming without uttering a sound. It is as if hundreds of deadly snakes were laying siege outside, marking off the house, slithering in through the walls, shoving themselves through every crack, and hissing through venomous fangs.

The old, rusty bed is made up but empty. The hard resting place waits for its wretched bedfellow.[1] The exertion and the exhaustion of the day have not brought him any nearer to sleep. The turmoil in his heart has pursued him. Alert, he sits by the little table, bent over a piece of paper, and guides his pen urgently over the page. He covers the white paper with fine dark markings, spilling out memories of times gone by, entrusting them with what he is now living through. Suddenly, his tired head jerks up. The pen falls from his hand. Ever vigilant, he tears himself from the table to which he seems to be grafted.

Emaciated and wasted, he looks like a sickly, scrawny kid. But above the exhausted, shrunken body, a high and clever brow proudly asserts itself, and beneath it, two deep-set, warm blue eyes gaze out. His long, lined, stricken face exudes endless grief and kindness, pain and

---

1 "I do not like to sleep at night because then I cannot sleep in the daytime. Bread and water taste better at night." "I sleep at night unwillingly – I prefer the daytime." Janusz Korczak, *Ghetto Diary* (New Haven, CT: Yale University Press, 2003).

The Last Night   163

affection. The old man with the shrunken body stands frozen in place. Only his head moves, slowly and fitfully. His short, thick beard trembles at each nod of his head. Two restless, searching eyes look around as if their penetrating glances could seek out the dangers behind the walls and so elude them.

The ghetto is sunk in the stillness of night. The silence is like the inheld breath of one in mortal danger hiding behind a wall from a pursuer close at hand. From time to time, the sound of a volley of arms rips through the calm of night.

The ghetto is wrapped in a thick fog of anguished terror. Over it hangs a dark, menacing sky. The August air is hot, humid, and suffocating, but people lie on their beds and in their hiding places, twisted up as if struck by an icy blast. Here and there a family has been left behind like a mutilated body from which the limbs have been hacked off. Entire houses have been emptied. Each day since the 22nd of July the ghetto has become even sparser. By six thousand or ten thousand a day.

In the daytime, death roams outside, revelling in the ghetto streets and courtyards; he savagely chases the beggars and the children, raging at anyone who pokes his head out. Death commands, calls them to come out to him voluntarily. He promises three kilos of bread and a kilo of marmalade to those who come forward freely.

The ghetto is fenced in, an enclosed hunting ground. Death has unleashed his hounds; they sniff about, putting their pointy muzzles into every den. Only the heaped Pinkert wagon, flowing with blood, courses about undisturbed. From morning till night, long caravans stretch out to the Umschlagplatz. The German Angel of Death takes his harvest only by day – until six o'clock, as is customary with the working day.

The ghetto is sunk in dreadful nocturnal silence, in anxious expectation. In attics and cellars people are lying in restless, nightmarish slumber. Dr. Janusz Korczak doesn't sleep. During the night Korczak remains vigilant. He writes, takes notes, listens to the menacing silence, tries to find a way to think things through. Around him, above him, and beside him, over two hundred children are sleeping. They believe in him. They have so much trust in him. They are sleeping the deep slumber of children. The chaos of the ghetto has not yet sunk in. Korczak doesn't allow dread and panic to settle in his house nor does he allow fear to weigh upon the children's innocent hearts. They appear calm, his children. What do they have to fear since the Doctor, their constant protector, is with them? Hasn't he kept hunger and sickness at bay? Fended off all calamities? In this hard, chaotic time, they feel secure with their Doctor. They are still asleep in their little beds.

164   Fables, Short Stories, and Historic Fiction

Janusz Korczak sleeps little at night. Now it seems to him that he hears the children breathing with difficulty. He sees their nightmarish dreams, feels how their eyes are turned to him. They reach out to him; they cling so very tightly. How should he continue to shelter and protect them? By what means? His throat constricts. He wants to scream, to call out for help, but to whom? To the world? He carries on a debate now, a silent debate. With the world, and with himself as well. With hands crossed behind his back and with a silent monologue on his lips, he slowly paces back and forth, bare feet hardly touching the floor.

You are deaf and blind, world. We scream, we call out to you, and you don't hear; we are bleeding to death and you don't see. We can no longer cry; our tears have dried up. We can't scream anymore with a human voice. We howl like hunted, wounded animals. Under the slaughterer's knife, we rattle in the throes of death. Does it not reach you? Or maybe you block your ears? Maybe? ... World, you are bankrupt! You have sealed your own fate. Your civilization, your high ideals, your ... your ... everything, entirely bankrupt, and I am bankrupt too, totally bankrupt. I've accumulated a lot of capital. I've built up the trust of the children, their belief in the good and the beautiful. So many words and concepts: humanity, dignity, knowledge, friendship, brotherly love ... How they sting, these words.

Several salvos have cut through the ghetto's summer air and interrupted the silent monologue. Korczak remains standing in the middle of the room. He raises his head and, with ears perked, listens closely to the black stillness that has returned. His eyes are as wide as those of a dying man. His searching glance falls on his own shadow as it steals across the wall. His shadow is restless. It moves awkwardly, jumps down, shrinks and grows big again.

Why is his shadow trembling so? Korczak studies it. Then for a while he closes his staring eyes. In place of his shadow, something appears. No, it's an old acquaintance ... It is ... it is Laocoön and his sons ... Giant serpents slither out from the walls – ocean waves whorl around their bodies, entwining them – biting into their flesh with their poisonous fangs, piercing them until the last drop of life has trickled away. He sees the father's face distorted in pain, the final jerking struggles of his sons. He tears open his eyes. The apparition is gone; the shadow remains. Is it his own shadow or Laocoön's? The Greek priest had two unfortunate children at his side. He himself has over two hundred. He knows what dangers lie in wait for them. He must shield them from the venomous snakes. But how? How? He wrings his hands in desperation.

What can be done to protect them? Ach, the powerlessness, the total powerlessness. There is nothing more terrifying than our powerlessness.

The Last Night   165

What to do? What can we devise? I've come up with so many fairy tales and now the mind can't muster anything. Ach, if one could only come up with storybook magic, with some kind of spell to give them magical wings that would take them over the ghetto walls under the veil of night, far away to safer places ... If only ... If only ...

Oy, you old fool. You're babbling, dreaming of fairy tales, even imagining protective wings. From whom? And maybe ... maybe they won't dare? Maybe the danger is the fiendish outgrowth of my sick mind? Stefa[2] says that it comes from lack of sleep and exhaustion. Dark thoughts, she says, come from exhaustion. Maybe she's right. I am like an old broken vessel. Like an old worn-out piece of clothing. Everything is torn, everything is fraying. Not one fibre of me is whole. Everything in me is breaking, the old body is falling apart. And the mind? No, the mind isn't sick. It still understands clearly. Yes, yes, the mind comprehends that behind us is death and before us is death. Death with a thousand faces on all sides. Where can we look for their rescue? How can we defend them against ...?

An immense sorrow spreads across his thin yellow face. Anguish and pain flood his entire being. His heart pounds as if it were about to smash, to spring out of his chest.

Stooped over and hunched, as if his thoughts have made him even smaller and thinner, he takes slow steps to his chair. His eyes are feverish. He lowers himself into the chair as though his legs have refused to hold him up any longer. He leans both arms on the table and rests his heavy head on them. In his brain an alarm clock goes off; his thoughts are racing, jockeying with one another. His ideas and thoughts break off from the noise in his mind just as, in a storm, branches and leaves are torn from a tree. The old thinker tries to gather his splintered thoughts and compel his mind to think of only one thing. He sets out the silent monologue.

At least to protect them ... from fear, from the suffering that terror brings. Maybe I can do this for them, only shield them in this way, help them get through ... to lessen the fear, the way we cause physical pain to atrophy. Help them to face the worst ... to take it with calm ... drive away their angst ... to spare them ... oy, how the mind races! A storm ... maybe I am exaggerating ... Stefa says ... from exhaustion ...

---

2 Stefania Wilcyńska worked with Korczak to establish the orphanage at Krochmalna Street and supported him in the fulfilment of his pedagogical vision. She too accompanied the children to their deaths at Treblinka. https://www.jhi.pl/en/articles/stefania-wilczynska-janusz-korczak,3461.

166   Fables, Short Stories, and Historic Fiction

exhaustion ... We have to leave Monish. In bed, fever ... Shlomka's drawing ... such talent ... vitamins ... I need to get, we have to have ... seriously wasting away ... What do they want from me? To think about those on the other side ... granted ... to get through, get through ... save oneself ... myself alone? Never! Help to get past the fear ... Stefa says these are dark thoughts ... not possible, they won't dare ... they will ... they won't ...

A persistent drowsiness clouds his thoughts and has ensnared them in dreams. His weary hands can no longer support the weight of his head and it hits the table. The exhausted body trembles. The dream ends abruptly.

The old doctor raises his head, looks around, slowly gets up. With an unsteady hand he turns down the weak light of the carbide lamp and makes his way quietly to bed. The old iron bed gives a slight groan. Korczak straightens his stiff limbs and exhales deeply. The weight pressing on his heart lets up. He feels lighter, as if he has found calmness in his thinking, as if his thoughts have chased off the dangers facing his children.

This time sleep comes quickly. It is a balm for the feeble body and for the strained, suffering mind. In sleep, the pale, grief-stricken face is even more anxious and pale. His skin is now thin and transparent. Asleep, he looks as if he is lying unconscious.

Korczak's sleep is fitful. At every rustle, he struggles as if against cobwebs. The summer night quickly flits away. The dark blind over the window gradually lightens as the dawn breaks. The blue of early morning pushes its way into the bedroom in a thin strip at the edge of the blind. The sleeping man wakes nervously in his bed, gets up suddenly, scans the walls where the poisonous snakes slithered out – no, they came out of the waves, threw themselves on Laocoön and his sons, bit and choked them, suffocated them. The line between dream and waking is so narrow, hardly even perceptible. At one moment the dream takes supremacy, and then, soon after, it is the waking reality. His right hand swipes nervously across his face, as if to drive the nightmarish vision from his imagination. His head falls exhausted on the pillow. His body and mind submit again to the salvation of sleep.

The sun has lifted off the horizon, moving along ever higher into the sky and, to spite the murderers, has sent its golden beams into the ghetto. Dr. Janusz Korczak is still sleeping this morning. His mind has emptied itself of nightmares. His sleep has become sounder, deeper, more solid. Like one famished, his body first swallowed, then devoured sleep, and relished it. Suddenly the sleeper trembles violently, as if rattled by a strong thunderclap. A savage whistle shriek has cut off his delicious

The Last Night 167

slumber. A beastly roaring drives him from his bed. Nervously he pulls on his trousers.[3] His hands are trembling. He runs to the window and pulls up the dark blind. Light pours into the room. Wild cries break in along with the light: *Juden heraus! Juden heraus! Schnell heraus!* In the silence that follows, a commotion is heard in the house.

Korczak quickly pulls his shoes out from under the bed and begins to put them on. But now the small, low door of the isolation room opens. Three eight- to ten-year-old invalids in their nightshirts fall into Korczak's room; their eyes are feverish from heat and fear. They cling to him. A little girl hurls questions at him.

"Doctor, what are they going to do with us? I'm so frightened!"

Korczak strokes her head and coaxes her:

"Nothing to be afraid of! You're a clever girl and you're acting so silly!"

A second sick girl snuggles into Korczak and asks:

"Doctor, where are they going to take us? Will the Doctor go with us?"

"Yes, yes. I'm going with you. Probably to a village. After all, it's summer."

He pulls the children down and chases them off.

"Go get dressed. Nothing to be afraid of."

A sickly boy of ten asks quietly:

"Doctor, will they take us to a village?"

"I've already said. Such big kids and you are behaving like babies. Go get dressed, hurry!"

"Do we have to take everything with us, Doctor? Our books? Our scribblers? Can we take a ball?"

Korczak does not appear to answer. Two nurses are already in the room leading the children away. Korczak pulls his jacket on hastily and gets ready to go out. But now the door opens on the left and Stefania Wilcynska comes in. She is pale but calm. Her voice wavers slightly. Clearly she is straining to keep control of herself. She speaks softly, her voice coming from somewhere far off. She gives him a satchel and helps him to pack his essentials. Korczak explains himself to her:

---

3 With this line, Berger begins an expansion of the ending that appeared in the version of the story published in *In Loyf fun tsayt*. In the original version there is no discussion with Stefa, no interaction with the children, and no encounter with "an unfamiliar man" who offers a reprieve. According to Newerly, there had been various times at which friends and supporters had tried without success to convince Korczak to accept assistance to flee the ghetto.

168   Fables, Short Stories, and Historic Fiction

"I left you on your own and yet you have come to help me. I slept late, and then the children barged in. I had to calm them; I didn't carry out my duties properly."

"You always carry out your duties. The children know that you are going with them. Everything is ready, no panic. Everything has been prepared as you wished. We are taking care of the sick children. Their bags are ready. The staff is assisting everyone down to the youngest children. You yourself prepared me so that everything is ready."

Packing his bag, Korczak asks Stefania to go to the children. He needs no one's help.

Now he is ready and joins the children.

"Are they calm? Not frightened?"

"Yes, calm. Not afraid. They know that you are travelling with them. Your presence gives them security."

"Safe with me. They still believe that I ..."

Stefania takes a few steps towards the door. Korczak throws down the towel that he was using to wipe his face and cries out in a strangled voice:

"Stefa ... It is to you ... I owe you so much!⁴ Forgive me! We won't be parted now."

For a moment Stefania looks lovingly at him. Her eyes fill with tears and without a word, she goes out.

Korczak takes his bundle and makes for the door. His way is blocked by an unfamiliar man.

"You are Dr. Janusz Korczak? Dr. Henryk Goldszmit?"⁵

"I am. But I haven't the time now. I have to be with the children."

"Don't hurry, Doctor. Your children's home is being moved."

"I know."

"I know that you know. But you can remain. You are a doctor. You are needed."

---

4 In this exchange Berger has Korczak begin to address Stefa with the formal *you /aykh* and then turn quickly to the informal *you / dir*.

5 In her *Yidishe shriften* article referring to Igor Newerly's newly published book *Lebedike ringen* (Żywe *wiązanie*), Berger cites a description of the day, 5 August 1942, when Korczak arrived at the Umschlagplatz at the head of a procession of the children from the Jewish orphanage. There was weeping among the bystanders, even those with the hardest of hearts, writes Berger. A German commandant asked his Jewish menials what the fuss was. They identified Korczak, and the commandant approached to ask him if he were the author of *The Bankruptcy of Little Jack*, a book that he had once read and thought very good. He then offered Korczak the chance to be removed from the transport and remain behind. The doctor refused. "Geven aza mench," *Yidishe Shriften* 12, no. 232 (December 1966): 5.

The Last Night 169

"I'm needed by my children. I've no time to waste."

"It's been arranged for you to stay right here."

"My place is with my children."

"Think about yourself, Doctor Goldszmit. There's still time, it's your last chance."

Korczak looks at him, tight-lipped, and doesn't answer. He wants to get away. The stranger takes him by the arm, attempts to persuade him.

"Think it over, Doctor Goldszmit."

"I've wasted too much time with you; I need to be with the children!"

Soon after, the stranger hears a cheerful fatherly voice through the open door. Korczak is organizing the children into lines. Holding hands with the youngest and with a song on his lips, he places himself at the front of the procession, shielding his children from the terror.

Translated by Judy Nisenholt
Ekhos fun a vaytn nekhtn, Tel Aviv 1993

Unfinished Pages: Excerpt

It's winter. The year 1940 is drawing to a close. Far from here, fall is just beginning. Here in remote Karaganda, the ground is white, covered in glittering, fluffy snow. It is a harsh winter. The burning frost tears through our tattered clothing, inflaming the skin. It jabs under our nails.

Far away, the world is at war, but there is war here too. Hunger, cold, and the dirty, infected barracks are at war with us internees. Just like bullets and bombs at the front, they maim and kill. And here am I, in this faraway white world, Esther Frumkin, now known as Marya Yakovlevna Frumkina, recently turned sixty. I, Esther, the name I took in my early revolutionary youth, am sixty. I feel as if I am many, many hundreds of years old and carrying thousands of years of my Jewish people's history. Maybe that's why the sixty years weigh so painfully and heavily on my shoulders.

Here, in exile, a person is naked, unarmed against the savage beast that is the camp. A sick old person is already in many ways naked and powerless. I don't say this out of resignation. Can there be resignation in camp? The animal instinct to live and the desire to hold out drive it away. But I know I won't hold out. The severe diabetes and its side-effects are getting worse. There is none of the necessary medicine. My legs are swollen to above the knees and wrapped in rags. It takes great exertion for me just to cross the camp.

But it is only my body that is impaired. Inside this wreck, there still lives a revolutionary spirit, an iron will to express the things I want to say. While I was in the prisons, I thought a great deal. Everything can be forbidden and stifled, but not one's thoughts. Ceaselessly, my mind was at work, thinking things through. My great desire is to have my reflections reach the living, those who are free. Would it not be an added punishment to take my words with me to the cold earth? Into a mass grave? I have always undertaken what is most difficult, even what seemed impossible. I have looked for and found – it seems to me – a means to speak my mind, express my nascent thoughts, and uncover the missteps on the dangerous path that I've trod for fifteen years.

Last night, when I was already in my bunk, Tatiana told me that when the convoy was taking them to work in the morning, along a different route than usual, she saw, not far from the camp zone, a heap of corpses. Neither the convoy nor the female slaves paid any attention to the bizarre scene: Rigid with frost, emaciated, they looked like a pile of huge frozen fish, Tatiana quietly told me.

The snow was covering them. On the way back, she saw no more than a snowy mound. Yesterday was bitterly cold and apparently the ground was too frozen to dig. Maybe it was also because Alexei, the digger was sick, laid low with a high fever? So, the dead need to wait to be hidden together in the earth, and for it be smoothed over, all traces wiped away. When is my turn? Who can say? Not even the doctor, an experienced internee. "Nature sometimes works miracles," he says: "It looks as if this one won't pull through and yet he goes on for a long while." That could still happen to me too; I may yet manage to write down a confession, to become the chronicler of my life.

I know that I want to undertake something like this, something that no one in these circumstances could do or dared to do. I want to achieve the unachievable. My former years in prison, my exile, my years of living illegally under tsarism, have taught me a little. Not that this present moment is the same. The past looks like an idyll compared to today. Experiences, as much as they pale by comparison, can nevertheless still be of service. The risk is incalculably great. But what do I risk? – a death sentence? Death is at my heels in any case. Nevertheless, you need to have superhuman strength and a will of steel, alone for hours in the barracks, to record thoughts and then to conceal them. First of all, you have to eradicate the fear, the terror that has taken root inside. Every minute you have to remind yourself that you are a human and not a beast, not the cattle that they have made you into. I have taken the first step: I have subjugated the terror and hidden two pencils in the hem of my coat. I stole a small notebook during my work in the office and stuck it in among my ragged clothing.

My neighbour in the bunk across from me, the fifty-three-year-old mathematician Yekaterina Vasilevna, recently said to me again, "You're lucky to be an invalid with aching, swollen legs; you don't have to go to hard labour every day, and get chased there and back over eight or ten verst." Maybe she's right. When the gong sounds at six in the morning and I see the bundles of rags rolling out of their bunks, worn out,

172   Fables, Short Stories, and Historic Fiction

moving with fatigue, a shudder goes through me. There are people in these bundles of *shmattes*, women who are waging a war to keep the spark of life from going out. When they come back at night I don't recognize them, deformed by cold, hunger, and the crushing drudgery. So, I have the "good luck" to be sick, to have been recognized as 100 per cent invalid, incapable of going to work outside the camp. This "luck" should be and must be used to a good end. I have always lived for some purpose, never for myself alone, always for a common good. Only too late did I grasp that the universal good can sometimes be false, like a counterfeit coin, tricking us with its outward appearance.

And another "bit of luck": I've persuaded them to let me work in the office for three or four hours in the morning. After midday, I stay in the barracks, taking the place of the so-called *dnyevalnaya*, the attendant on duty. There are days when my feet are so numb that it is even too difficult for me to go to the office. On the other hand, today, after the early morning shift, I walked across the yard of the camp, and the view of the snowy white world filled my eyes. I looked through the barbed wire into the distance. Gazing into the faraway whiteness, I felt as if I were on another planet, in a dead world. Yet it is beautiful, the dead white world – the kind of beauty that wrenches the heart to the point of suffering. A huge wild bird, probably an eagle of the steppes, swept by. Likely gone astray, or looking for food. He dropped down a bit, opened his thieving beak, and, seeing me, took fright, and flew off with wings spread wide. My appearance likely struck fear even into the heart of this bird of prey. I followed him on the wing. Won't he freeze? I had been told it happens that a little bird gone astray can freeze while in flight and drop down dead. Yet, gazing after him, I was jealous: he has wings, he is at liberty … what good fortune!

But I too am lucky – I have free time, I can write in solitude, keeping a record of all my thoughts. I stay on the alert in my barracks, like a creature in the fields during a hunt. I sit with ears pricked up beside a board that's fastened to the wall; it serves as a small table. The echo of footsteps, the sound of a door being opened and the pages and the pencil are quickly moved under the *shmattes* that cover me. Yesterday I began writing. A muffled echoing of steps knocked the pencil out of my hand.

My journalistic career now comes in handy. I always wrote quickly and easily, though I paid a lot of attention to the form. Now I don't: I write and let it stand, as long as it is quick, as long as I jot down everything tormenting me, percolating in me and leaving me restless. But will it ever reach the living? Surely not through me. I know, I'll undoubtedly remain among those that Tatiana saw yesterday, thrown onto a pile behind the camp's barbed wire. Others will survive and get out. Maybe someday they will bring it to the living, maybe to my daughter? My daughter, my one and only, where are you? You're the only one I've got left. But where? You have shared the same fate as me. Sooner than I did. But you are young and healthy – you will make it. I so want you to hold out. It is for you and because of you that I have been seized with the courage to risk doing what I now do. I am so much to blame for what has happened to you. I am to blame for all of it. When they dragged you off to some hellish torment, dear Freydl, I was still free, but paralysed by powerlessness. As powerless as I am now. I couldn't even find out what had become of you.

Today is the third day of my perilous project and I have just now realized that I am writing in Yiddish, in the language that I have not used for a good number of years and that I once loved so fiercely; I nursed it and fought for its full rights. Writing in Yiddish came on its own, as natural as having a tongue in one's mouth. Our tongue was ripped out, but since it was silenced, it has lived deep inside me. I have sinned against you, my Yiddish tongue; now you are back as before, a part of me, the most intimate part of me. Now, as I feel myself nearing the end of my life, I express myself in you, through you, my Yiddish language. You have come back to me, my most intimate voice, the most auspicious for expressing all the trembling of my heart and all the hidden places of the soul. A religious Jew makes confession in the holy tongue, so I will make my long confession in holy Yiddish. I see my current memoir as a confession. Yiddish is a fitting language for confession in this place. A language, like a person, becomes holy by being hunted and persecuted.

Yes, I see my writing now as a confession. In describing my life, I want to beg forgiveness and tell the truth about all my straying, all my harmful actions, all my sins. I do this with the hope that, if it reaches the living, it will be received with understanding by the Jewish public, by the Jewish working people. A distant memory has encouraged me. It was in the frightful Lefortovo Prison,[1] in isolation, in the "odinotchka."[2]

---

1 During the Great Purge, Lefortovo Prison was used by the NKVD for interrogations with torture. https://www.globalsecurity.org/intell/world/russia/lefortovo.htm.

2 This refers to a very tiny cell intended for solitary confinement.

174   Fables, Short Stories, and Historic Fiction

During the sleepless nights, and dull silent days, I would search through all the little recesses of my life, etch events in my memory, and recollect everything that I had once learned. I remembered too the excommunication of Rabbi Gershom. *Rabeynu Gershom, Meir HaGeulah, Light of the Redemption* as they called him in his time.[3] He issued Jews four rules: not to practise polygamy, not to read the letters of others, not to divorce a wife against her will, and also not to reproach or even remind a former convert of his conversion after he returns to his kin, to his people. I am returning. Yet, in heart and mind I returned a long time ago to myself, to my people. In truth, I never left them. I bind myself again *to* my beloved Yiddish, the language that I once fervently nurtured and defended.

Translated by Judy Nisenholt
Nisht farendikteh bletlekh, Tel Aviv 1982

---

3 Rabbi Gershom (960–1040).

The Debate between Paper and Letters: A Tale[1]

Paper and Letters have long-standing accounts to settle. On more than one occasion, they simply have not been able to bear one another. They would shake one another off quite happily, if they could. So, don't look to them to resolve their differences. The match has been made. Do what you will, they're a couple and there's no separating them!

It just so happened that this union did not work. In this world, anything can occur: Letters, arranged into words, trained and readied for partnering with white Paper, roused themselves as in revolt and dispersed. And as they scattered, so were the Letters discarded to meet upon the scrapheap of jettisoned, still virginal, Paper, as yet untouched by any black strokes.

At first, Letters and Paper greeted each other warmly. One can frequently bear a grudge, but carry on all the same, like old in-laws. And look how many decent and heaven-blessed pairings have emerged and continue to issue from the two of them. Yet one should never hide that which weighs heavily on one's heart. And so, having graciously received one another from the start, they both, calmly and

---

1 This tale exhibits Berger's talents as a wry fabulist. The convention of the two-animal fable featuring contending abstractions or attributes which serve to teach a moral lesson – in the tradition of Aesop, La Fontaine, and Krilov – is replaced here by two material things in dialogical opposition. Berger's tale echoes those in Eliezer Shteynbarg's volume *Mesholim* (Tshernovits: Komitet af aroystsugebn Eliezer Shteynbargs shriftn in tsvey bend. Band eyns. Mit holtsshnitn fun Artur Kolnik [Chernovits, the committee for the publication of Shteynbarg's book *Mesholim* (fables) in two volumes, with woodcuts by Artur Kolnik], 1932). Shteynbarg presents a host of inanimate objects to edify his reader. The title of his fable "The Debate," under the rubric "Letters" (233–4), corresponds with Berger's own, whether by influence or coincidence.

176 Fables, Short Stories, and Historic Fiction

tactfully, began to bare their souls. Each side laid out its respective complaints: Letters, quietly and politely, asked, "How can you, unspoiled white Paper, take on so many falsehoods, lies, obscenities, banal and altogether meaningless phrases? You were created to carry on your shoulders that which is most refined and most worthy, from generation to generation, for all eternity. Don't you see that through you they spread false messages and through you, as unsullied envoy, they smuggle dirty, contraband material? Oh, my dear Paper! How can you stand it?"

Paper's heart almost burst and, with a plaintive cry, it uttered these words: "Everything is thrown upon my weary, burdened shoulders! You, too, distinguished Letters, have your allegations but it is far easier to chastise someone else than to reproach oneself. From you, dear colleagues, Letters, this whole mess begins. One fashions out of you truly false discourse, most of which is trite, at best. No one sees his own handicap. Take a good, hard look at yourself in the mirror. See what an abomination your finely honed metaphors can often become – you so-called 'Letters.' Afterwards, I must forever bear the onus you thrust upon me, along with its back-breaking consequences. On top of that, you have the unmitigated gall to blame me, Paper!"

Letters grew dejected and began to respond in defence: "If only it depended upon us! We are but helpless and powerless. We are like clay: we are as malleable as the dough which may be kneaded as one wishes. We are also like bricks: we can be used to build equally a beautiful palace or a horrific prison. In experienced and noble hands one can wrest from us both authentic and sublime songs, and, most importantly, the true essence of life. Conversely, we can fall into the sloppy and unclean hands of a bungler who humiliates us, making of us a laughingstock, dragging our good name through the mud. The worst part happens when these fanatical souls undertake to strong-arm us into submission. Oh, how they disgrace us! Our incredulous eyes bulge out of our heads in shame and our hearts break in torment. And why deny that in that moment we are resentful of you, Oh, pristine white Paper, for taking on these odious goods, never, even occasionally, making a move to hurl them aside?

Paper began to defend itself all the more, changing its course to a full-frontal attack: "Is there a solution here? If you inflict such violence, you must bear the consequences. What choice does one have? Believe me, I would much prefer to deliver clever repartee and lofty rhetoric. If only I were able to cast off the idle talk and egregious lies that you invariably dump on me! Instead you hold me in a vise and press me into service at your bidding. You afflict me most forcibly! This misfortune originates with you, Oh, Letters. Yet you have the temerity to believe that you are always right!"

Letters painstakingly drew out a new argument in their defence: "We are indeed the instigators of this situation, but it is no easy thing for the bunglers to lay their soiled, fumbling hands on us. Nor do we allow ourselves to be so easily manipulated. Those who want to humiliate us have to sweat profusely and contort themselves with all manner of schemes and tricks until their printed matter is ready. You, my Paper colleague, quickly capitulate. You show them no resistance. Should they heap upon you a particularly loathsome load, you will inevitably accept it. Hence the truism, 'Paper can bear everything.'"

Paper was soon beside itself with anger: "You keep pouring salt on my wounds when you alone are the source of all my misery. This hackneyed prattle comes from you, I repeat, from you! People make of you what they want," Paper stammered in exasperation. Letters, emboldened, rebuked Paper for indiscriminately accepting everything: "Hold on, my partner Paper, we don't like this one bit. You are beginning to curse, a sure sign that that you are wrong."

An overgrown willow tree, bent with age, its swollen bark, like the skin of a wizened old man, stood close by and lent an ear to the debate. Finally, unable to hold back any longer, he broke into this war of words: "In vain, and without effect, you spew hateful bile."

"So you be the judge! Since you have been listening most attentively to all of this, you decide who has won the debate!" The venerable willow tree shook its clever old head and answered with Solomonic wisdom: "How can I possibly adjudicate this matter when you are both correct? The most difficult cases to settle are those where all embattled sides are right."

Warsaw 1960
Translated by Linda/Leye Lipsky
Ekhos fun a vaytn nekhtn, Tel Aviv 1993

EPILOGUE

EPILOGUE

Notes on the Underground: Lili Berger's Reflections on Marranism

While at the end of our sojourn into the vast and layered territory of Lili Berger's interests and capabilities, this afterword seeks to extend the reach of her polyglot erudition as imparted by the readings in this volume. It points the way to one further historical engagement, yet another literary proclivity, an additional window onto her world: Berger had a career-long interest in Marranism. Not just a passing fancy, but a deep and abiding concern, sustained throughout her oeuvre in essays, short stories, and travel literature. The critical effort to identify a Survivor-Marrano equivalence takes its lead from Berger's own recommendation of this correspondence at many junctures in her body of work.

For one who wore her Jewishness unapologetically and openly, Berger was empathetically interested in those who could not, by force of autocratic fiat, do the same. The Marrano paradigm of hiddenness has its analogous acts of concealment endured in the Holocaust. Among personal effects in these stories are ritual objects which stand, metonymically, for a Jewish identity, a Jewish sense of time, including the festivals which punctuate the Jewish year: "Dos khanike lempl" (The Hanukah lamp)[1] – in the series "Haynttsaytike Maranen" (Contemporary Marranos) – is hidden in a wall niche, out of the way, inconspicuous: "... dort vu Ane leygt op nisht noytike zakhn ... vi s'[dos lempl] volt oysbahaltn geven far a mentshlekh oyg" (... there where Anna places

---

1 *Opgerisine tsvaygn: Noveln un dertseylungen* (Severed branches: Short stories and tales) (Paris: Abexpress, 1970), 49–63. This collection contains a number of stories with Berger's designation "From the series 'Haynttsaytike Maranen.'" The opening story "Kolahoras eyniklekh" (9–33), despite its Marrano subject matter, is not officially in this series. Stories in the series are strewn throughout the volume, curiously, not under one rubric.

182   Epilogue

unnecessary things ... as if it were in refuge from the human gaze), to mislead her pursuers.

The phenomenon of the Marrano has engaged philosophers, historians, and critical thinkers alike, many of whom extend its domain well beyond the demographic of fifteenth- and sixteenth-century Iberian Jewry, its native geography, and language. Marranism has earned its "ism" through sheer force of its essentialist attributes of secrecy, duplicity, and outward compliance to an enforced conversion. Crypto-Jews remained inwardly faithful to their ancestral tradition.

Most "New Christians" embraced Catholicism and did not look back. Berger was far more interested in the clandestine cabal of believers who lived out their atavism furtively and disguised. Conversion created, as it necessitated, the precarious, often perfidious, lives of these Crypto-Jews, who ensured, through their hidden practices, that their Judaism be passed on to successive generations who would prove to be tethered – sometimes constrained, sometimes grounded – to their Jewishness through the ages.

The call of Marranism to ideological inquiry was answered belletristically by Berger with her typical mix of historical chronicle and imaginative narrative. Certainly her work was informed by historical research, as one can see irrefutably in her documentary appreciations of personages in this collection and in her piece on the Converso Uriel D'Acosta, discussed below. In her transcription of Marrano folkways and behaviour, a binary taxonomy emerges: figurative and philosophical. The reader of Berger's oeuvre might find these dual signposts instructive. The hiding of the "contraband" book *Tevye* in our volume bears a metaphoricity beyond what might be contained within the pages of the literal book. Her philosophical perspective on Marranism itself breaks down into contending paradigms of political collectivism/secular universalism versus Jewish or Yiddish particularism[2] of which Berger is so keenly aware and poignantly expressive.

---

2 According to Agata Bielik-Robson, who is a prolific commentator on the philosophy of Marranism, Hannah Arendt implicitly compared the great European thinkers and writers of Jewish origin to the Marranos who were permitted "to enter the realm of universality only on the condition of concealing their particular 'bias.'" "Bias" here is an encoded word for a brand of Jewish ethnocentrism. *The Marrano Phenomenon: Jewish "Hidden Tradition" and Modernity* (Basel: MDPI, 2019). Reprint of "Preface," *Religions Journal*, special issue, ed. Agata Bielik-Robson (2018–19): ix, https://www.mdpi .com/journal/religions/special issues/marrano, accessed 29 August 2022. Hannah Arendt, "The Jew as Pariah: A Hidden Tradition," in *The Jew as Pariah: Jewish Identity and Politics in the Modern Age*, edited by Ron H. Feldman, 67–90 (New York: Grove Press, 1944); originally in *Jewish Social Studies* 6 (April 1944): 99–122.

Notes on the Underground: Lili Berger's Reflections on Marranism   183

While it is beyond the scope of this afterword to address the panoply of critical exegeses on Marranism, Berger's meditation on Marrano-like dissent does bring to mind the work of Jacques Derrida, his recusant take on Marrano marginalism and his philosophical musings on his own Sephardic *marranismo*. In an essay written late in his career, "Circumfession," Derrida takes up a latitudinarian position, known as his "Toledo confession": "I am a kind of *marrane* of French Catholic culture."[3] Berger would have been puzzled by the oddity of this reversal but not by its spirit of pluralism. Derrida's Jewish selfhood is found somewhere at the juncture of Augustinian confession and the wound of covenant. In the Algerian community of Jews, many of whom are of Converso stock, circumcision is likened to baptism, Bar Mitsvah to communion. Derrida continues: "I am one of those Marranos who, even in the intimacy of their own hearts, do not admit to being Jewish."[4] As we shall see below, some of the latter-day Marranos in Berger's travelogue offer up a comparable evasion. This impulse to suspend Jewish identity by melding into the current and local matrix was repudiated by Berger, except in a situation *in extremis*.

For all that, Derrida admitted that the Marrano "Memory of Passover"[5] pervaded his work. Passover's objects, such as the Haggadah, seder plate, *afikomen* sac, and its distinctive foods, are all sensory catalysts to the memory of this rite of spring. Crypto-Jews did not travel light: along with the above inventory, they hauled supplications to the divine and instructions to the intellect collected in weighty volumes. In Berger's work, the resonances of Jewish memory found in holiday objects are in tacit alignment with Derrida's. Avrom Reyzen's poem "Zog Maran" (Tell Me, Marrano Brother)[6] is an evocative testimonial

---

3 "Circumfession," in *Jacques Derrida*, by Geoffrey Bennington and Jacques Derrida, translated by Geoffrey Bennington (Chicago: University of Chicago Press, 1993), 170.
4 Ibid., 160.
5 Derrida's answer to Hegel's "Memory of the Passion," which he developed in his essay "Glauben und Wissen." Jacques Derrida, "Foi et savoir" (Faith and knowledge), in *Acts of Religion*, trans. Gil Anidjar (New York and London: Routledge, 1994). See Agata Bielik-Robson's discussion in "The Marrano God: Abstraction, Messianicity, and Retreat in Derrida's 'Faith and Knowledge,'" *Religions* 10, no. 22 (2019), www.mdpi.com/journal/religions, accessed June 2022.
6 In Eleanor Gordon Mlotek and Joseph Mlotek, eds., *Pearls of Yiddish Song* (New York: Educational Department of the Workmen's Circle, 1988), 205. Set to music by Shmuel Bugatch. It is sung at third seder tables across the progressive Yiddish-speaking world. This tradition was instituted by the Arbeter Ring (Workmen's Circle) in 1920s America.

184   Epilogue

to the travails of Passover observance enacted underground. For the unenlightened Marrano, the connection might be merely to goods and chattels, abstracted from their devotional referent. Hence, in the way that Ahad Ha'am determined that the Sabbath has kept the Jews, not the other way around, so has the memory of Passover kept the Marranos close to their Judaism, at the very least, to its material culture. In Berger's work these memories of holiday customs, and Jewish traditions past, reveal themselves cumulatively, as shards of recollection.

This epilogue has a tripartite schema. Our collection *On the Waves of Destiny* does not contain a story or an essay dedicated wholesale to the Marranos, but there are both oblique and direct references to the paradigm of concealment and its satellite attributives on the spectrum of hiddenness: covert, clandestine, contraband, duplicitous, encrypted. This is mostly played out against the backdrop of the Holocaust, where suppression, smuggling, flight, and other acts analogous to Marrano camouflage are realized. Retrieving one's Jewishness and repatriating to Poland after the war meant that encoded Jewish values and practices emerged from hiding but the move "above ground" often left the survivors stunned by the light, exposed, and vulnerable. Berger writes in her preface to *Opgerisine tsvaygn* that the following themes are central to her Holocaust pieces: "... de[r] shtendik[er] umru, d[i] keseyderdike tserisnkeyt un di letste angstike tsaplenishn fun der kleyner sheyres hapleyte in Poyln" (... the sustained restlessness, the persistent vacillation, and the last angst-ridden death rattle of the small remnant of Holocaust survivors in Poland). These realities of concealment and expulsion echo to each other across time.

Next, from beyond our selected translations, we present Berger's interpretive travelogue of Iberian Jewry, inspired by George Sand's memoir of her visit to Mallorca. Finally, we offer excerpts from, and a discussion of, three critical reviews of Marrano-related works appearing in other volumes, demonstrating how this theme animates much of her writing.

Marranism in Our Collection

In the short story – from the series "Contemporary Marranos" – "Der farshpetikter Yid" (The Jew Who Came Late),[7] from the protagonist Henryk Grynsztajn's very first "hesitant steps" onto the scene, his

---

7 *Fun haynt un nekhtn* (Warsaw: Yiddish Bukh, 1965), 171–7. Reprinted in the series "Haynttsaytikte Maranen" in *Opgerisine tsvaygn*, 141–8. Please note that all English citations in this section derive from the work of the translators in our collection.

Notes on the Underground: Lili Berger's Reflections on Marranism 185

odd behaviour, executed with Marrano-like stealth, is meant to prevent onlookers from witnessing what will be a full disclosure of his identity. There is a choreography of diffidence, a letter of introduction with no return address, an appeal for charity with the proviso that the endowing organization not let on that it is a Jewish body,[8] a duplicitous "passing" as the blonde- haired "pure Aryan." There is the obligatory change of name to the Polish Catholic Sokołowski. At play here is the widespread onomastics of renaming, towards the end of assuming a new, counterfeit identity. Grynsztajn, who has spent the recent war years dissembling and avoiding discovery, could not "hold on to [his] secret," that he was "an old, broken Jew." Certainly, these ruses were no longer believed to be necessary, as the officious bureaucrat berates Grynsztajn: "[Y]ou continued to remain in hiding after the war ... why are you hiding?" Indeed such habits, born of historical necessity, die hard, as we will see in the refusal of the Marranos in Mallorca to own up to their heritage, a full four centuries after the start of the Inquisition. The mask one donned was not so easily jettisoned, well after the immediate threat had dissipated or repatriation had been achieved. Grynsztajn takes exception to the clerk's accusation that he was "not involved with Jewish people" with this remonstrance: "How does one know what a person is involved with on the inside, with what is going on in a person's heart?" In the end, the protagonist is alone in the world, untrusting, wounded to the core, "a hunted animal," eking out his meagre subsistence in a context of fear and dread, unmitigated by the passage of time.

The story "Mit Tevye dem milkhikn in untererd" (With Tevye the Dairyman in the Underground)[9] is replete with Marrano resonances: the volume of Sholem Aleichem's *Tevye der milkhiker* (Tevye the Dairyman) stands in the stead of a much-coveted ritual object. The Jewish cultural "artifact" is a Yiddish canonical book of almost totemic significance, which is spirited away and concealed in a "hope chest" for safekeeping: first in an oven, and later, in a false-bottomed basket. This sheltering of the "contraband" book is emblematic of all things and all people hidden. The protagonist is unnamed, to underscore, perhaps, the widespread, hence anonymous and unbranded, experience of holding on to one's Jewishness as one holds on to one's treasured book, that

---

8 Joint Distribution Committee. See footnote 1 in Judy Nisenholt's translation of this story.

9 *Fun vayt un fun noent: Noveln* (From far and near: Short stories) (Paris: SIPE, 1978), 72–82.

186 Epilogue

is, with unflinching tenacity. The protagonist feels like an "automaton," with paralytic survivor guilt: "... dear ones Aviva, Anka, Sara, Solyek, Lyonek, and Hershel. Why them and not me?" There are other ailments of the psyche: "Such nights, sinister, unkind, imprison the hunted and the homeless in an iron vise." The hunt, as in the hunting of game, is a fitting metaphor for both Grynsztajn and the narrator in this story. She runs through the streets and alleyways of Paris, teeming with "vendors and street girls," her tormenters – real or imagined – in hot pursuit. Wandering aimlessly through the streets and back alleys of Paris, the heroine knows something, somewhere, was hidden.

A sudden jolt of memory identifies the saga: the volume was entrusted to Sonyitchka, the Bessarabian, who hid *Tevye* in the stove, defeating efforts to make her home *Judenrein*. The book is contraband, *verboten*. The sole and favourite book saved by the protagonist, it is duly anthropomorphized: "Why not try to rescue *Tevye* again? Whatever would happen to me would also happen to 'him.'" Her efforts to retrieve the book fuel the narrative and echo Marrano intrigue. Berger taps into Sholem Aleichem's wry humour, buoying the tone: Sonya confuses the book with her brother of the same name; Sonya "agreed to postpone the execution [read: destroy the book] to the following morning ... She offered me the privilege of choosing the sentence ..." Sonya speculates that the heroine has become, unwittingly, a "thread" the Nazis "could follow to trap others." Covert and duplicitous actions ensue: suspicion, accusation of spying, "sidelong glances," conspiracy, stifling a child's cries, and an elaborate plan to effect a change of domicile to throw the Nazis off her scent: "Everyone looked suspicious to me"; "I had to convince myself that no one was following me." She has to run a gauntlet of probing looks as she passes the downstairs tenant to arrive at the street. What is more, this turmoil is an isolating and wounding one: "... loneliness and fear bit into [her] bones." The protagonist hid a "subtenant" – a baby, and the book, both equally precious. The protection of a contraband book in multiple acts of orchestrated subterfuge, is a redux of Marrano guile. Tevye himself, dressed, Joseph Papp-like, in "modern" guise, intrudes upon the narrative in a dream sequence, and with his signature sententious bravura, enjoins the protagonist, in this time of dark, Marrano-like concealment of a life "underground," to keep the faith. And that she does: In the end, this literary treasure, which had been hidden under a pile of Aryan papers, serves as a peace offering to a kind neighbour, the erstwhile "suspect" on the ground floor.

The volume *Tevye der milkhiker* is a touchstone of peoplehood, a repository of folkways, a lexicon of supplication. Jewish history, learning, ethics are offered up to the heroine by Sholem Aleichem's encyclopedic

Notes on the Underground: Lili Berger's Reflections on Marranism   187

knowledge, biblical command, and linguistic agility, all ventriloquized, in Berger's story, in the compelling person of Tevye. The protagonist of "With Tevye ..." is both uplifted and centred by his instruction.

In Berger's essay on Vasily Grossman, "Di geshikhte fun a bukh, oder der veg durkh payn tsu yidisher identitet" (The history of a book, or the path (through pain) to Jewish identity),[10] the fires of the Inquisition are directly named. Invoking the memory of Giordano Bruno, the Italian philosopher and heretic who was burnt at the stake, Berger reminds us of the important books and manuscripts that have been confiscated and torched. She alludes to "the stacks of Jewish holy books stashed away by the Spanish Inquisition when it compelled the local Jews to convert, burning Marranos at the stake in the central square."

Grossman was remote from his Jewish past before the war; after the war he assiduously researched the fate of the murdered Jews, co-authored the seminal "Black Book of Soviet Jewry," a copy of which was hidden, retrieved, and translated. His monumental novel *Life and Fate*, seized by the KGB, met a similar end. By clandestine means two manuscripts of this book escaped KGB detection and "saw the light of day" in Switzerland. A series of confiscations – *For a Just Cause* and an unnamed novel – ensued. Grossman denounced the Stalinist regime for enabling the Nazi war machine. It was the "totalitarian apparatus" which was "indifferent to human suffering and human need." Grossman, resourceful to the end, survived by both artfulness and cunning. His friends at the Jewish Anti-Fascist Committee were not so fortunate. Berger, upon rereading Grossman's novel, speculates that Grossman had never "introduced a Jewish character or taken account of any Jewish problems, but reversed course in what Berger calls the "epic ... fresco" of *Life and Fate*. The novel brought to the forefront defining Jewish values. Ideological and political disappointment, engendered by a Soviet dark nationalism, sent him to champion the cause of his fellow Jews. As was the case of many Marranos – whose holy or secular books were similarly confiscated or burned – Jewish identity, Jewish self-definition, repressed and dormant, lay in wait for an opportunity and historical context to express itself.

In Esther Frumkin's view from the barracks, that is, her fictionalized gulag diary, *Nisht farendikte bletelekh* (Unfinished pages),[11] the narrator notes her beast-like existence, forgoing her hitherto exclusive effort to

---

10 *Oyf di khvalyes fun goyrl: Noveln, dertseylungen, literarishe eseyen* (On the waves of destiny: Short stories, tales and literary essays) (Paris: IMPO, 1986), 268–81.

11 *A roman: Band* 1 (Tel Aviv: Yisroyl Bukh, 1982).

188   Epilogue

contribute to a "universal good" to focus her attention to the strife of her people. Again, not the concealed sacred objects, but implements of writing, tools of self-reflection, are redemptive for this Yiddish memoirist and chronicler of the tsarist and Stalinist abuses: "I have subjugated the terror and have hidden two pencils in the hem of my coat ... [and] a small notebook ... and stuck it in among my ragged clothing." These are the self-named "holy" tools with which she plies her trade and realizes her sacrosanct mission to commit her torment to paper; she leaves this written legacy for her daughter. At the dreaded sound of footsteps, she quickly moves the pencils and paper under a pile of *shmattes* (rags). Forbidden to speak "[her] beloved" Yiddish, the "tongue ripped from [her] mouth," Frumkin is determined to articulate her confession in this "intimate" language with renewed vigour: "A language, like a person, becomes holy by being hunted ... It presents "all the trembling of [her] heart and all the hidden places of the soul." Similarly, Marranos had to give up Ladino and Hebrew languages, rife with expressive and devotional capabilities.

The next three essays in our collection discussed below mark the centrality of the Warsaw Ghetto, its archive and its uprising, to Berger's character studies. She characterizes it as the "seven circles of hell," in "Der veg tsu zikh durkh payn: A dermonung anshtot blumen af a keyver" (The painful path to self-discovery: A memorial in place of flowers on a grave),[12] her portrait of Czajka. The Poland-loving, Jewishly "estranged" writer Izabela Gelbard was dubbed "Lieutenant Czajka," a military title, an affectionate diminutive, and a Yiddish/Polish "re-naming" or an "un-naming" of sorts, one that expunges her discernibly Jewish family name. Berger adjudges the "spirit infused" by Czajka's poetry to be an echo of Lamentations and of Job. Indeed the suffering to which her poetry gives voice is of biblical proportions. A poem emanates from the "fiery ashes and red flames" of the conflagration which burns "for centuries," a literalist's representation of both the crematoria and the Inquisitional *autos-da-fé*.

"A Polish writer, yet a Jew," Czajka appeals to Berger to translate her poems into Yiddish. These were acts of desperation, "sensing [as she did] the bitter winds approaching" (in postwar Poland]) Berger demurred, pointing out that she has never translated poetry, only prose (see footnote 25). At the end of this remembrance, Berger offers a poem of Czajka's in which she returns to her ancestral life, predating

---

12 *In gang fun tsayt: Eseyen* (In the course of time: Essays) (Paris: IMPO, 1976), 167–71.

Notes on the Underground: Lili Berger's Reflections on Marranism   189

her assimilated parents: "To you I swear, Zeyde [grandfather] / I hear your blood in my veins." This suggests a Crypto-Jewish-like testament to generations gone by and to the true denotative meaning of *tshuve*: a return, and a penance for her estrangement from the fold. This was fuelled by, in Czajka's case, "revenge," reified in the "pot-bellied vase with a large swastika on it" that sat at her bedside. She had repurposed it as a chamberpot.

Berger leads the way in the next study with the aphorism "We Jews are a people with a long memory." Hence the ready consonance of Holocaust anguish with Marrano suffering. In the essay "Tsum 90stn geboyrn-yor fun Dr. Emanuel Ringelblum: Zikhroynes un sakh-haklen" (On the ninetieth birthday of Dr. Emanuel Ringelblum: Recollections and summing up).[13] Berger notes her childhood memories of him as a revered teacher at her school in interbellum Warsaw and his efforts to introduce Jewish history into the Polish government–decreed curriculum of Jewish studies. Some years had elapsed between Berger's time at the gymnasium and her encounter with Ringelblum in 1937 Paris, when she was preparing for the International Jewish Culture Congress. Ringelblum was by that time engaged in writing an exhaustive historiography of Jews in Poland. Berger was teaching Yiddish in a supplementary school at that time. Shy and starstruck, she prepares her students to showcase their knowledge to best advantage for Ringelblum's visit. Language must be taught by the immigrant parents who speak broken French in the home, Berger offers.

During the war Ringelblum emboldened a cadre of militants for armed resistance. He expended the remainder of his efforts on creating an underground league of faithful researchers, chroniclers, and record keepers of the Warsaw Ghetto. Their moniker, Oyneg Shabes, was known to Jews alone, as if a page were copied from the Marrano playbook.

Radio bulletins were sent to the Polish government in London and then broadcast to the world. Ringelblum created an archive – cached in milk cans and later recovered – published in the volume *Ksovim fun geto* (Manuscripts from the ghetto), "amid the bloodiest persecution ... in every conceivable hiding place." After his apprehension by the Nazis he escaped, disguised as a railway worker, only later to be taken prisoner again and shot along with his righteous gentile colleagues.

---

13 *Ekhos fun a vaytn nekhtn: Dertseylungen, humesh-mayselekh, eseyen un skitsn* (Echoes of a remote past: Short stories, biblical tales, essays and sketches) (Tel Aviv: Farlag Yisroyl Bukh, 1993), 178–9.

190 Epilogue

Berger's essay "Der oysbahaltener kval fun kiem ha'ume: Vegn shafungen in getos un lagern" (The hidden source of a people's survival: Writings from the ghettos and camps)[14] abounds with references to a hidden life, a "mighty underground spring" from which issued "streams and rivulets ... unique in the history of human collectives." However, this uniqueness is qualified, as her discussion suggests that Marrano and other historical acts of intellectual resistance and demotic expression have their parallel in the Warsaw Ghetto. Berger posits here that ordinary people were not archivists, yet their vernacular writing is an enduring chronicle of their struggles. Among the documents culled from the Jewish Historical Institute in Warsaw is one named by Ber Mark,[15] *The Hidden Underground Source.*

Berger notes some of the literati, song writers, and photographers of Warsaw, including Alter Kacyzne, Berl Katsenelson, and Miriam Ulinover. Diarists wrote in "confined spaces," in basements and camps, on scraps of paper, a veritable corpus of folk literature – their own *Notes from Underground* – some of which were never recovered. The ethnographic collection of records of folklorist Shmuel Lehman is one such body of work. Some of the folk writings which survived were "primal": vengeful, angry, outraged. Berger quotes from poems which illustrate the power of the "underground current," which was a measure of "psychic resistance, a deeply interior provocation." The designation of "outcast" is often, for the Jewish intellectual, a badge of honour. Berger then goes on to expose as falsehood the notion that the Warsaw Ghetto Uprising was aided and encouraged by the Polish Resistance movement. This misapprehension was peddled by Wacław Poteranski in his 1968 study on the Warsaw Ghetto.[16] Berger counters that such "spiritual resistance" came only from "inner courage": "The ghetto inhabitant, the Jew in the camp, made a psychic revolt from the start." What is more,

---

14 *In loyf fun tsayt: Dertseylungen, noveln, eseyen* (Paris: Moderna-Fir, 1988), 146–59.
15 Ber Mark, colleague and friend, whose appreciation appears in this volume, uses the topic of this epilogue disparagingly for those who questioned his return to Poland after the war: "[They are] narrow-minded people, mostly from among those who might be called "Modern Marranos." Ber Mark, "Mir kumen tsurik," *Dos naye lebn* 10 (1946). Cited in Joanna Nalewajko-Kulikov, "Profiles: Three Colours: Grey, Bernard Mark's Portrait Sketch," *Holocaust Studies and Materials* 2: 216.
16 *Das Warschauer Getto. Zum 25. Jahrestag des bewaffnetten Kampfes im Getto. 1943* (Warsaw: Interpress-Verlag, 1968).

Notes on the Underground: Lili Berger's Reflections on Marranism   191

Berger confirms the broader truth, which she had implied or asserted throughout her career, that these acts were a testament to the expressive longevity of the Yiddish language. She ends this essay with an entreaty for the perseverance of Jewish historical memory (which includes the Marrano legacy) and against the revocation of national rights.

In Pursuit of Marranos and Crypto-Jews: A Mallorcan Travelogue

Berger's essay "Oyf di shpurn fun amolike Maranen" (In the footprints of yesterday's marranos)[17] establishes her interest in the Marrano legacy which dared not speak its name, passed down from generation to generation, irresistibly. Inspired by George Sand's[18] memoir, an autobiographical travel novel, *A Winter in Mallorca*,[19] Berger traced the tracks laid by the French author. Berger is intrigued by the interest Sand shows in the local "Jewish Catholic" populations. Taking her lead from Sand, Berger does some historical "excavation," in both Valldemossa and Palma, Mallorca's capital, in search of a Marrano presence. Her Converso and Crypto-Jew-sleuthing took place along alleyways, among marketplaces, jewellery shops, and cathedrals, repositories of a Jewish vestige and its cultural artifacts. Here Berger encounters both spectres of the Marrano past and their contemporary progeny. Indeed Berger gleaned many details about Marrano history directly from Sand's travelogue.

Berger's is a single-minded mission with a monolithic agenda: to trace the Jewish footsteps through the village streets. But these phantoms are reluctant participants in Berger's detective project. She meets up with – by coincidence or by appointment – a succession of diffident townsfolk who do not admit to their Jewish heritage, even when pressed. They often did not respond, or their words were not adequate to the task of addressing, much less identifying, their religious affiliations.

---

17 *Ekhos*, 125–37. This essay's companion piece in the same volume, "Geyresh shpanie mit 500 yor tsurik" (The Spanish expulsion of 500 years ago), 112–24, is a more rigorously documented historical chronicle of the Spanish expulsion and the fate of the "New Christians" than the essay under consideration here.

18 Pen name of French novelist and memoirist Amantine Lucile Aurore Dupin de Francueil.

19 Published in 1842, it first appeared in 1841 in the *Revue des deux mondes*, translated by Robert Graves (Wiltshire: Mount Orleans Press, 2022). Here Sand recounts her trips to the Balearic Islands and to the small village Valldemossa in the winter of 1838–9 with her companion Frédéric Chopin.

192 Epilogue

Jews fled Vespasian rule in 70 CE Jerusalem to the Balearic Islands. Mallorca had been colonized by Carthaginian, Roman, and Arab rule; Jews thrived under each regime, until the ascendancy of the Spanish Catholics during the Inquisition, which was instituted there in 1488. They gleefully oversaw forced conversions and group baptisms. Their moniker, "Individuos de la Calle," or Ghetto Folk, outlived their enforced seclusion, which ended in Mallorca and the Balearic Islands in 1782. Berger walked through this Jewish quarter, replete with *mikves* (ritual baths) and houses of worship, including La Sinagoga Balear. The *Judería*, as it was called in all Iberian countries, was not a circumscribed place, as Norman Simms has it: "Marranos inhabit a universe of discourse unbounded by geography. The *Judería* was no longer a place in the city but a state of mind."[20] Simms goes on to say that the double life which a Crypto-Jew must lead, whether "alternating or sequential or simultaneous articulations of biography," breeds a variety of collective madness. Indeed the people Berger tried to engage revealed a crippling paranoia about blowing their cover.

Berger was on an ethnographic mission. Most potential "informants," to borrow a term designated for interviewees in the field of folklore, were reluctant to speak, even after Berger identified herself as a Jew from Paris. A garrulous woman mentions an artist who, after centuries of deracination, wanted to reclaim these self-same Jewish roots to all of "*Yidntum*" (Jewry), no less. Berger herself remembers an old man of Moroccan descent, of dignified and elegant bearing, who confirmed that there are Jews living in Palma and that he will point out Jewish jewellery shops, whose mainstay are Mallorca pearls. Berger meets with shopkeepers whom she determined to have Jewish facial features. She does not mince words: "I am a Jew from France. Seems to me you look like a Jew." The obligatory denial is countered by a neighbour's wink. A watchmaker "with a dark Semitic face" from a "typical Polish shtetl" was another one, in fearful panic, to aver his Christian status. The more they objected, the more their faces would take on a Jewish cast, as Berger saw it.

A woman directs her to Jewish-owned businesses on Platería Street, where Berger concocts a false quest after the family Cohen. She is met with more agitated evasions, denials, more "ironic smiles." About to cook up another pretext, she is told not to wreak further havoc on these

---

20 Norman Simms, *Masks in the Mirror: Marranism in Jewish Experience* (New York: Peter Lang, 2006), 107.

Notes on the Underground: Lili Berger's Reflections on Marranism   193

poor souls. Her companion shows her the Plaza Major, where the *autos-da-fé* were carried out, burning at the stake "New Catholics" suspected of following *Halakha* (Jewish law) covertly. In 1495 blood ran in the streets. Today, as it has been for the last five centuries, they are all officially Catholic. Converted Jews lived and married endogamously, separate from the truly Catholic demographic. Most needed to hide their Jewish descent. Others did not.

Berger's efforts to interview these Jewish Catholics came to naught; the veil of secrecy could not be lifted. Her companion is curious about his own name, Miró. Indeed, he notes that the artist Joan Miró, a resident of Palma, was Jewish. Berger's companion uses the term "of Jewish descent" interchangeably with "true Jews." (Indeed Berger herself often unwittingly blurs the distinction between Marranos, Conversos, and Crypto-Jews.) They assume high positions in the city administration. The mayor of Palma, a well-known Socialist, is one such Jew. Berger visits a small *beys medresh* (study hall) where "Jewish" Jews and tourists gather and socialize on the sabbath and holidays. Efforts of some Mallorcan Jewish Catholics to convert back to Judaism met with procedural difficulties. Remarkably, she tells us, official tribunals of the Inquisition functioned until the early 1800s.

Berger ultimately visits a cathedral whose cellar is chock full of Jewish prayer books and a Dominican monastery, now converted into a casino, where Jews were imprisoned and tortured over the course of five centuries. This brings us back, Berger writes, to George Sand, who, in 1838, met a priest who spent seven years in this prison for his youthful heresy. While he was ultimately released, Berger speculates that those who practised Judaism undercover did not survive. Sand also cites a French writer and diplomat, Grasset de St. Sauveur, who noted that the Marranos did represent a reviled and ridiculed "underclass." He was horrified by the instruments of torture and the funeral pyres upon which Jews were burnt alive on the suspicion of practising their faith. Their ashes were cast to the wind. Berger ends with Sand's conclusion that in her day the disabling of the brutal ecclesiastical practices by the various liberalizing decrees of the prime minister of Spain, Juan Alvarez Mendizabal, himself a child of a Converso mother, was not as complete as one might assume. Mallorcan Jews and Marranos still suffered at the time of Sand's travels there. Berger ends with the notion that the Jews lived lives isolated and discrete from their "co-religionists." Catholic in name only, their fear lived on. She credits Sand with exposing and disseminating this truth. Berger saw for herself how some Jewish Catholics, at the time of her visit, still thought of themselves as

194 Epilogue

Jews, even those who attended church while abjuring their Jewish provenance.

Marrano Themes in Lili Berger's Oeuvre: Critical Reviews

(translated and adapted)

As addressed in our introduction, Berger's work garnered much critical attention; her reviewers note the wide contexts of her Euro-cosmopolitan aesthetic and political sensibilities. While the critics presented here show an interest in the deep contours of Berger's thought, they also attend to a more particular application in her work, that is, the recurrent Converso and Crypto-Jewish tropes. The story "Kolahoras eyniklekh" (Kolahoras' grandchildren) uncovers a Marrano demographic within Poland; the critics cited below grapple with this intriguing fact.

As noted earlier, the volume *Opgerisene tsvaygn* (Severed branches) contains a cycle of stories, "Haynttsaytike Maranen" (Contemporary Marranos), on which both Leyzer Domankevitsh and L. Bernard comment. Rifke Kope[21] reflects on the saga of Converso Uriel D'Acosta, in Berger's volume, *Fun vayt un fun noent* (From far and near). These critics, Berger's colleagues all, shared Socialist or Communist affiliation and similar trajectories of emigration from Poland to France, then, after the war, repatriation to Poland, then back to France. Their respective exegeses afford valuable insight into the life of Jews in postwar Poland. They engage variously with the phenomenon of Crypto-Judaism, which kept them, against all odds, Jewish by self-definition or, at the very least, aspiration.

In her review Rifke Kope singles out the story "Der untergehakter demb" (The felled oak tree) as it presents Berger's "dissertation-like"

---

21 What follows here are the reviewers' articles and the stories under consideration in each: Rifke Kope, "*Fun vayt un fun noent*: A nay bukh dertseylungen fun Lili Berger: variatsyes fun milkhome=khurbn" (*From far and from near*: A new book of Lili Berger's tales: Variations on the Holocaust), *Unzer vort* (Our word), April 1978, 6. *Fun vayt un fun noent*: "Der untergehakter demb," 7–36; "Shmelts," 51–64; "Er hot farshpetikt," 119–27. Leyzer Domankevitsh, "*Opgerisene tsvaygn*: Lili Bergers a nay bukh noveln" (Severed branches: Lili Berger's new book of short stories), *Unzer vort* (Our word, 22 October 1970, n.p.). *Opgerisine tsvaygn*: "Kolahoras eyniklekh," 9–33; "Af a shtiln dorf," 81–9. L. Bernard, "Ale doyres oyfgelebt mit a mol: Vegn Lili Bergers nay dershinen bukh, *Opgerisene tsvaygn*" (All generations brought to life at once: About Lili Berger's newly published book, *Severed Branches*) (Paris: *Naye Prese*, 1970), 2, 5.

Notes on the Underground: Lili Berger's Reflections on Marranism 195

reflections on the Converso Uriel D'Acosta, who educated Spinoza[22] to the value of philosophical scepticism and theological revisionism. According to Kope, D'Acosta was the "tortured prototype of the repressed Jew," whose attempt to return to his folk and to his ancestral Judaism was foiled by his censure of the barbarism enshrined in Jewish law. This invoked a *kheyrem* (excommunication) and the cruel rabbinical decree that D'Acosta be trodden upon, quite literally, in his synagogue. Berger's read of D'Acosta's legacy is that any manner of religious fanaticism, unmitigated by Jewish or Christian moral code, necessarily bears close scrutiny and almost certain repudiation. Kope notes that Berger gives the tale a literary turn, which addresses the constantly shifting terrain of D'Acosta's religious loyalties.

Kope then turns her attention to some "yet untold *khurbn* [Holocaust] fragments," which comprise some of the "endless supplements to the classical kaddish, the prayer for the dead, in the many Holocausts of the Jewish people." The story "Shmelts" (Scraps) revolves around a young woman, Dina, who lost her mother in the camps. Still reverberating hauntingly in the "deep fissure in her psyche" is the cruel directive, "left" or "right" in the Nazi *Selektion*. Here, as in almost all of Berger's Holocaust- and Marrano-themed stories, a scrap of faith endures. In the story "Er hot farshpetikt" (He arrived late), the survivor-protagonist, Izak Gelman, undertakes an act of spiritual self-appraisal in the face of existential annihilation. This introspective tendency of her protagonists – including some of the artists and writers in our volume – is a "model of Berger's own."

Concerning the story "Kolahoras eyniklekh" (Kolahoras' grandchildren),[23] Leyzer Domankevitsh notes the path taken by the Marranos – lonely, displaced, and uprooted – from Torquemada's expulsion to their "conversion" to Judaism in Poland. In fact, Poland itself has a history

---

22 Spinoza earned the Crypto-Jewishly resonant appellation "The Non-Jewish Jew" in Isaac Deutscher's lecture "The Message of the Non-Jewish Jew" (1958), later collected as an essay in his book *Non-Jewish Jew and Other* Essays (London: Oxford University Press, 1968). His coinage can be applied broadly to the faction of Marranos who rebuked both Jewish nationalism and orthodoxy, lessons Spinoza learned at D'Acosta's knee. Yirmiyahu Yovel named the Marrano the archetype of the non-Jewish Jew in *The Other Within: The Marranos: Split Identity and Emerging Modernity* (Princeton, NJ: Princeton University Press, 2009), 367.

23 Solomon Kolahora, of Spanish descent, was the much-beloved physician to King Stefan Bathory of Poland, of Transylvanian descent. The Kolahora family – including Talmudists, beadles, judges, rabbinical scholars – fled Spain during the Inquisition and took up roots in Kraków. "Cracow," *The Jewish Encyclopedia*, ed. Isidore Signer, 1901. https://www.studylight.org/encyclopedias/tje/c/cracow.html, accessed 5 May 2021.

196   Epilogue

of forced conversion.[24] The ancestors of the Kolahoras let their walking sticks lead them to countries and continents over the course of the many centuries. With borrowed names, these souls survived miraculously in concealment, as did their customs and practices. Domankevitsh holds that the "severed branches" of the title is a fitting rubric for each work in this volume; their roots had been ravaged "in the days of Hitler." These Jews were severed from the meagre remnant of their people, a much-diminished community. In postwar Poland's "new reality" they faced instances of classical antisemitism: Jewish students reviled and expelled, Jewish teachers ousted from their positions, Jewish PhDs dismissed from their government appointments, Jewish cemeteries desecrated.

In her story "Kolahora's Grandchildren," Berger illustrates the great disappointment in present-day Poland. While most *Anusim* (an alternative Hebrew term for Conversos) "embraced their newly gifted Slavic culture," the Polish government encouraged emigration to Palestine, thus indulging the Jews' Zionist fantasies, while gilding their exit and displacement. "Jews to Palestine!" was the enthusiastic, but deceitful, clarion call of the First Polish Republic.

Regarding Marranos in contemporary Poland, as Domankevitsh has it, there already exists a considerable literature. He cites here the characters in Adolf Rudnicki's novels, who, soon after war's end, are "just these present-day Marranos," Jews dressed in Polish garb.[25] This includes the fate of the Kolahora of Sephardic descent Artur Zavadzki,

---

24 Gershon Hundert writes about the "conversionary sermons" of Pope Gregory XIII and the papal bull of 1584, which were contemporary to Solomon Kolahora. Hundert notes the exhortations to revive this practice in the "conversionary efforts" of (Bishop) Francizek Kobielski in 1741. He issued an epistle which urged Jews to practise the "True Faith." More draconian measures followed, including the confiscation of books and punitive economic strictures. Gerson Hundert, *Jews in Poland-Lithuania in the Eighteenth Century: A Genealogy of Modernity* (Berkeley: University of California Press, 2004), 66–70.

25 See Berger's translation into Yiddish from the Polish of Rudnicki's *Der veg tsum himl* (Ascent to heaven) (Warsaw, 1962). Adolf Rudnicki was born Aron Hirschhorn. His depictions of Jewish traditions, rituals, and holidays abound, including Yom Kippur observances at the house of the tsadik of Ger. His stories allude to midrash and Jewish folk culture. Rudnicki sometimes reworked motifs from Yiddish literature, including Peretz's "Bontshe shvayg" (Bontshe the silent) and "Oyb nisht, nokh hekher" (If not, higher), in *Abel* (1960), and "Stara ściana" (The old wall, 1967). Eugenia Prokop-Janiec, *YIVO*, s.v. "Rudnicki, Adolf," 22 November 2010, https://yivoencyclopedia.org/article.aspx/Rudnicki_Adolf, accessed November 2021.

Notes on the Underground: Lili Berger's Reflections on Marranism 197

who survive the Jewish genocide only to suffer antisemitic indignities in Communist Poland. Domankevitsh states that "all Jews in contemporary Poland lived a Marrano-like existence" until they were unseated from their positions and fell victim to Christian false accusations.

The story "Oyf a shtiln dorf" (In a quiet village) offers another variation on a Polish tragedy. On a summer retreat to his family homestead, writer Arnold B. finds a concrete block in a niche, written in his sister Sorele's calligraphic script: "Mother and father are no more." Thus did his country idyll end. Berger presents, and Domankevitsh highlights, this cryptic, laconic, and private message. Domankevitsh ends this review: "Each [story] represents a variation on the despair ... of the last Jews in ... the Free Polish Republic. Lili Berger ... writes and speaks in the Jewish idiom. It has been many years since she emigrated from Poland and returned comfortably into the traditionally Jewish ranks. May this errand sustain her along her Jewish journey."

L. Bernard begins his review of *Severed Branches* with a similar assurance: "Let us immediately issue this warning: Lili Berger's Jewish soul has never known ambivalence about its identity," a valuable insight applicable to her entire oeuvre. It throws into high relief Berger's preoccupation with the Marrano inability to declare, much less to express, their faith. Bernard praises her "visceral sense of responsibility to shape the destiny" of her folk. In her consideration of these hidden Jews, Bernard suggests, "she was inspired by those heroes of rabbinic history who were tucked away in the caverns of Judea and Samaria." He notes that Berger lived the Polish Marrano existence vicariously while at the same time transcribing its "spiritual rupture" from its true native origin. Lili Berger "still and all, found within herself the necessary distance to confront boldly their Kafkaesque nightmares." This suggests the Marrano-Survivor congruence; the apt image of "severed branches" applies to both these populations.

Referring to Berger's influence, Bernard asks: "Which contemporary Polish Yiddish writers rouse their readership to greater redemption, to the historical consciousness needed to free themselves of all diasporic illusions? ... At the first opportunity after the Holocaust, she returned to Poland to build Socialism there ... and ... to help re-establish the destroyed Jewish cultural presence among the ruins, as far as one could." As was the case for the Crypto-Jews, the survivors' hope of living out their Jewishness was often a dream endlessly deferred.

Bernard offers his own history of the Kolahora lineage and its unhappy encounter with the Polish People's Republic. He notes that eight stories fall under the rubric "Contemporary Marranos" who are "invisible to the outside-gentile-Communist world, concealed also from

198 Epilogue

their own Jewish souls." In Bernard's view, the personages depicted in "Kolahora's Grandchildren" do not elicit the reader's sympathy, relinquishing as they do a sense of responsibility for their folk lineage. Artur Zavadzki, the famous architect, university professor, and adviser to the Polish Peoples' Republic, becomes in one fell swoop, both Matisyahu Kolahora and Arye Leyb Kolahora: "all generations of the Kolahoras are revived in him." Bernard renders censorious judgment on their "sudden reacquaintance with their origins." Yet he concedes, they "never did stop being what they are: Jews, transgressive and slanderous Jews, yet Jews nonetheless." If they repent, as Berger writes in the story, "with divine consent and with consent of the congregation," their children will be the "progeny of the best Jews."

Bernard observes that *Opgerisene tsvaygn* is an important testimony to the "exodus" from Poland. "Her language is honest and cautious; Lili Berger strides ever forward, from strength to strength. And we, her readers, wish: May this strength be emboldened into perpetuity."

By Linda/Leye Lipsky

Cultural Figures Named in the Text

The following list includes cultural figures not footnoted in the text. The reader can easily locate biographic details using the online sources listed in the bibliography.

Aberdam, Alfred (1894–1963)
Adlen, Michel (1898–1980)
Adler, Yankl (1895–1949)
Anielewicz, Mordekhai (1920?–1943)
Aronson, Naum (1872–1943)
Ashkenazy, Szymon (1866–1935)
Balaban, Meir (Mayer/Majer) (1877–1942)
Ben-Adir (Abraham Rozin) (1878–1942)
Benn (Bension Rabinowicz) (1905–1989)
Berenshteyn (*possibly* Yitzhak Bernstein) (1900–1943)
Bergelson, Dovid (1884–1952)
Berlewi, Henryk (1894–1967)
Berman, Adolf (1906–1978)
Bialik, Chaim Nachman (1873–1934)
Botwin, Naftali (1905–1925)
Breza, Tadeusz (1905–1970)
Broderzon, Moyshe (1890–1956)
Broniewski, Władisław (1897–1962)
Buchbinder, Szymon (1853–1908)
Drozdzynski, Aleksander (1925–1981)
Ehrenburg, Ilya (1891–1967)
Fefer, Itsik (1900–1952)
Feldhorn, Juliusz (1901–1943)

200 Cultural Figures Named in the Text

Feldman, Wilhelm (1868–1919)
Ficowska, Wanda (1929–2013)
Ficowski, Jerzy (1924–2006)
Fiszgrund, Salo Henryk (?–1971)
Fleg, Edmond (Flegenheimer) (1874–1963)
Frug, Shimen Shmuel (1860–1916)
Gajzler, Irena (Geisler, Gayzler) (??)
Garfinkel, Fayvl (1896–1944)
Gebirtig, Mordkhe (1847–1942)
Gilinsky, Shloyme (1888–1961)
Glicenstein, Henryk (1870–1942)
Glik, Hirsh (1922–1944)
Gomulicki, Wiktor (1848–1919)
Gottlieb, Maurycy (1856–1879)
Hirschbein, Peretz (1880–1948)
Infeld, Leopold (1898–1968)
Jarecka, Gustawa (1908–1943)
Joselewicz, Berek (1764–1809)
Kacyzne, Alter (Alter Sholem Katsizne) (1885–1941)
Kaczerginski, Shmerke (1908–1954)
Karp, Esther (1897–1970)
Katz, Emmanuel-Mane (1894–1962)
Katzenelson Yitshak (1885–1944)
Kirman, Yosef (1896–1943)
Kisling, Moise (1891–1953)
Kiveliovitch, Michel (Mikhail)
Klaczko, Julian (1825–1906)
Kolnik, Arthur (1890–1972)
Konopnicka, Maria (1842–1910)
Kowalska, Chana (1907–1942)
Kramsztyk, Roman (1885–1942)
Kraushar, Aleksander (1843–1931)
Krochmal, Nahman (1785–1840)
Kulback, Moyshe (1896–1937)
Kuna, Henryk (1879–1945)
Kvitko, Leyb (1890 or 1893–1952)
Lange, Antoni (1861–1929)
Lastik, Salomon (Shlomo, Shloyme) (1907–1977)
Lazowert, Henryka (1909–1942)

Cultural Figures Named in the Text 201

Lehman, Shmuel (1886–1941)
Lejbowicz, Lejb. (refer to YIVO entry Lejbowicz Herszek)
Lekert, Hirsh (1879–1902)
Lerer, Yekhiel (1910–1943)
Leśmian, Bolesław (1837–1937)
Lesser, Aleksander (1814–1884)
Levartovski, Jozef (Lewartowski, Joseph) (1895–1942)
Levi Yitzchak of Berdichev (1740–1809)
Lis, Kalmen (1903–1942)
Mahler, Raphael (1899–1977)
Manger, Itsik (1901–1969)
Markish, Peretz (1895–1952)
Markowicz, Artur (1872–1934)
Mickiewicz, Adam (1798–1855)
Mikhoels, Solomon (1890–1948)
Mortkowicz-Olczakowa, Hanna (1905–1968)
Nałkowska, Zofia (1884–1954)
Nadir, Moyshe (1885–1943)
Nadler, Munye (Shmuel) (1908–1942)
Nusinov, Yitskhok (1889–1950)
Olitski, Borekh (1907–1941)
Opoczynski, Peretz (1895–1943)
Orzeszkowa, Eliza (1841–1910)
Ostrzega, Abraham (1889–1942)
Pacanowska, Felicia (1915–2002)
Peretz, I.L. (1852–1915)
Perle, Yehoshua (Shyie/Joshua) (1888–1942)
Pilichowski, Leopold (1869–1933)
Pitoeff, Ludmilla (1896–1951)
Priłucki, Noah (Prilutski, Noyekh) (1882–1941)
Ravitch, Melech (Meylekh Ravitch) (1893–1976)
Reyzen, Zalmen (1887–1941?)
Robina, Chana (1890–1980)
Rosenfeld, Morris (1862–1923)
Rubinstein, Arthur (1887–1982)
Rudnicki, Adolf (Aron Hirszhorn) (1909–1990)
Segal, Chaim ben Isaac (Circa 1740)
Seksztajn, Gela (1907–1943)
Shneour, Zalman (1886–1959)

202   Cultural Figures Named in the Text

Shtern, Avraham (Abraham Stern) (1769–1842)
Shtern, Yisroel (1894–1942)
Skalov, Zalman (Y. Sluskalovski) (?–1942)
Sloves, Chaim (1905–?)
Sochaczewski, Aleksander (1843–1923)
Soutine, Chaim (1893–1943)
Szlengel, Władysław (1912–1943)
Szmidt, Andrzej (Pinkus Kartin) (1914–1942)
Tuwim, Julian (1894–1953)
Ulinover, Miryem (1890–1944)
Vaysenberg, I.M. (Weissenberg) (1881–1938)
Vogel, Debora (1900–1942)
Wachtel, Wilhelm (1875–1942)
Warshawski, Mark (Varshavski) (1848–1907)
Weinles, Jakub (1870–1938)
Wienawski, Henryk (1835–1880)
Wienawski, Jozef (1837–1912)
Zamenhof, Ludwig (1859–1917)
Zeitlin, Hillel (1872–1942)
Zuskin, Benjamin (1899–1952)

Biographies of Editors and Translators

Frieda Johles Forman (1937–2024) was involved in a number of publications, including *The Exile Book of Yiddish Women Writers* (2013, editor, translator, for which she was awarded the Canadian Jewish Book Award for Yiddish Translation in 2014); *Found Treasures: Stories by Yiddish Women Writers* (1994, researcher, co-editor, translator); *Taking Our Time: Feminist Perspectives on Temporality* (1989, editor); *Jewish Refugees in Switzerland During the Holocaust: A Memoir of Childhood and History* (2009). She was a contributor to the encyclopedia *Jewish Women in America* (1997). She was the founder and director of the Women's Educational Resources Centre at OISE/UT, 1974–98.

Sam Blatt grew up in the Yiddish-speaking immigrant community of Montreal: Yiddish was his first language. He was a founding member of the Dora Wasserman Yiddish Drama Group. Upon retirement, he taught Yiddish to adults for the Toronto Jewish Federation on a volunteer basis. He was a contributing researcher to *Found Treasures: Stories by Yiddish Women Writers* and a translator in *The Exile Book of Yiddish Women Writers*. He continues to be active in Yiddish cultural activities, and as a writer and translator.

Vivian Felsen is a Toronto-based independent scholar and award-winning translator of both French and Yiddish into English. With a background in modern history, modern languages, and law, her published translations include books on Canadian Jewish history, Holocaust memoirs, and short stories, mostly by Yiddish women writers.

Books she translated from Yiddish include *Montreal of Yesterday: Jewish Life in Montreal*, 1900–1920, by Israel Medres, which received a Canadian Jewish Book Award in 2001, and *Between the Wars: Canadian Jews in Transition*, also by Medres, for which she won a prestigious J.I. Segal Award in 2004.

204 Biographies of Editors and Translators

Among the Holocaust memoirs she has translated from Yiddish are the historically significant *Memoirs of the Lodz Ghetto*, by Yankl Nirenberg (2003), and *The Vale of Tears*, by Rabbi Pinchas Hirschprung (2016). In 2018 her English translation of the latter was awarded a gold medal in the autobiography/memoir category of the Independent Publisher Book Awards, as well as another J.I. Segal award.

Her translations of short stories by Yiddish women writers have been published most notably in the award-winning *The Exile Book of Yiddish Women Writers* (2013), edited by Freida Johles Forman, to which Felsen contributed her translations of two of Lili Berger's short stories.

Felsen's translations from French include *The Veiled Sun: From Auschwitz to New Beginnings* (2015), by Paul Schaffer with an introduction by Simone Veil and a foreword by Serge Klarsfeld, as well as *J.I. Segal (1896–1954): A Montreal Yiddish Poet and His Milieu*, by Pierre Anctil. For the latter, she was named a finalist for the Governor General's Literary Award for translation (French to English) in 2018. The book also contains over twenty of Segal's poems, which Felsen translated into English directly from the original Yiddish.

Vivian Felsen's essays on the subject of Yiddish translation appeared in *New Readings of Yiddish Montreal*, edited by P. Anctil, N. Ravvin, and S. Simon (2007), and *Kanade, di Goldene Medine? Perspectives on Canadian-Jewish Literature and Culture*, edited by K. Majer, J. Fruzińska, J. Kwaterko, and N. Ravvin (2018). She is the author of the entry for Lili Berger in the *Shalvi/Hyman Encyclopedia of Jewish Women* and the *Encyclopaedia Judaica*.

Ronnee Jaeger has been involved in Yiddish poetry, literature, and translation since her arrival in Toronto in 1970. She participated as a translator in *Found Treasures: Stories by Yiddish Women Writers* (1994) and her work has also appeared on the internet in Jewish Fiction.net. Her translation *The Rebbetzin's Sense of Justice* was selected for the anthology *18 Jewish Stories Translated from 18 Languages*. She served as the Jerusalem culture/political correspondent for *Outlook Magazine* (Vancouver) from 2005 to 2015.

Linda/Leye Lipsky is a co-translator with Joshua A. Fogel of I.J. Singer's novella *Willy* (2020). Her entry on Avrom Liessin appears in *The Encyclopedia of the Bible and Its Reception* (2018). She has written critical appreciations of Beyle Schaechter-Gottesman in the proceedings of the conference "Czernowitz at 100," edited by Joshua A. Fogel and Kalman Weiser (2010), *Afn Shvel* (2006), and *Jewish Women's Archive* (1999). She has published Yiddish poetry in *Afn Shvel* (2013) and in *Vidervuks: A*

Biographies of Editors and Translators 205

naye dor yidishe shrayber (1989). Among the courses she has taught at York University in Toronto are Yiddish Modernist Poetry, Modern Yiddish Fiction, and Modernism across the Arts.

Sylvia Lustgarten (1926–2023) inherited a rich and vibrant Yiddish literature in her home and in the wider Jewish immigrant community of Montreal. Director of the Committee for Yiddish for ten creative years, she developed and nurtured major projects such as heritage language programs for children, teacher training classes, and numerous study groups. Her translations appeared in the *Exile Book of Yiddish Women Writers* (2013). At the time of her passing, she was still an active member of our group.

Judy Nisenholt grew up in a Yiddish-speaking family and was educated in Winnipeg's I.L. Peretz Folk Shul. She has built upon the foundation of her Jewish day school learning through Yiddish reading groups. She has worked on the translation of handwritten Yiddish memoir and letters. Her translations have appeared in the *Exile Book of Yiddish Women Writers* (2013), Jewish Fiction.net in 2018, and in the Pakn Treger digital translation issue of 2022. She was a Yiddish Book Center translation fellow in 2023–4. As a teacher of English as a Second Language to both international and domestic college students, she specializes in English for academic purposes.

Books by Lili Berger

In Yiddish

Eseyen un skitsn (Essays and sketches). Warsaw: Yidish bukh, 1965.
Fun haynt un nekhtn (Of today and yesterday). Warsaw: Yidish bukh, 1965. *Nokhn mabl* (After the flood) Warsaw: Yidish bukh, 1967.
Opgerisen tsvaygn, noveln un dertseylungen (Severed branches, novellas and short stories). Paris, 1970.
Tsvishn shturems, roman (Between storms: A novel.) Buenos Aires: Fraynshaft, 1974.
In gang fun tsayt, eseyen (In the course of time: Essays). Paris, 1976.
Fun vayt un fun noent, noveln un dramaturgishe skitse vegn yanush kortshak (From near and far, short stories and a dramatic sketch concerning Janusz Korczak). Paris, 1978.
Nisht-farendikte bletlekh (Unfinished pages). (A novel concerning the life of Esther Frumkin.) Tel Aviv: Yisroel bukh, 1982.
Oyf di khvalyes fun goyrl, noveln, dertseylungen, literarishe eseyen. (On the waves of destiny, Novellas, stories, literary essays.) Paris, 1986.
In loyf fun tsayt: Dertseylungen, noveln, eseyen (With the passage of time: Short stories, novellas, essays.) Paris, 1988.
Geshtaltn un pasirungen, dertseylungen, noveln, eseyen (Vies et Destins) (Portraits and events: Short stories, novellas, essays). Paris, 1991.
Ekhos fun a vaytn nekhtn, dertseylungen, khumesh maysalekh, eseyen un skitsn. (Echoes of a distant past: Stories, Bible tales, essays, and sketches). Tel Aviv: Yisroel Bukh, 1993.

Selected Translations

Ethel and Julius Rosenberg, *Briv fun toytn-hoyz* (Death house letters). Warsaw, 1953.
Adolf Rudnicki, *Der Veg tsum himl* (The ascent to heaven: The selected works of Adolf Rudnicki). Warsaw: Yidish bukh, 1962.

208 Books by Lili Berger

In Polish

Zwyciestwo Narodu Wietnamskiego (The Vietnamese people in struggle).
 Warsaw: Książka i viedza, 1954; published under the name L. Gronowska.
Polacu we Francuskim Ruchu Oporu (Poles in the French Resistance). Warsaw:
 Książka i viedza, 1959; published under the name L. Gronowski.

In French

Korczak, un homme, un symbole (Korczak, the man and the symbol). Paris: Magnard,
 1990.

Bibliography

CPL: Adam Mickiewicz Institute. Entries in "Artists and Works." Available at https://culture.pl/en/artists.

JWE: Jewish Women's Archive. Entries in *The Shalvi/Hyman Encyclopedia of Jewish Women*. Available at https://jwa.org/encyclopedia.

N-K: Nalewajko-Kulikov, Joanna. "Profiles: Three Colours: Grey. Bernard Mark's Portrait Sketch." In *Holocaust Studies and Materials* (2010): 205–26. Available at https//www. ceeol.com/search/article-detail?id=35122.

YL: Fogel, Joshua, trans. Entries from *Yiddish Leksikon*. Translation of *Leksikon fun der Nayer Yidisher Literatur* (Biographical Dictionary of Modern Yiddish Literature]. 8 vols. New York, 1956–1981, and *Leksikon fun yidish-shraybers/yidishe shraybers* (Biographical Dictionary of Yiddish Writers). New York, 1986. Available at http://yleksikon.blogspot.com.

YIVO: Hundert, Gershon David, ed. Entries from *The YIVO Enyclopedia of Jews in Eastern Europe*. Online edition. Available at https://yivoencyclopedia .org/default.aspx.

Abramski, Shimen, ed. *The Jews in Poland*. Blackwell, 1996.

Adamczyk-Grabowska, Monika, et al. *Jewish Presence in Absence: The Aftermath of the Holocaust in Poland, 1944–2010*. Jerusalem: Yad Vashem, the International Institute for Holocaust Research, 2014.

Auerbach, Karen, and Nick Underwood. "Yiddish in the City." *East European Jewish Affairs* 50, nos. 1–2 (2020).

Avishai, Bernard. *The Tragedy of Zionism: Revolution and Democracy in the Land of Israel*. New York: Farrar, Straus and Giroux, 1985.

Chandler, Robert. Introduction. In Vasily Grossman, *Life and Fate*. New York: New York Review Books, 2006.

Cohen, Nathan. "The Renewed Association of Yiddish Writers and Journalists in Poland, 1945–48." *The Mendele Review: Yiddish Literature and Language* (A Companion to Mendele) 9, no. 4 (15 March 2005).

210 Bibliography

Curtis, Glenn E., ed. *Poland: A Country Study*. Washington, DC: GPO for the Library of Congress, 1992.

Estraikh, Gennady. *In Harness: Yiddish Writers' Romance with Communism*. Syracuse: Syracuse University Press, 2005.

Ficowski, Jerzy. *Regions of the Great Heresy: Bruno Schulz, A Biographical Portrait*. Trans. and ed. Theodosia Robertson. New York: W.W. Norton, 2002

Gronowski Brunot, Louis. *Le dernier grand soir: Un juif de Pologne*. Paris: Éditions du Seuil, 1980.

Grozinger, Elvira, and Magdalena Ruta. *Under the Red Banner: Yiddish Culture in the Communist countries in the Postwar Era*. Wiesbaden: Harrassowitz Verlag, 2008.

Gutman, Y., and G. Greif, eds. *The Historiography of the Holocaust Period: Proceedings of the Fifth Yad Vashem International Historical Conference, Jerusalem, March 1983*. Jerusalem: Yad Vashem, 1988.

Kassow, Samuel D. *Who Will Write Our History?: Emanuel Ringelblum, the Warsaw Ghetto, and the Oyneg Shabes Archive*, Bloomington: Indiana University Press, 2007.

Klepfisz, Irena. "Queens of Contradiction: A Feminist Introduction to Yiddish Women Writers," in F. Forman, E. Raicus, et al., eds., *Found Treasures: Stories by Yiddish Women Writers*. Toronto: Second Story Press, 1994.

Korczak, Janusz. *Ghetto Diary*. New Haven, CT: Yale University Press, 2003.

Kuhn-Kennedy, Fleur. "Les Territoires de Lili Berger." In A. Kichielewski, J. Lyon-Caer, et al., eds, *Les Polonais et Le Shoah: Une nouvelle école historique*. Paris: CNRS éditions, 2019.

Mark, Bernard. *Di umgekumene shrayber fun di getos un lagern un zeyere verk* (The murdered writers of the ghettos and camps and their work). Warsaw: Yidish-Bukh, 1954.

Mark, Bernard. *Der oyfshtand in Bialystoker geto* (The uprising in the Bialystok Ghetto). Warsaw: ZIH, 1950. 2nd ed. Buenos Ayres: Ikuf, 1953.

Mark, Bernard. *Der oyfshtand in varshever geto*. (The uprising in the Warsaw Ghetto) Moscow: Der Emes, 1947.

Mark, Bernard. *Dokumentn un materyaln vegn oyfshtand in Varshever geto* (Documents and materials about the Warsaw Ghetto Uprising). Warsaw: Yidish-Bukh, 1953.

Marrus, Michael, and Robert Paxton. *Vichy France and the Jews*. Stanford, CA: Stanford University Press, 2019.

Nalewajko-Kulikov, Joanna. "Profiles: Three Colours: Grey. Bernard Mark's Portrait Sketch." *Holocaust Studies and Materials* 2: 205–26. https//www .ceeol.com/search/article-detail?id=35122.

Nesselrodt, Markus. "I bled like you, brother although I was a thousand miles away: Postwar Yiddish Sources on the Experience of Polish Jews in Soviet Exile during World War II." *Eastern European Jewish Affairs* 46, no. 1 (2016).

Netzer, S. "The Holocaust of Polish Jewry in Jewish Historiography." In Y. Gutman et al., eds., *Historiography of the Holocaust Period* (1988), 133–40. Cited in https://www.jewishvirtuallibrary.org/jewish-historical-institute-warsaw.

Opalski, Magdalena, and Israel Bartal. *Poles and Jews: A Failed Brotherhood.* Walthan, MA: Brandeis University Press, 1992.

Polonsky, Antony. *Poles, Jews, Socialists: The Failure of anIideal.* Oxford: Oxford University Press, Littman Library of Jewish Civilization, 2008.

Polonsky, Antony, et al. *New Directions in the History of the Jews in the Polish Lands.* Boston: Academic Studies Press, 2018.

Poznanski, Renee. *Jews in France during World War II.* Waltham, MA: Brandeis University Press, 2001.

Ravine, Jacques. *In gerangl kegn natsishn soyne*: Der organizirter vidershtand fun di yidn in frankraykh (The struggle against the Nazi enemy: The organized resistance of the Jews in France). Paris: Farlag Oyfsnay, 1970.

Reinhartz, Jehuda. *The Road to September 1939: Polish Jews, Zionists, and the Yishuv on the Eve of World War II.* Waltham, MA: Brandeis University Press, 2018.

Roskies, David G. *Against the Apocalypse: Responses to Catastrophe in Modern Jewish Culture.* Cambridge, MA: Harvard University Press, 1984.

Ruta, Magdalena. *Without Jews?: Yiddish Literature in the People's Republic of Poland on the Holocaust, Poland, and Communism.* New York: Columbia University Press, 2018.

Sakwa, George. "The Polish 'October': A Re-appraisal through Historiography." *The Polish Review* 23, no. 3 (1978).

Stola, Dariusz. "Jewish Emigration from Communist Poland: The Decline of Polish Jewry in the Aftermath of the Holocaust." *Eastern European Jewish Affairs* 47, nos. 2–3 (2017).

Trunk, Yehiel Yeshaia. *Poyln: My Life within Jewish Life in Poland, Sketches and Images.* Toronto: University of Toronto Press, 2007.

Tumarkin Goodman, Susan. *Russian Jewish Artists in a Century of Change, 1890–1990.* New York and Munich: Prestel, 1995.

Turski, Miriam. *Polish Witnesses to the Shoah.* London: Vallentine Mitchell, 2010.

Van Tendeloo, Dorothée. "Paper Treasures: An Introduction to the Life and Work of the Yiddish Novelist, Literary Critic and Essayist Lili Berger (1916–1996)." Masters thesis, School of Oriental and African Studies, University of London, 2000.

Wolff, Frank. *Yiddish Revolutionaries in Migration: The Transnational History of the Jewish Labor Bund.* Boston: Brill, 2020.

Zucotti, Susan. *The Holocaust, the French, and the Jews.* Lincoln: University of Nebraska Press, 1999.